Ronald Reagan
and the Politics of
Immigration Reform

Ronald Reagan and the Politics of Immigration Reform

NICHOLAS LAHAM

 PRAEGER

Westport, Connecticut
London

Library of Congress Cataloging-in-Publication Data

Laham, Nicholas.
    Ronald Reagan and the politics of immigration reform / Nicholas Laham.
        p.   cm.
    Includes bibliographical references and index.
    ISBN 0–275–96723–9 (alk. paper)
    1. Reagan, Ronald.   2. United States—Emigration and immigration—Government policy.
3. Emigration and immigration law—United States.   4. United States—Politics and
government—1981–1989.   I. Title.
    JV6455.L335   2000
    325.73'09'048—dc21   99–045987

British Library Cataloguing in Publication Data is available.

Library of Congress Catalog Card Number: 99–045987
ISBN: 0–275–96723–9

First published in 2000

Praeger Publishers, 88 Post Road West, Westport, CT 06881
An imprint of Greenwood Publishing Group, Inc.
www.praeger.com

Printed in the United States of America

The paper used in this book complies with the
Permanent Paper Standard issued by the National
Information Standards Organization (Z39.48–1984).

10 9 8 7 6 5 4 3 2 1

Contents

Preface

When Ronald Reagan entered the White House on January 20, 1981, the two most pressing items on his agenda were restoring noninflationary economic growth and rebuilding America's shattered defenses. Concerns over the American economic and military decline, which marred the Carter presidency, were the dominant issues determining the outcome of the 1980 presidential election. It is understandable that Reagan would devote top priority to the economy and defense, which, after all, were the issues most responsible for his election to the presidency.[1]

However, presidents cannot completely control the national agenda. Issues of concern to members of Congress and the public often rise to the top of the national agenda, even if those problems are of lesser interest to the incumbent president. Presidents can set in motion processes, which elevate an issue of concern to them to the top of the national agenda, after they have left office. This was certainly the case with immigration.

Reagan was disinterested in immigration and did not intend to devote his attention to this issue when he entered the White House. However, as a result of processes set in motion by his predecessor, Jimmy Carter, he soon found it impossible to ignore this issue. By the late 1970s, immigration had emerged as a top issue on the national agenda as a result of the unprecedented levels of immigration, both legal and illegal, which the Immigration Act of 1965 unleashed.

Since passage of the Immigration Act of 1924, the United States had maintained a highly restrictive immigration policy. The Immigration Act of 1965 substantially expanded and liberalized federal immigration law, resulting in a significant rise in levels of legal immigration, which was accompanied by a flood of illegal immigration to the United States.[2] While supporting the high levels of legal immigration existing since 1965, every president who has served in office since Jimmy Carter, as well as virtually all members of Congress, have strongly opposed illegal immigration and supported measures to deter aliens from residing in this nation without authentic documentation.[3] In an effort to translate this consensus against illegal immigration into public policy, in 1977 Carter made recommendations to Congress to address the problem of illegal immigration.[4]

However, Congress failed to act upon Carter's recommendations. Instead, in 1978 Congress established the Select Commission on Immigration and Refugee Policy (SCIRP), which was charged with the responsibility of proposing measures to achieve comprehensive immigration reform. Unlike Carter's recommendations, which were limited to addressing the problem of illegal immigration, Congress granted SCIRP a broader mandate to review the entire immigration policy of the federal government, including legal immigration.

SCIRP had not yet issued the final report, containing its recommendations on immigration reform, by the time Carter left the White House on January 20, 1981. Reagan was forced to confront the issue once those proposals were finally released, five weeks after his inauguration. Five days following the issuance of the report, Reagan established the President's Task Force on Immigration and Refugee Policy. He directed the Task Force to present recommendations on immigration reform to him, which he would subsequently consider proposing to Congress.

The release of SCIRP's final report, and Reagan's establishment of the Task Force on Immigration and Refugee Policy, triggered efforts in Congress to pass comprehensive immigration reform legislation, which continue to this very day. Those efforts have culminated thus far in passage of three immigration reform bills: the Immigration Reform and Control Act (IRCA) of 1986, the Immigration Act of 1990, and the Illegal Immigrant Reform and Immigrant Responsibility Act (IIRIRA) of 1996. The Reagan presidency represents a milestone in the history of immigration policy, insofar as it marks the beginning of a two-decades-long, ongoing effort to achieve comprehensive immigration reform.

Since immigration reform efforts began in Congress in 1981, the fundamental challenge, which every president since Reagan has faced on this issue, can be summarized as follows: The levels of immigration, both legal and illegal, existing since 1965 are excessive and unsustainable. The United States lacks the resources to support the millions of poor aliens who have immigrated to this nation since 1965, and the millions more who will immigrate through the foreseeable future, barring major reforms in immigration policy. Poor immigrants, like poor native-born Americans, require a vast and costly array of social services to meet their basic needs. However, as a result of the severe constraints upon the growth of the welfare system, which Congress has imposed through successive reforms in the budget and means-tested entitlement programs its members have undertaken since 1981, the federal government lacks the resources to finance those social services. In the era of welfare reform and shrinking budgets for social services at the federal and state levels, the immigration of millions of poor aliens is a luxury which the United States can no longer afford. At some point, Congress will have to impose major restrictions on immigration if a massive growth in welfare spending, to support America's burgeoning population of poor immigrants, is to be averted.

This book addresses Reagan's conduct of immigration policy. It uses information on the economic consequences of mass immigration, which has been produced since Reagan left the White House, in order to assess the credibility and effectiveness of his immigration policy. Immigration is an issue which has significant political, economic, fiscal, social, cultural, demographic, and environmental consequences for the United States. As a result, immigration represents an important issue by which to measure the performance of every president who has served in office since immigration reform emerged as a top priority on the national agenda in 1981.

This book concludes that Reagan demonstrated gross ineptitude in his conduct of immigration policy. He failed to press for much-needed reforms in legal immigration, believing instead that the United States has benefited from the high levels of legal immigration existing since 1965. His belief was based upon the simplistic assumption that legal immigrants represent hard-working, enterprising individuals who make substantial contributions to the American economy. He failed to recognize that the benefits of legal immigration are dependent upon the socioeconomic status of the immigrant population: While the United States certainly benefits from the immigration of well-educated, highly skilled foreign-born workers, the same is not true in the case of their poorly educated and unskilled counterparts.

In addition to his inability to comprehend the problems associated with the high levels of legal immigration existing since 1965, Reagan failed miserably to achieve the single, central, overriding goal of his immigration policy: to stem the flow of illegal immigration, which was an unintended consequence of the Immigration Act of 1965. He supported the establishment of a fraud-ridden employer-sanctions regime which has had no discernible effect in achieving its goal of stemming the flow of illegal immigration to the United States. He failed to take the first step toward establishment of a fraud-resistant worker verification system, which would enable the employer-sanctions provisions of IRCA to be effectively enforced, as he was authorized to do under the bill. He supported passage of the amnesty provisions of IRCA which granted permanent legal residence to 2.7 million poorly educated, unskilled, and low-wage illegal aliens, many of whom have become dependent upon the welfare system.

Reagan bequeathed a legacy of failure on immigration policy, requiring Congress to revisit the issue of immigration reform during the Bush and Clinton administrations. George Bush and Bill Clinton have had to address the two single, central, overriding problems in immigration policy which Reagan had to confront during his presidency: how to curtail the excessive and unsustainable levels of legal immigration existing since 1965 while imposing effective measures to deter further illegal immigration to the United States. To be sure, Bush and Clinton have been no more successful than Reagan in confronting those problems. Indeed, the two immigration reform bills Bush and Clinton signed— the Immigration Act of 1990 and the IIRIRA, respectively—have been no more effective than IRCA in addressing those problems. As a result, the excessive and unsustainable levels of immigration, both legal and illegal, continue to this very day—clear evidence that none of the three presidents who have served in office since immigration reform efforts in Congress began in 1981 have effec- tively addressed the challenges posed by mass immigration to the United States.

The lack of presidential leadership on immigration policy that has existed since 1981 is difficult to dispute. The real question is why such leadership has been lacking. The most likely answer is interest-group politics. Indeed, immi- gration is an issue which has attracted the intense interest and involvement of two major groups: immigrant ethnic constituencies, whose members have a strong personal interest in perpetuating the mass immigration existing since 1965, and the liberation community, which is philosophically committed to the preservation of an open and liberal immigration policy. Those two interest groups have successfully lobbied Congress since 1981 against any effort to curtail the high levels of immigration, both legal and illegal, resulting from the Immigration Act of 1965.[5]

On the surface, one could assume that the White House has been subject to the same special-interest pressures that have thwarted passage of comprehensive immigration reform legislation in Congress. Indeed, investigations into the cam- paign finance scandals surrounding the 1996 presidential contest reveal that Clinton's opposition to efforts within the 104th Congress to reduce levels of legal immigration may have been directly influenced by the substantial financial contributions to the Democratic National Committee made by the Asian- American community, whose members have a strong personal stake in contin- uing the mass immigration. As we will see in Chapter 1, the evidence strongly suggests that Clinton shaped immigration policy to conform to the wishes of immigrant ethnic groups opposed to comprehensive immigration reform.

Could Reagan have been motivated by the same corrupt intent which seems to have guided Clinton in his conduct of immigration policy? Was Reagan's own support for the mass immigration the result of special-interest pressures? The answer to those questions is a definite no.

No evidence of any kind exists among the voluminous documents on the Reagan administration's conduct of immigration policy to suggest that the pres- ident addressed this issue in a manner designed to satisfy the desires of interest groups opposed to comprehensive immigration reform. Indeed, the record shows a moderate, though hardly overwhelming, amount of lobbying activity directed at the Reagan White House over immigration on both sides of this issue. More- over, there is no evidence to suggest that Reagan was motivated in his conduct of immigration policy by any consideration other than his desire to serve the national interest. Indeed, Reagan made every effort to develop an immigration policy to conform to the national interest, and he remained very immune to the relatively weak special-interest pressures which were exerted against the White House to influence his handling of the issue. Accordingly, while Clinton may very well have operated out of corrupt intent in his conduct of immigration policy, Reagan functioned under a directly opposite motive: his desire to shape immigration policy to serve the national interest.

Nevertheless, however honest Reagan's intent, it is difficult to dispute the argument that he provided ineffective leadership in confronting the challenge posed by mass immigration. If Reagan's motives are beyond reproach, we are still left with the question of why the president was so ineffectual in his conduct of immigration policy. Our answer to this question is that the Reagan administration was crippled in its ability to develop a sound and effective immigration policy by two factors: first, the lack of accurate and reliable information existing on this issue, especially as it pertains to the economic consequences of mass immigration; and second, the president's ideological opposition to big government, which impeded the ability of Congress to develop a workable and effective employer-sanctions regime capable of achieving its goal of stemming the flow of illegal immigration to the United States.

Presidents obviously cannot develop sound and viable public policy unless they possess a substantial body of accurate and reliable information. Such information is essential in enabling the president to identify relevant problems and choose from a range of options which can effectively address those problems. Information on the economic impact of mass immigration upon the United States was simply unavailable during the Reagan administration. Such information that did exist tended to confirm the prevailing consensus among the experts on the economics of immigration that mass immigration has had a positive economic impact upon the United States. Based upon that information, Reagan saw no need to recommend reductions in the high levels of legal immigration that had existed since 1965. However, the information on immigration that has been developed since Reagan left the White House casts doubt upon whether mass immigration has indeed been economically beneficial to the United States.

Immigrants have traditionally arrived in the United States with less education and skills than the native-born population, and limited fluency in English. However, immigrants have traditionally overcome those socioeconomic impediments through their commitment to hard work and entrepreneurial activity. This has allowed immigrants to achieve rapid upward socioeconomic mobility. They have generally been able to earn incomes which are equivalent to, if not in excess of, those of native-born Americans within a generation.

However, the economic performance of immigrants has deteriorated drastically since 1970. This is due to the change in the ethnic composition of the immigrant population. The Immigration Act of 1924 limited immigration largely to Europeans and Canadians, who generally tend to have high levels of education and skills, perfect fluency in English, and relatively high incomes. However, the Immigration Act of 1965 eliminated the barriers to immigration among non-

Europeans, which resulted in a flood of immigration from Latin America and
Asia. Immigration has been especially heavy from Mexico, Central America,
and Indochina, whose citizens suffer from extremely low levels of education
and skills, poor fluency in English, and abysmally low incomes.

Due to the dramatic transformation in the ethnic composition of the immigrant
population since 1965, the overwhelming majority of legal immigrants who have
been admitted to the United States during the last three decades lack the minimal
education and skills necessary to find decent-paying jobs. This has resulted in
substantial welfare participation among America's burgeoning population of
poor and unskilled immigrants. The open and liberal immigration policy pursued
since 1965 has inflicted harm upon the United States, insofar as it has failed to
meet the labor needs of the American economy, while imposing substantial
financial burdens upon the welfare system. Accordingly, current immigration
policy has failed to serve the national economic interest.

The economic harm to the United States is the direct result of Congress's
decision to allow large numbers of poorly educated, unskilled, and low-income
aliens to immigrate to this nation illegally, while providing incentives for many
other foreign-born individuals with similar human capital endowments to do so
illegally, through passage of the Immigration Act of 1965. Since the bill was
passed fifteen years before Reagan entered the White House, one would assume
that the president should have known about the negative economic consequences
of post-1965 mass immigration, and recommended much-needed reforms in legal immigration. However, the empirical evidence did not become apparent until
the 1990s. As a result, Reagan cannot be held responsible for the mistake he
made in supporting the mass immigration, since he had no reason to believe
that this policy was inflicting economic harm upon the United States. A president
can only be held responsible for the information existing at the time he resided
in the White House; and the information available to Reagan was that post-1965
mass immigration was having the same economically beneficial impact upon the
United States as previous waves of immigration to this nation.

In addition to lacking accurate and reliable information on the economic impact of mass immigration upon the United States, Reagan was also crippled in
his ability to develop a sound and credible immigration policy by his ideological
aversion to big government. Since Reagan supported the high levels of legal
immigration existing since 1965, his immigration reform efforts were concentrated on the more narrow issue of illegal immigration. Consistent with SCIRP's
recommendations, the Reagan administration endorsed the imposition of federal
civil and criminal sanctions upon employers who knowingly hire illegal aliens.

The purpose of employer sanctions is to deprive illegal aliens of jobs. Aliens
immigrate to the United States illegally primarily in search of employment. By
depriving illegal aliens of jobs, employer sanctions are designed to eliminate the
incentives which foreign-born individuals have to immigrate to the United States
without authentic documentation, thereby stemming the flow of illegal immigration to this nation. Accordingly, a central element of IRCA is the imposition

of an employer-sanctions regime designed to deter further illegal immigration by prohibiting firms from hiring undocumented individuals.

IRCA requires employers to solicit documents from individuals, whom they wish to hire, which verify their eligibility to work in the United States. Employers are only legally permitted to hire individuals who can present these documents. Employer compliance with the worker verification provisions of IRCA would presumably deny illegal aliens jobs, since they carry no such documents which are valid. However, illegal aliens have been able to circumvent employer sanctions by providing their employers with fraudulent documents which falsely purport to verify their eligibility to work in the United States.

Firms cannot comply with their legal obligations under the employer-sanctions provisions of IRCA unless they have a secure and reliable means to determine the authenticity of the documents presented to them by individuals. This would enable firms to detect and crack down upon document fraud in order to assure that such individuals are eligible to work in the United States. Congress authorized Reagan to establish worker verification pilot projects in order to determine their effectiveness as a means of eliminating document fraud. To accomplish this objective, Congress also authorized Reagan to recommend reforms in the worker verification provisions of IRCA. However, Reagan failed to exercise this authority.

In the absence of a credible worker verification system, employer sanctions have been rendered almost completely ineffective as a means to deprive illegal aliens of jobs. With an abundant supply of jobs readily available to them, aliens have every incentive to continue to immigrate to the United States illegally. Indeed, employer sanctions have had no discernible effect in stemming the flow of illegal immigration since they went into effect in 1987.

In order to be workable and effective, employer sanctions have to be coupled with a fraud-resistant worker verification system, which would enable firms to use a single document, preferably the Social Security card, as a secure and reliable means to establish the identity of individuals who seek employment. This procedure would assure that only individuals who carry valid Social Security cards and can verify that they are the rightful owners of those cards would be allowed employment, thereby enabling firms to detect and crack down upon document fraud.

However, the Reagan administration strongly opposed the establishment of a fraud-resistant worker verification system. The administration feared that such a system would result in the transformation of the Social Security card into a de facto national identity card, which would represent a threat to individual privacy. Use of the Social Security card as a secure and reliable means of individual identification would require the federal government to maintain personal records on every individual eligible to work in the United States. The federal government would make those records available to employers in enabling them to meet their legal obligations under the employer-sanctions provisions of IRCA. The Reagan administration feared that such control and dissemination of personal information by the federal government would result in an invasion of individual privacy. The administration also believed that it would be too costly for the federal government to convert the Social Security card into a secure and reliable means to establish the identity of individuals who seek employment. The administration's ideological opposition to the establishment of a credible and effective worker verification system, especially one involving the use of the Social Security card, prevented Congress from developing an enforceable employer-sanctions regime.

Reagan's failure to address the challenges posed by mass immigration was not due to any corrupt intent he may have had to twist and pervert immigration policy to serve his own political interests, as members of Congress have routinely done. Rather, Reagan's failure was due to a gross lack of accurate and reliable information on immigration, which would have made it practically impossible for any president who served in office during the 1980s to develop a sound and lasting immigration policy; and by his own ideological aversion to big government, which prevented him from taking the practical steps necessary to make the employer-sanctions provisions of IRCA effective and workable. Clinton has had access to far more accurate and reliable information on immigration, and is in a substantially better position to confront this issue than Reagan was. Moreover, Clinton is better equipped ideologically than Reagan to confront the failures of employer sanctions, since the forty-second president lacks the philosophical aversion to big government which impeded the ability of his predecessor to effectively address this issue. This makes Clinton's own failures to confront the economic challenges posed by mass immigration to be stronger evidence of a dereliction of presidential duty than was the case with Reagan.

Indeed, the fact that Clinton's immigration policy may have been influenced by the substantial financial contributions to the Democratic National Committee which the Asian-American community made during the 1996 presidential campaign only heightens suspicion that the president was motivated by the need to protect his political interests. This is especially true given the fact that Clinton has access to sufficient information to develop a sound and viable immigration policy, a luxury Reagan never enjoyed. The fact that Reagan, in contrast to Clinton, was well-intended in his response to the economic challenges posed by mass immigration leads us to have a positive view of the fortieth president, despite his failures on this issue. Indeed, it is difficult to sustain censure of a president who was motivated to do what is in the best national interest, however failed his policies may have been.

This book is almost entirely based upon research I conducted at the Ronald Reagan Presidential Library in Simi Valley, California. All presidential records cited in this book were opened to the public pursuant to the Freedom of Information Act and the Presidential Records Act of 1978. This book is based upon research into two major holdings at the Reagan Library: the first, pertaining to the President's Task Force on Immigration and Refugee Policy, containing 6,600 pages of documents; and the second, relating to the congressional passage and presidential signing of IRCA, containing 2,110 pages of documents.

The Presidential Records Act of 1978 makes all official White House records, beginning on January 20, 1981, the day Reagan was inaugurated as Chief Executive, the property of the federal government. Those White House records, existing at the Ronald Reagan Presidential Library, consist of two different types of holdings: the official files of over 600 individuals who served on Reagan's White House staff and the files of the White House Records of Office and Management (WHORM). WHORM files are organized either in alphabetical order (Alpha File) or according to subject (Subject File). The WHORM Subject File consists of fifty-eight different subject categories.

Research for this book was mostly limited to the files of a single member of Reagan's White House staff—Francis S. M. Hodsoll. The Hodsoll files contain an extensive record of the President's Task Force, established on March 6, 1981. In addition, research for this book was based upon a review of a single WHORM Subject File, pertaining to immigration, which is cited in the notes listed at the end of this book under the abreviation IM.

This is the second consecutive book I have written which is based upon research conducted at the Ronald Reagan Presidential Library. As has been the case in the past, my research benefited from the generous and unfailing assistance I received from the excellent archival staff at the Reagan Library. I would like to extend my appreciation to the following archivists, who assisted me in the location of files which are the subject for research of this book, and supervised my review and photocopying of over 1,000 pages of presidential records: David Bridge, Michael Duggan, and Catherine Sewell. Each of those archivists spent several hours with me providing their invaluable assistance on the several research trips I made to the Reagan Library. Needless to say, this book could not have been written without their assistance, for which I am very grateful. I would also like to extend a special word of thanks to Lisa Vitt, an archivist at the Reagan Library, for having located and photocopied for me fifty-five pages of presidential records pertaining to IRCA, which were opened just prior to my completion of this book.

In addition to the invaluable assistance I received from the fine archival staff at the Ronald Reagan Presidential Library, I wish to acknowlege the debt of gratitude I owe to other individuals, without whose support this book could not have been published. I am especially grateful to James T. Sabin, the senior acquisitions editor at Greenwood Publishing Group, who granted his expeditious attention and approval to this manuscript when I first submitted it to him for consideration. This is the second consecutive book I have written under the editorial guidance and supervision of Dr. Sabin, and I have consistently found the opportunity to work with him to be an extremely rewarding and enjoyable experience. I would also like to thank John Donohue, the production editor for this book. This is my second consecutive book which Mr. Donohue has produced, and its completion was made that much easier by the unique combination of professionalism and personableness which he brings to his job.

I am especially grateful to my mother, Nadia Laham, my aunt, Laure Abu-Haydar, and my sister, Martha Laham, for the moral and financial support they provided me during the course of writing this book. It could not have been written without the patience and understanding my family provided me, and I hope it proves worthy of their support.

Chapter 1

The Assumptions Influencing the Development of the Reagan Administration's Immigration Policy

During the 1980s. . . . the movement to a much more expansive immigration
policy, stymied for so long, occurred with remarkable speed.[1]
—Peter H. Schuck, professor, Yale Law School

Immigration reform represented, at best, only a marginal priority on Reagan's
agenda when he entered the White House on January 20, 1981. Rather, Reagan's
two most pressing priorities when he was inaugurated as president were to restore noninflationary economic growth while rebuidling America's shattered defenses. Reagan entered the White House at a time when the United States was
suffering an economic and military decline. The Carter years had been marked
by an economic malaise, involving a particularly virulent combination of low
levels of economic growth and high rates of inflation. The defense posture of
the United States had been adversely affected by a precipitous decline in American military power and prestige which followed the American defeat in the
Vietnam War. Given the severe erosion in American economic and military
power during the Carter administration, it is understandable that the economy
and defense represented the two most pressing issues which confronted Reagan
when he entered the White House.

However, Reagan could not escape the issue of immigration reform when he
assumed the presidency. In 1965, Congress passed the Immigration Act, designed to dismantle the discriminatory barriers which prevented all but a token
number of non-Europeans, born in the Eastern Hemisphere, from immigrating
to the United States. However, the bill had the unintended effect of unleashing
a wave of immigration, both legal and illegal, to the United States. By the late
1970s, immigration policy had fallen into complete disarray. Legal immigration

had risen to excessive and unsustainable levels. In the meantime, federal immigration law was being flouted and flagrantly abused as a result of the massive and unprecedented levels of illegal immigration to the United States since 1965.[2]

SCIRP ISSUES ITS RECOMMENDATIONS ON IMMIGRATION REFORM

With immigration policy falling into increasing disrepair, in 1978 Congress passed amendments to the Immigration Act of 1965, which, among other things, established the Select Commission on Immigration and Refugee Policy (SCIRP).[3] The bill required President Jimmy Carter to appoint sixteen individuals to serve as members of SCIRP, four of whom must be the attorney general and the secretaries of Health and Human Services, Labor, and State, respectively.[4]

On March 1, 1981, SCIRP issued its final report, which recommended reforms in legal immigration, and measures to deter further illegal immigration to the United States. As the chairman of SCIRP, the Reverend Theodore M. Hesburgh, president of the University of Notre Dame, put it, the purpose of the report was "to bring illegal immigration under control, while setting up a rational system for legal immigration." The members of SCIRP strongly supported the high levels of legal immigration established under the Immigration Act of 1965. As Hesburgh put it, "we believe that there are many benefits which immigrants bring to U.S. society." However, Hesburgh also noted that "we believe that there are limits to the ability of this country to absorb immigrants in much larger numbers effectively."[5] Consistent with their qualified support for mass immigration, the members of SCIRP recommended a moderate increase in the annual number of legal immigrants admitted to the United States.

The Immigration Act of 1965 established a seven-category preference system, which governed the admission of legal immigrants to the United States.[6] A total of 290,000 legal immigrants were admitted annually under the preference system.[7] By a vote of twelve to four, the members of SCIRP recommended that this number be raised to 350,000.

SCIRP also recommended that an additional 100,000 legal immigrants be admitted to the United States during the next five years in order to relieve the backlog of aliens waiting in line to obtain permanent legal residence in the United States.[8] Such a backlog resulted from the fact that the Immigration Act of 1965 imposed a ceiling, which limited the annual number of legal immigrants admitted from any single foreign nation to 20,000.[9] With the number of aliens who desired to immigrate to United States substantially exceeding 20,000 in many foreign nations, a large backlog of foreign-born individuals, waiting for permission to obtain permanent legal residence, had developed.

The Immigration Act of 1965 excludes the immediate family members of American citizens, including their spouses, nonadult children, and parents, from the annual ceiling on legal immigration which the bill imposed; they are admitted to the United States in unlimited numbers.[10] As a result, the bill contained no annual numerical ceiling which limited total legal immigration to the United States. Rather, the ceiling of 290,000 on the number of legal immigrants admitted covered only aliens who entered under the preference system which governed legal immigration to the United States.

Accordingly, the annual levels of legal immigration have substantially exceeded the nominal ceiling of 290,000 which the Immigration Act of 1965 imposed. In fiscal 1981, the year SCIRP issued the final report containing its recommendations on immigration reform, 596,600 legal immigrants were admitted to the United States, more than double the number allowed to do so under the annual ceiling which the bill imposed.[11] By a vote of fifteen to one, members of SCIRP decided to oppose the imposition of an annual numerical ceiling on total legal immigration to the United States. Instead, SCIRP recommended that the immediate family members of American citizens be allowed to continue to immigrate to the United States in unlimited numbers.[12]

Six of the seven preference categories, established under the Immigration Act of 1965, governed the legal immigration of nonrefugee aliens to the United States. Four of those preference categories were reserved for family-based immigrants. Three of the four preference categories were reserved for the single adult children, married children, and siblings of American citizens, respectively. The fourth category was reserved for the spouses and single children of permanent legal residents. Seventy-four percent of the 290,000 visas allotted to legal immigrants admitted under the preference system, which the Immigration Act of 1965 established, were reserved for family-based immigrants.[13]

SCIRP recommended a number of changes in the preference system which governed family-based immigration to the United States. By a vote of fourteen to two, members of SCIRP recommended the removal of single adult children of American citizens from the preference system; instead, they would be admitted to the United States in unlimited numbers. The Immigration Act of 1965 reserved no visas for the grandparents of American citizens. By a vote of thirteen to three, SCIRP recommended that the grandparents of American citizens also be admitted to the United States in unlimited numbers. Finally, SCIRP recommended that the other preference categories for family-based immigrants, established under the Immigration Act of 1965, be retained; and that a new category be added for the elderly parents of permanent legal residents, who have no children residing outside the United States.[14]

In addition to the four preference categories reserved for family-based immigrants, the Immigration Act of 1965 established two preference categories for employment-based immigrants: the first was reserved for professionals, scientists, and artists of exceptional ability; and the second for skilled and unskilled workers, who could fill domestic labor shortages existing in the United States. Twenty percent of the 290,000 visas allotted annually under the Immigration Act of 1965 would be reserved for legal immigrants who fall into either one of those two categories.[15]

SCIRP recommended that employment-based immigration be replaced by a new system of independent immigration. Two preference categories for independent immigrants would be created: one for those with exeptional qualifications and another for certain investors. A third preference category would be created for independent immigrants who neither possess exceptional qualifications nor have assets to invest in the United States. An unspecified annual number of visas would be allotted to independent immigrants.[16]

In addition to recommending a modest increase in levels of legal immigration, SCIRP also proposed measures to address the problem of illegal immigration. Aliens reside in the United States illegally primarily through two means: they either enter the United States without inspection or they arrive in this nation legally, but subsequently violate the terms of their visas, either by remaining in this nation beyond the authorized time limit or violating the terms of their visas by taking a job when they lack authorization to work in this nation. In 1995, 60 percent of all aliens who resided in the United States illegally entered this nation without inspection, with the remaining 40 percent having arrived in this nation legally, but subsequently violated the terms of their visas.[17]

Practically all illegal aliens who enter the United States without inspection do so by crossing the Mexican border. In fiscal 1981, the year SCIRP issued its recommendations on immigration reform, 975,789 illegal aliens were apprehended by the Immigration and Naturalization Service (INS), which is responsible for the enforcement of federal immigration law.[18] Ninety to 95 percent of all illegal aliens apprehended by the INS annually are Mexicans physically caught either crossing, or in close proximity to, the American border.[19]

To curtail the flow of illegal immigration across the Mexican border, members of SCIRP unanimously voted, with only one abstention, to beef up the Border Patrol. However, the members recognized that beefing up the Border Patrol by itself could not effectively curtail the flow of illegal immigration to the United States. Rather, aliens immigrate to the United States illegally primarily in search of employment. Jobs in the United States are particularly attractive to immigrants, both because employment opportunities in this nation substantially exceed those of developing nations, which serve as the primary sources of illegal immigration, and because wages in this nation are many times greater than they are in Third World countries. As a result, aliens, who do not qualify to immigrate to the United States legally, have every incentive to do so illegally in order to obtain employment, which can provide them with a substantially higher standard of living than they are capable of attaining in their native nations.

To deter further illegal immigration, aliens must be deprived of incentives to reside in the United States illegally. Since jobs are the primary magnet drawing illegal immigration to the United States, aliens will only be deprived of such incentives when they are denied employment. To deprive illegal aliens of jobs, members of SCIRP, by a vote of fourteen to two, recommended that Congress pass legislation prohibiting employers from knowingly hiring illegal aliens. The legislation would require employers to solicit documents from individuals whom they wish to hire which verify their eligibility to work in the United States. Only individuals who presented such documents would be permitted employment. However, members of SCIRP fully recognized the ability of illegal aliens to circumvent employer sanctions, in illegally obtaining jobs, by presenting their employers fraudulent documents which falsely purport to verify their eligibility to work in the United States.

To enable employers to detect and crack down on document fraud, members of SCIRP recommended that employers use a reliable method of identification to verify the eligibility of individuals. However, the members could not agree on the precise method of identification employers should use. By a vote of nine to seven, the members recommended that employers use existing documents to verify the eligibility of individuals. By another vote of eight to seven, with one abstention, the members recommended that the federal government develop a more secure worker verification system as an alternative to employer solicitation and inspection of existing documents in order to enable firms to comply with their legal obligations under employer sanctions legislation. Members of SCIRP were unable to define the specific worker verification system they wanted Congress to establish; and the commission remained equally divided concerning even the vaguely defined worker verification proposals which a slim majority of its members recommended.[20]

Deterring further illegal immigration represented only half the problem of illegal immigration. The other half of the problem concerned what to do with the millions of illegal aliens who resided in the United States. In 1980, the year before SCIRP issued its recommendations on immigration reform, the Urban Institute estimated that between 2.5 million and 3.5 million illegal aliens resided in the United States.[21] Members of SCIRP believed that it was neither politically practical nor morally acceptable to engage in the mass deportation of those illegal aliens to their native nations. Rather, many, if not most, of those illegal aliens had demonstrated their capacity to become productive, law-abiding American citizens through their years of residence in the United States.

As a result, members of SCIRP believed that the only practical and humane solution to the problem of the millions of illegal aliens who resided in the United States was to grant amnesty to those undocumented individuals who had demonstrated their capability to become productive, law-abiding American citizens. To this end, the members unanimously recommended the granting of amnesty to illegal aliens who had resided in the United States since prior to January 1, 1980, and had lived in this nation continuously for a minimum period to be determined by Congress.[22]

REAGAN ESTABLISHES THE PRESIDENT'S TASK FORCE ON IMMIGRATION AND REFUGEE POLICY

The release of SCIRP's final report, containing its recommendations on immigration reform, forced Reagan to shift his attention to the issue of immigration reform. Members of Congress were sure to respond to the report by attempting to pass legislation implementing SCIRP's recommendations. Since the president is responsible for the enforcement of federal immigration law, he must play a role, at least equal to that of Congress, in the development of immigration policy. A strong president cannot allow Congress to dictate the federal laws he must enforce, without participating in the development of those laws. This is no less true on immigration than it is on any other issue governed by federal law.

Reagan was determined to be a major player in the development of immigration reform legislation, which was sure to arise from SCIRP's recommendations. To this end, on March 6, 1981, just five days after SCIRP released its final report, Reagan sent a memo to eight cabinet members, the director of the Office of Management and Budget (OMB), and the director of the Federal Emergency Management Agency (FEMA) announcing that he was appointing them to serve as members of the newly established President's Task Force on Immigration and Refugee Policy. Reagan directed the Task Force to conduct a thorough and comprehensive review of immigration policy in order to present recommendations on immigration reform to him, which he would consider proposing to Congress. Reagan appointed Attorney General William French Smith to serve as chairman of the Task Force. Reagan also sent his memo to Francis S. M. Hodsoll, Deputy Assistant to the President and Deputy to the Chief of Staff, informing him that he would represent the White House as a member of the Task Force.

In his memo, Reagan stated:

The Task Force should review the entire range of immigration and refugee policies and programs and report to me by the first week of May with recommendations or alternatives on the basis of which we can make progress. The Task Force's work should include consideration of new international approaches, the adequacy of the U.S. legal framework, and improved methods for the control of illegal immigration and the handling of mass asylum or immigration crises. I have separately asked our White House staff and OMB to look at the question of Executive Branch organization to deal with these problems.

Please give the Attorney General your cooperation in this effort. Our review will require rapid action and close cooperation with Congress.[23]

THE KEY ASSUMPTIONS GOVERNING THE REAGAN ADMINISTRATION IN ITS DEVELOPMENT OF IMMIGRATION POLICY

The President's Task Force on Immigration and Refugee Policy conducted a four-month review of immigration policy before presenting its recommendations to Reagan on July 1, 1981. Responding to those recommendations, on July 30 the Justice Department, Reagan, and Smith issued separate statements, respectively, which defined the administration's immigration policy. In developing its immigration policy, the Reagan administration operated within the prevailing consensus on this issue, existing since the late 1970s, which differentiates between legal and illegal immigration: viewing legal immigration as good, and illegal immigration as bad.

Congress has generally supported the high levels of legal immigration existing since 1965. The Reagan administration shared Congress's support for mass legal immigration. By contrast, Congress has strongly opposed illegal immigration, viewing it as an abuse of federal immigration law, and a subversion of America's sovereign right to control its borders and determine the criteria in which aliens are to be lawfully admitted to the United States. Once again, the Reagan administration joined Congress in its opposition to illegal immigration.

The political consensus, which the Reagan administration and Congress shared in support of the high levels of legal immigration, was based upon the widely held view among the experts that mass immigration is economically beneficial to the United States.[24] It was widely recognized, as early as the late 1970s, that the bulk of the immigrant population, who had entered the United States since 1965, was composed of poorly educated and unskilled individuals. Income is largely derived from the education and skills possessed by each worker; the greater the amount of education and skills, the higher the income each worker tends to earn. This has been especially true since the early 1970s, as the United States has made the transition from an economy based upon the production of goods to one dependent upon the dissemination of information. The newly emergent information-based economy demands a labor force with substantially greater education and skills than the old industrial economy.[25] Accordingly, given their generally low levels of education and skills, post-1965 immigrants might have been expected to fare poorly in America's newly emergent information-based economy.

However, experts on the economics of immigration generally believed that post-1965 immigrants would do well economically, despite their generally low levels of education and skills. The assumption was that immigrants represent hard-working, enterprising individuals who contribute to the American economy. Given their industriousness, even the poorest immigrants enjoy a high rate of economic assimilation: that is, though they may begin life in the United States at the very bottom of the economic ladder, immigrants, through their hard work and entrepreneurship, achieve rapid upward socioeconomic mobility. As a result, immigrants tend to overtake native-born Americans, in terms of income, after residing in the United States for less than a generation.

A primary exponent of the view that immigrants enjoy a high rate of economic assimilation was Barry R. Chiswick, a prominent expert on the economics of immigration. In a highly influential study of the economics of immigration, published in 1978, Chiswick declared unequivocally that immigrants were achieving unparalleled economic success in the United States: "Immigrants start with earnings about 17 percent below that of natives, but after 10–15 years working in the U.S. they tend to 'overtake' the average wage level and thereafter rise above the average wage."[26]

The prevailing consensus that mass immigration is economically beneficial to the United States was fully embraced by the Reagan administration. In its 1985 annual Economic Report of the President, the Council of Economic Advisers (CEA) extolled the economic benefits of mass immigration.

On the whole, international migrants appear to pay their own way from a public finance standpoint. Most come to the United States to work, and government benefits do not appear to be a major attraction. Some immigrants arrive with fairly high educational levels, and their training imposes no substantial costs on the public. Their rising levels of income produce a rising stream of tax payments to all levels of government. Their initial dependence on welfare benefits is usually limited, and they finance their participation in Social Security retirement benefits with years of contributions.[27]

THE REAGAN ADMINISTRATION'S ASSUMPTIONS ON IMMIGRATION COME UNDER CHALLENGE

However, since the CEA made its ringing declaration in 1985, which affirmed the economic benefits of mass immigration, each of its three major assumptions regarding the economic value of mass immigration—that immigrants experience rising levels of income; pay their own way, in terms of their fiscal impact upon the government; and do not impose substantial financial burdens upon the welfare system—have come under sharp challenge. The view that immigrants experience rising incomes has been challenged by George J. Borjas, perhaps America's preeminent expert on the economics of immigration. In an article published in 1994, Borjas found that the average income of nonelderly male immigrants has declined substantially, in relation to their native-born counterparts.

Using census data, Borjas found that in 1970 the average income of nonelderly male immigrants actually exceeded that of their native-born American counterparts by 0.9 percent. However, since 1970, the average income of immigrants has deteriorated substantially, falling well below that of native-born Americans. The average income of nonelderly male immigrants was 9.2 percent less than that of their native-born American counterparts in 1980, and 15.2 percent less in 1990.

The decline in the average income of immigrants is due to the fact that more recent immigrants earn substantially lower wages than their earlier counterparts. The average income of nonelderly male immigrants, who entered the United States during the previous five years, was 16.6 percent lower than their native-born counterparts in 1970, 27.6 percent lower in 1980, and 31.7 percent lower in 1990. The average income of newly arrived immigrants is so low that Borjas concludes, ''It is extremely unlikely that the earnings of recent cohorts will ever reach parity (let alone overtake) the earnings of American-born workers.''[28] Borjas notes that ''The process of economic assimilation [for immigrants] takes place mainly in the first two decades after arrival [in the United States] and narrows the wage gap by about 10 percentage points. This rate of assimilation allowed earlier immigrants, for whom the wage gap was less than 20 percent, to almost catch up with natives, but it is not sufficient to permit recent immigrants, for whom the wage gap starts at more than 30 percent, to reach economic parity.''[29]

Why has the average income of immigrants, relative to that of native-born Americans, declined substantially since 1970? The answer to this question lies in the ethnic composition of the immigrant population. Prior to 1965, the immigrant population was composed overwhelmingly of Europeans and Canadians, who tend to be well-educated and highly skilled, and earn incomes substantially in excess of those of native-born Americans.

From 1951 through 1960, 66 percent of all legal immigrants admitted to the United States were born in Europe and Canada. Latin America and especially Asia served as only marginal sources of legal immigration to the United States prior to 1965. From 1951 through 1960, only 26 percent of all legal immigrants admitted to the United States were born in Latin America and 6 percent in Asia.[30] The European and Canadian dominance of the pre-1965 immigrant population was due to the national origins quota system, imposed under the Immigration Act of 1924, which limited legal immigration to the United States almost exclusively to Europe and Canada, and prohibited all but a token level of legal immigration from the non-European nations of the Eastern Hemisphere.[31]

The national origins quota system imposed racist criteria governing legal immigration to the United States, which discriminated against citizens of the non-European nations of the Eastern Hemisphere. This was especially true among citizens of the Asian-Pacific Rim. During the late nineteenth and early twentieth centuries, Congress passed legislation which specifically prohibited all legal immigration from China and Japan, and admitted only a token number of Filipinos to the United States.[32]

As a complement to the civil rights laws passed during the 1960s, the Immigration Act of 1965 abolished the national origins quota system, and granted, for the first time in American history, the citizens of all nations an equal opportunity to immigrate to the United States, regardless of race or national origin.[33] This resulted in a flood of legal immigration from Latin America and Asia. Since 1968, Latin America and Asia have emerged as the primary sources of legal immigration to the United States. From 1968 to 1993, 46.7 percent of all legal immigrants admitted to the United States were born in Latin America, and 33.8 percent in Asia. In the meantime, Europe and Canada have been reduced to marginal sources of legal immigration. From 1968 to 1993, only 14.3 percent of all legal immigrants admitted to the United States were born in Europe, and 2.6 percent in Canada.[34]

Much of the legal immigration from Latin America and Asia is from nations with poorly educated and unskilled populations, especially Mexico, Central America, and Indochina. From 1989 to 1993, 21.2 percent of all legal immigrants admitted to the United States were born in only four nations—Mexico, El Salvador, Guatemala, and Vietnam.[35] With legal immigration from Mexico, Central America, and Indochina rising, aliens born in those poor areas of the world are increasingly comprising a dominant segment of the immigrant populations.

As the segment of the immigrant population born in Mexico, Central America, and Indochina has risen, the average income of aliens has declined substantially, relative to that of native-born Americans. With well-educated and highly skilled Europeans and Canadians increasingly being replaced by poorly educated and unskilled Mexicans, Central Americans, and Indochinese, in comprising the dominant segment of the post-1970 immigrant population, it is little wonder that the average income of aliens has declined substantially, relative to that of native-born Americans, during the last three decades. As Kevin F. McCarthy and Georges Vernez put it,

While the average earnings of immigrants have declined over 15 percent between 1970 and 1990, this decline is due to two developments during that period. First, immigrants from Mexico and Central America have markedly increased their share of the total immigrant population, and second, their wages have declined relative to those of native-born workers. The average earnings of all other [immigrant] groups have actually increased relative to those of natives. . . . The one exception to this improvement is the Indochinese refugee population, whose wages continue to lag well behind those of natives.[36]

As their incomes have declined, immigrants have become increasingly dependent upon the welfare system. The prevailing consensus among experts on the economics of immigration during the 1980s was that immigrants were less prone to use welfare benefits than native-born Americans.[37] However, like the notion concerning the economic success of immigrants, this assumption has also been challenged by Borjas. To be sure, immigrants were less prone to use welfare benefits than native-born Americans as late as 1970. This reflected the fact that, as late as 1970, the average income of immigrants exceeded that of native-born Americans.

However, in an article published in 1997, Borjas uses census data to measure the welfare participation rates between immigrant and native-born American households. A household was classified as immigrant if its head was born in a foreign nation, and native if its head was born in the United States. The welfare participation rate was defined as the share of households which used at least one of three means-tested income transfer programs—Aid to Families with Dependent Children, Supplemental Security Income (SSI), and general assistance.

In 1970 the welfare participation rate among immigrant households was 5.9 percent, compared with 6 percent for native-born American families. However, the welfare participation rate among immigrant households has risen substantially since 1970, exceeding that of native-born American families, consistent with the significant decline in the average income of aliens which has occurred during the last three decades. In 1980 the welfare participation rate among immigrant households was 8.7 percent, compared to 7.9 percent for native-born American families. In 1990 the welfare participation rate was 9.1 percent among immigrant households, compared to 7.4 percent for native-born American families.[38]

The welfare participation rate is limited to measuring the use of means-tested income transfer programs. Analyzing the use of all means-tested entitlement programs, including noncash transfers, Borjas finds that a substantially higher share of immigrants use welfare benefits than native-born Americans. Utilizing data from the 1990–1991 Survey of Income and Program Participation (SIPP), Borjas finds that 26.1 percent of immigrant households used at least one means-tested entitlement program, compared to 16.3 percent of native-born American families.[39] Immigrant households comprised 8.8 percent of the population of the United States, but accounted for 13.8 spending on means-tested entitlement programs.[40]

As the Reagan administration was proclaiming in 1985 that immigrants were achieving rising levels of incomes, and were imposing only a modest financial burden upon the welfare system, the opposite was in fact true; since 1970, immigrants have experienced a substantial decline in income, relative to native-born Americans, and have become increasingly dependent upon the welfare system. The third argument, which the administration made in support of mass immigration, was that aliens pay their own way in terms of the fiscal impact they have upon the government. This argument remains unproven.

During the 1990s, experts on the economics of immigration undertook substantial research to determine the fiscal impact of mass immigration upon the United States. No consensus among the experts has been reached thus far. Estimates of the net fiscal impact of mass immigration, measured in terms of the taxes paid by immigrants and the cost of providing social services to them, vary substantially, from an annual per-immigrant surplus of $1,400 to a deficit of $1,600. Reliable information concerning the actual use and cost of providing social services to immigrants and the sources and amount of taxes paid by them is simply unavailable, making it impossible to make any conclusive determination concerning the fiscal impact of mass immigration upon the United States.[41]

CHISWICK RECOMMENDS TO REAGAN REFORMS IN IMMIGRATION POLICY

While experts on the economics of immigration generally believed during the 1980s that mass immigration was economically beneficial to the United States, they were not unequivocal in their support of this view. Indeed, even some experts who held this view believed that mass immigration would produce negative economic consequences. One such expert was Barry R. Chiswick. It was

Chiswick's 1978 pioneering study affirming the high rate of economic assimilation among immigrants which helped shape the consensus among the experts during the 1980s that mass immigration is economically beneficial to the United States.[42]

However, unlike other immigration enthusiasts within the economics profession, Chiswick was not an uncritical supporter of the open and liberal immigration policy pursued since 1965. Rather, Chiswick believed that the mass immigration existing since 1965 had negative economic consequences for the United States. Chiswick's critique of post-1965 mass immigration was contained in a paper entitled "Guidelines for the Reform of Immigration Policy," released on April 15, 1981 under the auspices of the American Enterprise Institute. Chiswick sent a copy of his paper to Reagan upon its release.

The paper challenged the prevailing tendency to view immigrants monolithically when attempting to measure their economic performance. Rather, Chiswick argued that immigrants should be divided into two categories for the purposes of economic analysis: family-based and employment-based immigrants. Family-based immigrants are those who have been admitted to the United States to be reunited with family members who reside in this nation legally. Employment-based immigrants are those who have been admitted to the United States primarily because they possess skills in critical demand. As we have seen, the Immigration Act of 1965 made family reunification the cornerstone of immigration policy. Practically three-quarters of all visas allocated under the preference categories, which the bill established, were reserved for family reunification, and only one-fifth of all visas were earmarked for employment.[43]

The overwhelming majority of legal aliens who have immigrated to the United States since 1965 have done so to be reunited with family members who reside in this nation. Only a small fraction of post-1965 legal immigrants have been admitted to the United States as a result of skills they possess which are in critical demand. From 1965 to 1994, 58 percent of all legal aliens admitted to the United States were family-based immigrants, and only 12 percent were skill-based immigrants.

The preference categories reserved for skill-based immigrants include both skill-based immigrants and their family members. Family members of skill-based immigrants are admitted to the United States not on the basis of any skills which they possess, but on their desire to accompany their skilled relatives to this nation. As a result, many, if not most, of the legal aliens who have been admitted to the United States under the preference categories reserved for skill-based immigrants are actually family-based immigrants. Accordingly, the share of all legal aliens who have been admitted to the United States as skill-based immigrants since 1965 is less than 12 percent.[44]

Family-based immigrants are admitted to the United States without regard to their education and skills, and most such immigrants tend to be poorly educated and unskilled. By contrast, most employment-based immigrants are admitted to the United States because they are highly educated and possess skills which are in critical demand. It is a well-established economic fact that income is largely linked to the possession of education and skills; the greater the education and skills a worker possesses, the higher his or her income tends to be, and vice versa. Employment-based immigrants tend to have substantially higher levels of education and skills than family-based immigrants. As a result, the incomes of employment-based immigrants tend to be substantially higher than those of family-based immigrants.

Chiswick argued that mass immigration has had negative economic consequences, since it has resulted in a massive influx of poorly educated, unskilled foreign-born workers who enter the labor market to compete against native-born Americans with similar human capital endowments. The surplus in low-skilled labor arising from mass immigration has resulted in wage depression among low-skilled workers. Employers of low-wage labor have profited from the wage depression resulting from mass immigration. This results in a transfer of income from low-wage workers to their employers, which leads to greater inequality in the distribution of income. Unable to earn a decent income, low-wage workers have become more heavily dependent upon the welfare system. Accordingly, Chiswick concluded that the mass immigration of poorly educated, unskilled, low-wage foreign-born workers to the United States has aggravated the plight of the working poor, worsened the inequality in the distribution of income, and imposed increased financial burdens upon the welfare system. As a result, comprehensive immigration reform is in order.

Chiswick recommended that Congress eliminate family reunification as the cornerstone of immigration policy and restrict family-based immigration to the immediate family members of American citizens. As an alternative to family reunification, Congress should limit legal immigration to the United States only to those aliens who possess the highest levels of education and skills. A skill-based immigration policy would be an improvement over the current family-based immigration policy, insofar as it would result in an immigrant population with substantially higher levels of education and skills, and therefore significantly greater incomes than those which currently exist.

Family-based immigrants are admitted to the United States regardless of how little education and skills they possess. By linking immigration to family reunification, the Immigration Act of 1965 triggered the immigration of a flood of poorly educated and unskilled aliens to the United States. The elimination of family reunification as the cornerstone of federal immigration policy, and the restriction of family-based immigration only to the immediate family members of American citizens, would also substantially reduce the number of poorly educated, unskilled, low-wage foreign-born workers admitted to the United States. This would in turn significantly reduce the existing surplus of low-skilled labor and alleviate the downward pressure on the wages of low-skilled workers. By shoring up the wages of low-skilled workers, a policy which linked immigration to skills and prevented large numbers of unskilled foreign-born workers from immigrating to the United States, the inequality in the distribution of income would be reduced, as would the financial burdens imposed upon the welfare system.

Chiswick attacked the recommendations on immigration reform SCIRP made, which urged an expansion and liberalization of family-based immigration. Chiswick argued that SCIRP's recommendations would only exacerbate the socioeconomic dislocations which the massive influx of poorly educated, unskilled, low-wage foreign-born workers has created.[45] On April 27, 1981, Chiswick sent a letter with a copy of his paper to Reagan. In his letter, Chiskwick urged Reagan to recommend the elimination of family reunification as the cornerstone of immigration policy, and link future immigration to the United States to the possession of skills. This recommendation was fully consistent with the findings of Chiswick's study, which argued that the economic benefits of mass immigration to the United States could be optimized by replacing family reunification with the possession of skills as the primary criterion governing legal immigration to the United States.

My study reviews current immigration policy, as well as what is known on the economic progress and economic impact of immigrants. It shows that current policies, and even more so the recommendations of the Select Commission on Immigration and Refugee Policy, are not consistent with your administration's efforts to reduce the size of the income transfer system and promote rapid economic growth. I propose an alternative rationing system that focuses on the skills of visa applicants that is consistent with your administration's domestic policy objectives.[46]

Chiswick's conclusions concerning the downward pressure which mass immigration has exerted upon the wages of native-born low-skilled workers has been confirmed by research conducted during the 1990s. Indeed, the CEA endorsed those conclusions in its 1994 annual Economic Report to the President, which argued that "immigration has increased the relative supply of less-educated labor and appears to have contributed to the increasing inequality of income" in the United States. A 1995 Bureau of Labor Statistics study found that "immigration accounted for approximately 20 to 25 percent of the increase in the wage gap between low- and high-skilled workers during the 1980s in the fifty largest metropolitan areas of the United States," and half the decline in real wages for native-born high school dropouts.[47]

Chiswick's paper represented a sound and reasoned critique of the mass immigration which the Immigration Act of 1965 unleashed. Immigration should serve the national economic interest by improving the quality, productivity, and competitiveness of the American labor force. This requires that immigration be limited only to the best-educated and most highly skilled foreign-born workers, as Chiswick argued. To achieve this result, Congress needs to eliminate family reunification as the cornerstone of immigration policy.

In his letter to Reagan, Chiswick invited the White House to engage in discussion with him on immigration policy: "I welcome any comments you or your staff may have on this paper, and would be willing to discuss immigration policy in greater detail with your staff.''[48] However, there is no evidence that any such discussion took place. In fact, the White House failed to even extend to Chiswick the courtesy of a presidential reply, which many, if not most, correspondents with Reagan received. Chiswick's recommendations on immigration reform fell upon deaf ears at the White House.

CHISWICK FAILS TO MAKE A PERSUASIVE CASE FOR COMPREHENSIVE IMMIGRATION REFORM

The White House certainly needed to consider the critique of immigration policy Chiswick made in his paper. That critique was based upon sound and reasoned arguments concerning the economic harm which family-based immigration has caused. Accordingly, why did the White House ignore Chiswick's paper? The most likely answer is that Chiswick's arguments, though economically sound, were neither politically persuasive nor supported by sufficient empirical evidence.

Chiswick recommended that the Reagan administration propose major reforms in immigration policy which would eliminate family reunification, and replace it with the possession of skills as the primary criterion governing legal immigration to the United States. However, neither of Chiswick's two grounds for reforming immigration policy are politically persuasive.

Chiswick's social case for comprehensive immigration reform rested upon the argument that family-based immigration has had negative socioeconomic consequences, not for American society as a whole, but for one, single, narrow constituency—the working poor. Chiswick based his recommendations for immigration reform largely upon the need to improve the lot of the working poor and reduce the inequality in the distribution of income. However, the Reagan administration was not about to consider any major reforms in immigration policy, such as those which Chiswick recommended, to advance some social agenda: in his case to respond to the economic needs of the working poor, who represent a politically marginal constituency. Rather, the administration could only be expected to consider such reforms on economic grounds, if it could be shown that mass immigration has undermined the national economic interest.

To be sure, Chiswick did advance an economic argument for comprehensive immigration reform to compliment the social case for such action he had made: that a skill-based immigration policy would yield greater economic dividends for the United States than the current family-based immigration policy. However, this argument is insufficient: Chiswick needed to go further than this, and show that mass immigration is, on balance, harmful to the American economy, and has undermined the national economic interest in the most flagrant manner. To prove this, Chiswick needed to show that immigrants are faring poorly, in economic terms, in relation to native-born Americans.

The purpose of any rational and credible immigration policy, which serves the national economic interest, is to admit only well-educated foreign-born workers, who can provide the critical skills necessary to improve the productivity of the labor force and maintain the competitiveness of the United States in the global market.

Accordingly, the key to determining whether immigration policy serves the national economic interest is to analyze the data measuring the average income of immigrants in relation to native-born Americans. If the data shows immigrants to have a higher average income than native-born Americans, then this is a good indicator that immigration policy is serving the national economic interest. If the data shows the opposite, then the reverse conclusion concerning immigration policy is the case.

To demonstrate that family-based immigration is not serving the national economic interest, and to make an effective case for comprehensive immigration reform, Chiswick needed to present data which showed that the average income of immigrants was lagging behind that of native-born Americans. However, Chiswick never showed this, because empirical evidence to this effect did not exist in 1981, when his paper was written. To be sure, such evidence now exists, as a result of the pioneering work on the economic consequences of mass immigration which Borjas undertook during the 1990s. However, this evidence is based upon rigorous and systematic analysis of the 1980 and 1990 census data, which Chiswick could obviously not have undertaken when he wrote his paper in 1981.

Indeed, in the paper he presented to Reagan, Chiswick never challenged the argument made in his highly influential 1978 study, which claimed that immigrants enjoy a high rate of economic assimilation. Chiswick simply did not have access to the data, based upon the adverse economic experience which immigrants have confronted since 1970, to defend his argument that comprehensive immigration reform was needed.

Rather, Chiswick only shows that employment-based immigrants, due to their generally higher levels of education and skills, are faring better economically than family-based immigrants. However, for mass immigration to be placed into serious question, Chiswick needed to show that family-based immigrants are faring poorly, in relation not just to employment-based immigrants, but to native-born Americans as well. Employment-based immigrants can be expected to fare, in economic terms, far better than native-born Americans, let alone family-based immigrants. To say, as Chiswick did, that employer-based immigrants fare better economically than family-based immigrants is to express the obvious.

One prominent expert on the economics of immigration, Vernon M. Briggs, Jr., has shown how family-based immigration has undermined the national economic interest. In his pioneering 1996 book on the economic consequences of mass immigration, Briggs notes that ''The evidence clearly shows that the jobs that are increasing in number are those with the highest educational and skill requirements, while jobs that are declining are overwhelmingly those that require the least in terms of human-capital endowment. . . . In this economic environment, an immigration policy designed to admit a flexible number of highly-skilled and educated workers is what is required."[49]

At a time when the American economy is increasingly demanding a well-educated and highly skilled labor force, federal immigration law is permitting a massive influx of poorly educated and unskilled aliens to the United States. In 1990, 26 percent of immigrants aged 25 or older had less than nine years of education, compared to only 9 percent of their native-born American counterparts.[50] In 1996, 36 percent of immigrants aged 25 or older lacked a high school diploma, compared to only 16 percent of their native-born American counterparts.

To be sure, the share of immigrants with bachelor's and graduate degrees is almost identical to that of native-born Americans. In 1996, 16 percent of immigrants aged 25 or older had a bachelor's degree, compared to 15 percent of their native-born American counterparts. Eight percent of immigrants aged 25 or older had a graudate degree, compared to 9 percent of their native-born American counterparts.[51] However, despite the fact that many immigrants are well-educated, the overwhelming majority of aliens are not. As the data presented shows, in 1996, 84 percent of immigrants aged 25 or older had a high school diploma or less, and were qualified only for the rapidly diminishing number of jobs which require such low levels of education.

As a result, family-based immigration has undermined the national economic interest, insofar as it has resulted in a massive influx of poorly educated and unskilled foreign-born workers, at a time when the supply of jobs available to them is rapidly shrinking. As Briggs puts it, "Just at the time when every labor market indicator shows that the nation needs a more highly-skilled and better-educated labor force, its immigration policy is pouring largely numbers of un-skilled, poorly-educated workers with limited English-speaking ability into the central cities of many of its major urban labor markets. The perpetuation of such an incongruence cannot possibly be in the national interest."[52]

Briggs notes that the massive influx of poorly educated and unskilled foreign-born workers is the result of a policy which links immigration to family re-unification, and admits immigrants to be reunited with family members, who reside in the United States legally, without regard to their levels of education and skills. With family reunification, rather than the possession of skills serving as the cornerstone of immigration policy under the Immigration Act of 1965, Briggs charges that "nepotism . . . became the driving force of the legal admissions system. Moreover, whatever human-capital characteristics the vast majority of legal immigrants possessed at the time of their entry is purely incidental to the reason why they were admitted."[53]

To assure that immigration policy serves the national economic interest, Briggs, like Chiswick, recommended the elimination of family reunification and its replacement with the possession of skills as the primary criterion governing legal immigration to the United States. As Briggs puts it, "Legal entry should be restricted to skilled and educated immigrants, because the United States has an abundance of unskilled and poorly prepared would-be workers. . . . Already having an abundance of unskilled and poorly-educated adults, the last thing the nation needs is to continue to allow unskilled and poorly-educated persons to continue to immigrate to the United States.''[54]

Had Chiswick made the same kind of argument in support of a skill-based immigration policy that Briggs advanced over a decade later, the White House would have been expected to take his paper more seriously. However, Briggs's argument is based upon data taken from 1978 to 1990, which clearly shows a dramatic shift in the labor market from low- to high-skill jobs. This data, published in 1991, was obviously unavailable to Chiswick a decade earlier, when he sent his paper to Reagan.[55] Such a finding was essential if Chiswick was to support his argument that far-reaching reforms in immigration policy were in order. The data showing the negative economic consequences of mass immigration has become clear during the 1990s; and Briggs has effectively used this data to support Chiswick's argument that family reunification should be replaced with the possession of skills as the primary criterion governing immigration to the United States.

During the Reagan administration, the prevailing consensus among experts on the economics of immigration was that mass immigration is economically beneficial to the United States. Leading this consensus was Chiswick himself, whose influential 1978 study seemed to prove conclusively that immigrants enjoy a high rate of economic assimilation. By 1981, Chiswick had second thoughts about the economic benefits of mass immigration, as the paper he sent to Reagan illustrates.

However, Chiswick failed to frame his arguments in a politically persuasive manner, and his paper lacked the critical data necessary for him to make an effective case for comprehensive immigration reform. Moreover, the White House was disinclined to reconsider its unequivocal support for mass immigration, content in the prevailing consensus that it is economically beneficial to the United States. With Chiswick unable to make a politically persuasive case for comprehensive immigration reform, the data to support this case unavailable, and the White House unwilling to challenge the prevailing consensus that mass immigration is economically beneficial to the United States, the economist's call for a reexamination of immigration policy went unanswered by the Reagan administration. Instead, the White House filed Chiswick's paper away in its archive, never to see the light of day again.

THE POLITICAL OBSTACLES TO COMPREHENSIVE IMMIGRATION REFORM

The only possibility that Congress might seriously consider imposing additional restrictions on family-based immigration is if clear and compelling evidence exists that it has undermined the national economic interest in some fundamental way. Such evidence exists today, due in large part to the pioneering work on this issue which Borjas conducted during the 1990s.

Congress is strongly disinclined to pass comprehensive immigration legislation, due to the powerful political opposition such action is certain to provoke. Indeed, the elimination of family reunification as the primary criterion governing legal immigration is certain to provoke powerful opposition from America's burgeoning immigrant community. Many immigrants wish to be reunited with family members who reside in their native nations. Chiswick's recommendation that family-based immigration be restricted to the immediate family members of American citizens would foreclose the opportunity for citizen immigrants to be reunited with extended family members who reside in their native nations. In addition, Chiswick's recommendation would prohibit permanent legal residents from being reunited with immediate family members, who live in their native nations, until they obtain American citizenship.

The number of immigrants has been rising rapidly since the expansion and liberalization of legal immigration which the Immigration Act of 1965 imposed. The share of the population who are immigrants has risen from 4.7 percent in 1970 to 8.7 percent in 1994.[56] Many immigrants are citizens and have the right to vote. In 1990, 33 percent of all immigrants were citizens.[57] In addition, the American-born children of immigrants are automatically entitled to citizenship under the Fourteenth Amendment, and have the right to vote when they reach the age of eighteen.[58]

To be sure, the share of immigrants who are citizens has increased dramatically in response to the rising political backlash against aliens, which occurred during the 1990s. Immigrants are obtaining citizenship in record numbers for two reasons: first, to defend their political interests in response to this backlash, through the exercise of the right to vote; and second, to gain entitlement to SSI and Food Stamp benefits, which most noncitizen legal immigrants are no longer eligible for as a result of passage of the Personal Responsibility and Work Opportunity Reconciliation Act (PRWORA) of 1996.[59] Strengthened by a rising number of voters, immigrants are more politically powerful and better organized today than they were when Reagan resided in the White House. Nevertheless, citizen immigrants were sufficiently numerous to exercise considerable political clout during the 1980s.

Immigrants who wish to be reunited with family members residing in their native nations would strongly oppose any effort in Congress to impose additional restrictions on family-based immigration. Immigrants and their American-born children are likely to organize and target for defeat any member of Congress who supports legislation to impose such restrictions. Organizations which represent various immigrant ethnic groups have the capacity to mobilize their constituencies to vote against members of Congress who seek to impose such restrictions. Given the fact that immigrants represent a large and growing community, they are sufficiently numerous, when joined with other voting blocs, to retain the potential capacity to defeat House members who represent congressional districts with large alien populations, especially in such states as California, New York, Texas, Florida, New Jersey, and Illinois. Seventy-two percent of all immigrants reside in those six states, which are represented by 39 percent of all House members.[60]

Given the political backlash any effort to impose additional restrictions on family-based immigration is likely to provoke among America's burgeoning immigrant community, members of Congress are highly reluctant to seriously consider instituting such restrictions. This is especially true of members of Congress who represent the six states where nearly three-quarters of the immigrant population resides. As Kenneth K. Lee puts it, "The vast majority of immigrants reside in six states: California, New York, Texas, Florida, New Jersey, and Illinois. And immigrants are further concentrated in certain (mainly urban) areas of those states. So, for example, a Congressman in districts with a high foreign-born population (such as Los Angeles) may feel intense pressure to vote against restrictionist [immigration] legislation, lest he appear nativist and alienate his many foreign-born constituents."[61]

Indeed, legislation to impose additional restrictions on family-based immigration was introduced in both houses of Congress during the 1980s and 1990s. However, while the Senate passed this legislation during the 1980s, the House did not; and the Senate and House rejected similar bills when they were introduced in both houses of the 104th Congress.

The effort to reform legal immigration in Congress during the 1980s was in response to the introduction of the Immigration Reform and Control Act (IRCA), designed to implement the recommendations of SCIRP contained in its final report issued on March 1, 1981. The versions of the IRCA, which the Senate passed in 1982 and 1983, respectively, would have imposed an annual ceiling which limited the total number of nonrefugee immigrants admitted to the United States to 425,000. A separate annual ceiling would have been imposed, which limited the number of family-based immigrants admitted to the United States to 350,000. This would have been accomplished primarily by eliminating the preference category which admits the siblings of American citizens to the United States, and granting priority in the allocation of visas to the immediate family members of American citizens. Any unused visas not claimed by the immediate family members of American citizens would have been allocated to legal aliens admitted to the United States under the remaining preference categories for family-based immigrants.[62]

In addition to the Senate, efforts to reform legal immigration were undertaken in the House during the 1980s. In 1983, Representatives F. James Sensenbrenner, Jr. of Wisconsin and Carlos Moorhead of California introduced amendments to IRCA in the House Judiciary Committee, which would have imposed annual numerical ceilings on total legal immigration to the United States. The Sensenbrenner amendment would have imposed an annual ceiling which limited the total number of legal immigrants admitted to the United States to a range of between 300,000 and 420,000. The Moorhead amendment would have imposed an annual ceiling which limited the number of nonrefugee immigrants admitted to the United States to 450,000.

However, the House Judiciary Committee rejected the Moorhead and Sensenbrenner amendments.[63] To be sure, on June 12, 1984, Moorhead bypassed the committee and introduced his amendment during the debate on IRCA on the House floor. However, the House rejected the amendment by an overwhelming margin of 231 to 168. The House vote on the amendment fell largely along party lines, with most Democrats opposing it and most Republicans supporting it. A total of 185 Democrats opposed the amendment and 111 Republicans supported it. Fifty-seven Democrats crossed party lines to support the amendment; 46 Republicans did the same to oppose it.[64]

The House's rejection of the Moorhead amendment ended all further efforts to include reforms in legal immigration in IRCA. The Democratic majority in the House was completely unwilling to accept any such reforms. In opposing such reforms, House Democrats were responding to the interests of the Latino community. One major interest group representing the Latino community, the Mexican American Legal Defense and Education Fund (MALDEF), made clear its support for the retention of family reunification as the cornerstone of immigration policy, in a statement which its president, Vilma S. Martinez, issued during her appearance before a joint hearing of the immigration subcommittees of the Senate and House, respectively, on May 6, 1981: "Family reunification has for several decades been an underlying theme of American immigration policy. Family reunification is favored so that U.S. citizens and permanent residents need not exile themselves [from] members of their families. . . . This policy is both humane and prudent in knitting the fabric of a stable, orderly society. . . . The Select Commission endorsed the family reunification policy and recommends that it play 'a major and important role in U.S. immigration policy.' . . . We emphatically agree."[65]

It is understandable that MALDEF would support family-based immigration, given the fact that it has allowed many Mexican immigrants who reside in the United States legally to be reunited with their family members living in Mexico. As the leading interest group representing the Mexican-American community, which constitutes the fastest-growing ethnic group in the United States, MALDEF had the political resources, when combined with those of other members of the pro-immigration lobby, to prevent any restrictions in family-based immigration, and may have been in a position to singlehandedly prevent such reforms. As Peter Skerry notes, "With headquarters in San Francisco and regional offices in Los Angeles, San Antonio, Chicago, Denver, and Washington, MALDEF was the only Mexican-American organization with the expertise and resources to wage a national campaign in Congress and the media against immigration restriction."[66]

Indeed, MALDEF had close ties to the liberal wing of the Democratic Party which dominated the House. An overwhelming majority of House members, especially Democrats, did in fact reject the imposition of additional restrictions on family-based immigration, as the vote on the Moorhead amendment clearly shows. The House's steadfast opposition to reforms in family-based immigration, which reflected in part the political power of MALDEF and the rapidly growing Mexican-American community, clearly illustrates the difficulties the Reagan administration would have encountered had it actively attempted to recommend such reforms.

Immigrants, and the interest groups which represent foreign-born Americans, have consistently opposed any effort within Congress to impose additional restrictions on family-based immigration. Responding to pressure from the pro-immigration lobby, members of Congress, especially those philosphically supportive of an open and liberal immigration policy, have refused to grant serious consideration to legislation which imposed such restrictions. Such legislation is sure to provoke a strong political backlash from immigrants, organized immigrant ethnic groups, and pro-immigration members of Congress.

Reagan could not have acted upon Chiswick's recommendation that family reunification be replaced by the possession of skills as the primary criterion governing legal immigration to the United States. Congress would not have seriously considered making such reforms in immigration policy unless Reagan was able to present a clear and compelling case for such action. Chiswick's argument that such reforms are desirable because they would yield greater economic benefits to the United States than current immigration policy is insufficient: He needed to demonstrate that family-based immigration had undermined the national economic interest. Chiswick presented no such argument.

Lacking any strong evidence to question the wisdom of mass immigration, and with Congress unwilling to seriously consider any reforms in immigration policy, Reagan had no political basis to recommend any substantial changes in immigration policy. Reagan would have been politically unwise to have recommended the far-reaching reforms in immigration policy which Chiswick proposed, unless he could present to Congress strong evidence that mass immigration was undermining the national economic interest. Congress needed a persuasive reason to make far-reaching reforms in immigration policy, and the only such reason which could pass political muster was that mass immigration was undermining the national economic interest, making comprehensive immigration reform a political imperative.

Chiswick offered Reagan no evidence that mass immigration represented a threat to the national economic interest. This made it politically irrational for Reagan to have acted upon Chiswick's recommendation that he spearhead a drive to pass comprehensive immigration reform legislation. The pro-immigration lobby remains a potent political force on Capitol Hill which has succeeded in preventing passage of every comprehensive immigration reform bill introduced in Congress since 1981. It would have been a politically daunting task for any president serving in office since that year to overcome the power of the pro-immigration lobby, which is why Reagan and his successors have shunned the pursuit of such a task.

THE DIFFICULTIES CONFRONTING THE REAGAN ADMINISTRATION IN FORMULATING IMMIGRATION POLICY

We can conclude that the Reagan administration's ability to develop a sound and viable immigration policy which reflected the national economic interest was crippled from the very moment the president established his Task Force on Immigration and Refugee Policy on March 6, 1981. To be sure, the inability of the administration to develop such an immigration policy was not due to any lack of genuine intent to serve the national economic interest. No evidence exists among the voluminous documents on the Reagan administration's conduct of immigration policy to suggest that the president was motivated by anything other than a desire to address this issue in a manner consistent with the national economic interest. However, to achieve this objective the administration needed accurate and reliable information concerning the economic consequences of mass immigration. If the economic consequences were positive, then no major change in immigration policy was in order; if they were negative, then major change was warranted.

However, the information which the Reagan administration needed to develop sound and coherent immigration policy was lacking. Instead, the administration accepted without question the consensus prevailing among the experts during the 1980s that mass immigration is economically beneficial to the United States. Indeed, as we will see, the administration generally supported an open and liberal immigration policy. This was based upon studies conducted during the 1980s which affirmed the economic benefits of mass immigration to the United States. A White House document issued on July 9, 1986 noted the existence of a number of such studies.

A study by the Urban Institute covering the period 1970–83 in California concluded that immigrants . . . did not take jobs or depress wages of Americans and . . . did not cause an excessive burden on the infrastructure or social services of the area. Another recent study by the RAND Corporation showed that immigrants provided an economic boost to California. Another study conducted in Texas during 1982–83 determined that tax revenues received from illegal immigrants by state government exceed the cost of public services provided to them.[67]

We now know that many of the claims concerning the economic benefits of mass immigration to the United States are simply not true. Indeed, the information which has developed since Reagan left the White House clearly disputes the widely held belief that immigrants are enjoying rising levels of income and low rates of welfare participation. While this was the case prior to 1970, it has not been true since.

Indeed, as the pioneering work by Borjas clearly shows, the average income of immigrants, relative to that of native-born Americans, has declined substantially since 1970. As a result, welfare participation among immigrant households has been rising more rapidly than among native-born American families since 1970. Moreover, the Reagan administration, without any empirical evidence, assumed that mass immigration was having a positive fiscal impact upon the United States. The empirical evidence developed since Reagan departed from the White House leaves that argument open to question; the information needed to answer this question is simply unavailable.

This does not mean that the Reagan administration bears no responsibility for its failure to develop a sound and viable immigration policy. Even as early as 1981, the administration had reason to be concerned about the wisdom of continuing the mass immigration existing since 1965, as Chiswick's paper clearly shows. The administration had legitimate grounds to be wary of making family reunification the cornerstone of immigration policy, for the reasons spelled out in Chiswick's paper.

In addition to the political obstacles to comprehensive immigration reform, the Reagan administration based its immigration policy on either mistaken or unproven assumptions, which saw mass immigration as economically beneficial to the United States. This led the administration to reject granting any serious consideration to reforming legal immigration. The administration recommended no reduction in the high levels of legal immigration existing since 1965, and no elimination of family reunification as the cornerstone of immigration policy.

Given the negative economic consequences of mass immigration, which we now know, the Reagan administration's failure to recommend any reforms in legal immigration was a serious mistake. Such reforms are clearly in order, as Briggs's arguments illustrate. Because of the Reagan administration's failure to recommend such reforms, Congress has been forced to revisit the issue of immigration during the Bush and Clinton presidencies. This is clearly the result of the Reagan administration's failure to adequately address immigration through the recommendations on this issue which the White House ultimately made.

To be sure, Reagan cannot be held responsible for his administration's failures in immigration policy. Those failures were due to factors outside his control, and relate to the substantial lack of information concerning the economic consequences of mass immigration upon the United States. Reagan could not develop a sound and rational immigration policy unless he understood what the economic consequences of mass immigration were. We do know substantially more about the economic consequences of mass immigration than we did during the 1980s, and Clinton has been in a far stronger position to make sound immigration policy than was the case with Reagan.

Indeed, Clinton has had the benefit of the recommendations of the Commission on Immigration Reform (CIR) which Congress established under the Immigration Act of 1990. Congress passed the bill nearly a decade after SCIRP issued its final report in 1981, which contained its recommendations on immigration reform. As a result, Congress believed that the time was ripe to establish yet another commission to take a fresh look at the issue of immigration reform, resulting in its decision to establish the CIR. The Immigration Act of 1990 required President George Bush to appoint the nine members of the CIR.[68]

Substantial information had been gathered on the economic effects of mass immigration between the time SCIRP issued its final report in 1981 and the time the CIR did the same in 1995. As we have seen, the information available during the 1980s suggested that mass immigration is economically beneficial to the United States. Based upon this information, SCIRP explicitly rejected the imposition of any numerical ceiling on total legal immigration, and recommended instead an expansion and liberalization of immigration in its final report in 1981.

However, the information gathered during the 1990s suggested that mass immigration is economically harmful to the United States. This is due to the declining levels of education and skills and lower incomes of more recent immigrants, in relation to their precedessors. Based upon this information, the CIR recommended the adoption of a more restrictive immigration policy in its interim report on legal immigration, issued in 1995.

By a vote of eight to one, the members of the CIR recommended the imposition of an annual numerical ceiling which limited the total number of legal immigrants admitted to the United States to 550,000. Strict limits would be imposed on the annual allocation of visas, reserving 400,000 for family-based immigrants, 100,000 for skill-based immigrants, and 50,000 for refugees. Family-based immigration would be limited only to the immediate family members of American citizens and permanent legal residents, including their spouses, nonadult children, and parents. The preference categories, existing under federal immigration law, which reserved a specified number of visas for the adult children and siblings of American citizens and the single adult children of permanent legal residents, would be eliminated.[69]

In fiscal 1994, the year prior to the CIR's issuance of its interim report on legal immigration, 804,416 aliens immigrated to the United States legally, of whom 463,608 did so to be reunited with family members who resided in this nation.[70] Accordingly, the CIR's recommendations would have resulted in a substantial reduction in levels of legal immigration, with a somewhat more modest cut in the volume of family-based immigration.

The CIR's recommendation that levels of legal and family-based immigration be reduced stands in sharp contrast to SCIRP's earlier proposals for an increase in the volume of legal and family-based immigration. SCIRP's recommendations were consistent with the prevailing consensus among the experts during the 1980s that mass immigration is economically beneficial to the United States. However, as the evidence accumulated that mass immigration is actually economically harmful to the United States, the consensus among the experts changed, from support for an open and liberal immigration policy during the

1980s to backing for a more restrictive immigration policy in the following decade. The CIR's recommendation that Congress adopt a more restrictive immigration policy is fully consistent with that new consensus.

To be sure, strong support for an open and liberal immigration policy continues to exist among some experts on this issue. However, that support is largely limited to two pro-immigration think tanks—the Urban Institute and the Cato Institute.[71] Moreover, the support for an open and liberal immigration policy by those two groups is based more on the ideological orientation of its scholars than on the empirical evidence. The Urban Institute is a liberal think tank, and the Cato Institute a libertarian think tank. The liberal and libertarian communities represent the strongest sources of support for an open and liberal immigration policy: liberals, because they believe the United States has a moral obligation to provide the poor of the world an opportunity to immigrate to this nation in search of a better life; and libertarians, because they are philosophically committed to maintaining an open border with the rest of the world. However, reputable experts on the economics of immigration, such as Borjas and Briggs, who base their judgments on the empirical evidence rather than their ideological leanings, tend to conclude that mass immigration has been economically harmful to the United States.[72] That consensus among the reputable experts on the economics of immigration prevails, despite the pro-immigration views of more ideologically motivated, and less scholastically inclined, think tanks such as the Urban and Cato Institutes.

In 1995, Alan K. Simpson of Wyoming and Lamar Smith of Texas, who served as chairmen of the immigration subcommittees of the Senate and House, respectively, introduced legislation to implement the CIR's recommendations. The Simpson and Smith bills would have imposed separate annual numerical ceilings on legal and family-based immigration, respectively. Family-based immigration would have been restricted to the spouses, nonadult children, and parents of American citizens and the spouses and nonadult children of permanent legal residents. This would have resulted in the elimination of several preference categories for family-based immigrants, including the adult children and siblings of American citizens and the single adult children of permanent legal residents.[73]

IMMIGRATION POLICY AND INTEREST-GROUP POLITICS

President Bill Clinton initially endorsed the CIR's recommendations on legal immigration, declaring that they ''were consistent with [his] own views'' on this issue. On February 11, 1996, Clinton reiterated his support for ''lowering the level of legal immigration.'' However, eight days after Clinton made those remarks, he attended a fund-raising event sponsored by Asian Americans, in which he raised over $1.1 million in campaign contributions for the Democratic National Committee. According to the Boston Globe, in a memo which he sent to Clinton following the event, John Huang, a fund-raiser for the Democratic National Committee, informed the president that opposition to efforts in Congress to impose additional restrictions on family-based immigration represented a "top priority" on the agenda of the Asian-American community.[74] The Asian-American community had good reason to oppose such restrictions, since 62 percent of its members were immigrants in 1994.[75]

Many, if not most, Asian immigrants wish to be reunited with family members who reside in their native nations. By sharply restricting family-based immigration, the Simpson and Smith bills were sure to undermine the ability of Asian immigrants to be reunited with their family members. As a result, the Asian-American community lobbied the White House to oppose the Simpson and Smith bills. Accordingly, on March 20, 1996, Clinton reversed himself and announced his opposition to any reforms in legal immigration, including those contained in the Simpson and Smith bills.

Clinton's decision to reverse himself on the issue of legal immigration came just one day before the House was to vote on an amendment, introduced by Representative Dick Chrysler of Michigan, which deleted the provisions pertaining to reforms in legal immigration from the Smith bill. Had Clinton continued his support for the Smith bill, a sufficient number of Democrats probably would have followed the president's lead and voted against the Chrysler amendment in order to assure its defeat on the House floor. However, by announcing his opposition to reforms in legal immigration, Clinton influenced a sufficient number of Democrats to oppose the measure in guaranteeing House passage of the Chrysler amendment. As Smith lamented in an interview, "The White House reversed its position 180 degrees [on legal immigration reform], and we lost [the vote on] this crucial amendment by twenty votes. We might have defeated that amendment had the administration not reversed its position and given [Democrats] some political cover [to support the amendment]."[76]

Unlike Clinton, Reagan's failures on immigration policy were not due to special-interest pressures. Indeed, such pressures upon the Reagan White House were minimal, as will be seen in the next chapter. Rather than the corrupt intent which seems to have influenced Clinton's immigration policy, Reagan's motives on this issue are beyond reproach: He genuinely wanted to design an immigration policy which served the national interest. While no definitive conclusions can be reached concerning Clinton's handling of the issue of immigration, since all the facts have yet to be uncovered, the evidence suggests that the forty-second president may have corrupted and perverted immigration policy to suit his political interests. This was definitely not the case with Reagan, who cannot be blamed for the mistakes he made in his conduct of immigration policy which were errors arising out of factors beyond his control, rather than corrupt intent and ill-conceived motives.

The Reagan administration's decision not to recommend any major reforms in legal immigration meant that any proposals on immigration reform would be limited to the more narrow issue of illegal immigration. Indeed, the administration was eager to recommend reforms to address the problem of illegal immigration, especially as they pertained to measures to deter further illegal immigration to the United States. The administration shared the prevailing view among members of Congress that illegal immigration represents a flagrant abuse of federal immigration law, and a subversion of America's sovereign right to control its own borders and determine the criteria by which aliens are lawfully admitted to the United States. Accordingly, a major priority of the President's Task Force on Immigration Reform was the recommendation of effective measures to curtail the flow of illegal immigration to the United States.

THE PLAN OF THIS BOOK

The remainder of this book analyzes the efforts within Congress to pass comprehensive immigration reform legislation during the Reagan administration, which culminated in enactment of the Immigration Reform and Control Act (IRCA) into federal law in 1986. Chapter 2 examines the lobbying efforts directed at the White House by interest groups and members of Congress on opposing sides of the immigration debate. Chapter 3 turns to the work of the Task Force on Immigration and Refugee Policy, resulting in the statements which the Justice Department, the president, and Smith, respectively, issued on July 30, 1981, defining the Reagan administration's immigration policy. Chapters 4 and 5 explore the two key provisions of IRCA designed to address the problem of illegal immigration—employer sanctions and amnesty, respectively. Chapter 6 concludes with an analysis of Reagan's conduct of immigration policy.

This book concludes that Reagan made a substantial contribution to the persistent mishandling of immigration policy, which the three presidents who have served in office since 1981, as well as Congress, have engaged in. However, Reagan's failures on immigration policy, unlike Clinton's, were not due to any corrupt intent. Reagan was not intent on developing immigration policy to satisfy the desires of the dense network of special interests, which have a vital stake in this issue. Rather, his failures on immigration policy were the result of a lack of accurate and reliable information on this issue, which crippled his ability to effectively address the challenges to the national economic interest posed by the mass immigration existing since 1965. Reagan, unlike Clinton, certainly wanted to develop an immigration policy which served the national economic interest.

Reagan relied on either incomplete or inaccurate information concerning immigration, which led him to support the continuation of the mass immigration existing since 1965, based upon the prevailing consensus that it is economically beneficial to the United States. That consensus made sense during the Reagan administration, given the fact that the evidence seemed to indicate that mass immigration is indeed economically beneficial to the United States. However, that consensus has evaporated since Reagan left the White House, as evidence has accumulated that, far from being beneficial, mass immigration has been economically harmful to the United States.

However, Reagan cannot take the blame for the mistakes he made in addressing the issue of immigration. Rather, Clinton and future presidents will have to take the blame for continuing the mass immigration existing since 1965, given the fact that there is powerful and overwhelming evidence that it has undermined the national economic interest. A president who is well-intentioned cannot be held accountable for making mistakes when the information needed to make the right decisions is unavailable. However, a president who has ill-conceived motives should be held accountable for making mistakes when he has access to the information needed to make the right decisions but chooses other options because he finds them more politically expedient.

The mistakes made in immigration policy during the 1980s were due to the actions of a well-intentioned president, Ronald Reagan, who lacked the information to make the right decisions. The mistakes made in immigration policy during the 1990s were due to the actions of a president, Bill Clinton, who had access to the information needed to make the right decisions but was unable to do so because of corrupt motives he seems to have possessed. If blame is to be assessed for the persistent presidential mishandling of immigration policy which has occurred since 1981, that blame rests squarely on the shoulders of Clinton and all future presidents who seek to emulate his conduct of immigration policy, and not on Reagan, a basically decent and well-intentioned Chief Executive who was operating in the dark on this issue as a result of factors well beyond his control.

Chapter 2

Interest Groups and Members of Congress Lobby the White House to Influence the Development of Immigration Policy

Immigration . . . is an area of public policymaking that has been captured by special-interest groups with private agendas that simply ignore any concern for the national interest. . . . Congress [has] elected to appease these special-interest groups.[1]
——Vernon M. Briggs, Jr., economist

Reagan's decision to establish the President's Task Force on Immigration and Refugee Policy placed the White House squarely in the middle of the intense debate on immigration reform, which Congress triggered when it established SCIRP in 1978. This debate has been especially heated, given the extreme importance of immigration as an issue in governing the future of the United States. Indeed, it is not an exaggeration to say that no single policy which Congress has pursued since 1965, when it passed the Immigration Act, has had a greater impact upon the United States than immigration.

Accordingly, it is not surprising that immigration would become the focus of such heated and intense debate, as has been the case since the establishment of SCIRP. Opponents of mass immigration argue that it has had negative consequences for the United States—politically, economically, fiscally, socially, culturally, demographically, and environmentally; supporters argue the opposite.[2] With Reagan having injected his administration squarely into the debate on immigration through his decision to establish the President's Task Force on Immigration and Refugee Policy, interest groups on opposing sides of the issue lobbied the White House to influence the recommendations on immigration reform which the White House planned to make in the coming months. They were joined by members of Congress, especially those supporting a more restrictionist immigration policy, who also lobbied the White House in order to influence those recommendations.

SIMPSON AND MAZZOLI LOBBY THE WHITE HOUSE ON IMMIGRATION POLICY

Reagan's decision to establish the President's Task Force on Immigration and Refugee Policy was welcomed by Alan K. Simpson of Wyoming and Romano L. Mazzoli of Kentucky, chairmen of the immigration subcommittees of the Senate and House, respectively. As the leading immigration policymakers in Congress, both Simpson and Mazzoli had served as members of SCIRP. They were committed to co-sponsoring legislation implementing SCIRP's recommendations. Passage of such legislation obviously depended upon the success of Simpson and Mazzoli in winning White House support for their immigration reform agenda. To assure such support, Simpson and Mazzoli actively lobbied the White House in an effort to assure that the recommendations of the President's Task Force on Immigration and Refugee Policy reflected the views of the two chairmen of the immigration subcommittees of the Senate and House, respectively. Simpson and Mazzoli generally favored a more restrictive immigration policy than the other members of SCIRP, who supported the high levels of legal immigration existing since 1965.

Mazzoli Contacts the White House to Discuss Immigration Policy

Mazzoli wasted no time contacting the White House following Reagan's decision to establish the President's Task Force on Immigration and Refugee Policy. On March 9, 1981, just three days after Reagan announced this decision, Mazzoli and the staff of the Subcommittee on Immigration, Refugees, and International Law of the House Judiciary Committee, which he chaired, met with Hodsoll to discuss the recommendations on immigration reform which the Reagan administration planned to make in the coming months. The day following the meeting, Mazzoli wrote Hodsoll:

Thank you for taking the time to meet with me and the subcommittee staff on Monday to discuss the administration's plans to study the immigration and refugee issue. I am pleased to learn that the Attorney General and other members of the Task Force intend to move quickly with their examination of the significant issues.

As I said in our meeting, I believe that only through ongoing cooperation among the House, the Senate, and the administration, can we expect to develop a workable set of changes in our immigration and refugee policies. I look forward to continued close coordination with you as the administration joins me and my subcommittee in tackling this tough matter.[3]

The Senate Immigration Subcommittee Introduces the White House to Simpson's Views on This Issue

Joining Mazzoli in welcoming the establishment of the President's Task Force on Immigration and Refugee Policy was Richard W. Day, staff director of the Subcommittee on Immigration and Refugee Policy of the Senate Judiciary Committee. Day made an active effort to acquaint the White House with the views of Simpson, who served as chairman of the subcommittee. As we saw in the previous chapter, the overwhelming majority of the members of SCIRP supported the high levels of legal immigration experienced since 1965, even recommending a 20 percent increase in the annual ceiling on the number of legal immigrants admitted to the United States.

With only one dissenting vote, the members of SCIRP rejected the imposition of an annual numerical ceiling on total legal immigration to the United States. Rather, the members recommended preservation of the immigration system established under the Immigration Act of 1965. This included the preservation of an annual ceiling on the number of legal immigrants admitted to the United States under the preference system which governed legal immigration. The immediate family members of American citizens would remain excluded from this preference system; they would continue to be admitted to the United States in unlimited numbers.

However, the lone dissenting voice within SCIRP to its opposition to the imposition of an annual numerical ceiling on total legal immigration was that of Simpson. He believed that legal immigration had risen to excessive and unsustainable levels as a result of the Immigration Act of 1965. Simpson especially opposed provisions of the bill which made family reunification the cornerstone of immigration policy, and allowed the immediate family members of American citizens to be admitted to the United States in unlimited numbers.

By making family reunification the cornerstone of immigration policy, the Immigration Act of 1965 triggered a never-ending cycle of chain immigration. Legal immigrants who reside in the United States sponsor the admission of their immediate and extended family members to this nation, who do the same for their immediate and extended family members, and so on. The effect of chain immigration has been to trigger a flood of legal immigration from Latin America and Asia, as legal immigrants born in those regions have sponsored the admission of their immediate or close family members to the United States, who have done the same for their immediate and extended family members, and so on. As we saw in the previous chapter, nearly half of all legal immigrants who have been admitted to the United States since 1968 were born in Latin America, and one-third in Asia.

Simpson supported reducing levels of legal immigration by restricting family-based immigration mostly to the immediate family members of American citizens and permanent legal residents. To assure that the President's Task Force on Immigration and Refugee Policy would take Simpson's views into account in making its recommendations on immigration reform, on March 18, 1981, Day wrote Hodsoll. Attached to Day's letter was a statement, which Simpson issued on SCIRP's final report, containing its recommendations on immigration reform, released on March 1. In his letter, Day emphasized the desire of Simpson and Mazzoli to work with the White House in pursuing their efforts to pass comprehensive immigration reform legislation. Day noted that Simpson wanted the White House to adopt a more restrictive immigration policy, in sharp contrast to SCIRP's support for a continuation of the open and liberal immigration policy pursued since 1965.

Senator Simpson, as you can see from his supplemental views, did not concur with all the recommendations of the Select Commission. Although we were vitally interested in getting legislation passed, and toward that end, want to work as closely as practical with Congressman Mazzoli's people in attempting to reach some sort of consensus, I did want you to know that Senator Simpson is rather conservative in his position concerning many aspects of the problem.

[Simpson's] views [on] the Select Commission report . . . clearly set forth his position on [its] many recommendations.[4]

In his statement commenting on SCIRP's final report, Simpson took strong exception to the commission's support for continuing the mass immigration existing since 1965. Simpson's opposition to mass immigration was largely based upon demographic and economic considerations. Simpson argued that mass immigration was having an adverse demographic impact upon the United States. Simpson based his claim on a report issued by Lee Bouvier, a demographic adviser to SCIRP. Bouvier argued that mass immigration was driving population growth in the United States to excessive and unsustainable levels. To illustrate his point, Bouvier projected that if net annual immigration, both legal and illegal, continues at the post-1965 level of 750,000, and the fertility rate remains constant, the population of the United States would rise to 300 million by 2080, a third of whom would consist of post-1979 immigrants and their descendants.[5]

Bouvier has recently released a study which shows that mass immigration will drive population growth in the United States substantially higher than the predictions he made when he was a demographic adviser to SCIRP. Bouvier now predicts that if net annual immigration and the fertility rate remain unchanged, then the population of the United States will rise to 392 million by 2050, 36 percent of whom will consist of post-1970 immigrants and their descendants, respresenting 139 million individuals.[6] Bouvier estimates that immigration accounted for half the growth in the population of the United States from 1970 to 1995, and will represent 90 percent of the population growth from 1995 to 2050.[7]

Simpson argued that mass immigration, in the long term, was sure to drive population growth in the United States to excessive and unsustainable levels, resulting in a substantial decline in the American standard of living.

The problems which may be caused by excessive population growth include the following: additional cost of government services, not merely transfer programs, such as welfare and health care, but also on all services, which depend upon the size of the population served, such as education, fire fighting, law enforcement, and sanitation; overcrowding of scarce public facilities, such as parks and roads; increased cost and scarcity of commodities of limited supply, such as urban housing and domestic natural resources; greater environmental damage; greater use of imported oil and other natural resources, with accompanying national security risks; higher food consumption and, therefore, a decrease in food exports and in the associated diplomatic and balance of payments deficits.

In addition to triggering excessive and unsustainable population growth in the United States, Simpson charged that mass immigration was having an adverse economic impact upon American workers. Immigrants compete against native-born American workers for a limited supply of jobs. Immigrants are often willing to work for lower wages and in less safe and healthful working conditions than native-born Americans. As a result, employers profit from hiring immigrants, who represent a vital source of cheap labor. Immigrants are generally grateful for the opportunity to work, and are unlikely to complain about being paid less than the minimum wage, or having to work in unsafe and unhealthful workplaces. Accordingly, employers of immigrants can avoid having to spend substantial sums paying their alien workers the minimum wage, and bringing their workplaces into compliance with federal occupational safety and health regulations.

Because they save substantial sums in lower labor costs and avoiding the expenditures in having to meet federal occupational safety and health regulations when they employ immigrants, employers tend to prefer hiring aliens as an alternative to native-born Americans. Accordingly, Simpson charged that mass immigration results in substantial job displacement of American workers. As we saw in the previous chapter, the overwhelming majority of immigrants are poorly educated and unskilled. As a result, poorly educated and unskilled native-born American workers are most vulnerable to competition from immigrants, and they must bear the brunt of the job displacement which results from mass immigration.

Adverse economic impacts do occur—not only because of illegal immigrants, but also due to refugees and legal immigrants who are admitted under family reunification preferences, who do not require a screening for labor market impact. Adverse impacts include unemployment and less favorable working conditions for U.S. workers, together with the related costs, such as welfare or other transfer payments to adversely affect U.S. workers and their families. . . .

Adverse job impacts are most likely to affect low-skilled Americans, who are most likely to face direct competition. Direct or indirect job displacement of low-skilled Americans, a very high percentage of whom are now unemployed, is a very serious issue. Not only does such unemployment bring economic distress upon the displaced Americans and their families, but it may also be a source of increased social tension within our society.

Obviously many, perhaps most, goods and services could be sold in the United States at a lower price if employers are able to employ anyone from abroad willing to work for less. This can also result in exploitation. If there were no restrictions on this practice, the adverse impacts described would occur to a much greater degree than at present.[8]

Simpson's charge that the mass immigration existing since 1965 has resulted in substantial job displacement of American workers is false. The empirical evidence clearly shows that the job displacement arising from mass immigration has been minimal. Consider the case of California, the state with the single largest immigrant population, which served as home to 32.7 percent of all foreign-born individuals who resided in the United States in 1995.[9] In a book which RAND published in 1997, Thomas F. McCarthy and Georges Vernez estimate that in 1990 between 128,000 and 195,000 native-born Americans who resided in California were either unemployed or had withdrawn from the labor force as a result of competition from immigrants, representing between 1 percent and 1.3 percent of all nonelderly native-born Americans living in the state. McCarthy and Vernez estimated that between four and six native-born American workers have either been unemployed or withdrawn from the labor force for every 100 immigrants who entered the labor force.[10]

Why is there little evidence of job displacement arising from mass immigration? The answer lies in the fact that there is clear segmentation within the labor market between immigrants and native-born Americans. Because they tend to have substantially lower levels of education and skills than native-born Americans, immigrants are largely confined to low-wage, menial jobs, which Americans generally shun. Accordingly, American workers are largely insulated from having to compete with immigrants for employment, and they suffer little job displacement as a result of mass immigration.[11] Immigrants, both legal and illegal, pose very little threat to the jobs of native-born Americans, contrary to the arguments which immigration restrictionists, like Simpson, have made.[12]

To relieve the United States of the socioeconomic dislocations created by excessive and unsustainable population growth and alleged job displacement, Simpson recommended that Congress pass legislation which imposed an annual numerical ceiling limiting the total number of legal immigrants admitted to the United States to a range of between 400,000 and 550,000. Simpson suggested that the bottom figure of this range—400,000—be adopted until Congress had imposed effective measures to stem the flow of illegal immigration to the United States. As we saw in the previous chapter, in fiscal 1981, the year SCIRP issued the final report containing its recommendations on immigration reform, 596,600 legal immigrants were admitted to the United States. Had Congress imposed an annual ceiling which limited the number of legal immigrants admitted to the

United States to 400,000, then such action would have reduced levels of legal immigration by a third.

Bouvier estimated that if net annual immigration were reduced to 500,000, and the fertility rate remained constant, then the population of the United States would rise to 270 million by 2080.[13] However, net annual immigration since 1981 has stood at roughly 900,000, nearly double the level Simpson recommended.[14] As a result, the population of the United States currently stands at just short of 270 million, having reached that level eighty years ahead of the time which it would have taken had Congress adopted Simpson's recommendations in 1981.

To maintain his proposed annual ceiling of 550,000 on the total number of legal immigrants admitted to the United States, Simpson recommended that family-based immigration be limited to the spouses and children of American citizens and the spouses and nonadult children of permanent legal residents. The preference categories, established under the Immigration Act of 1965, which admits the siblings of American citizens and the single adult children of permanent legal residents to the United States, would be eliminated.

Simpson's recommendation to substantially reduce levels of legal immigration stood in sharp contrast to the other members of SCIRP, who supported a continuation of the mass immigration existing since 1965. However, Simpson's views on illegal immigration were much closer to those of the other members of SCIRP. Simpson supported the two-pronged approach, which SCIRP adopted, to address the problem of illegal immigration: the granting of amnesty to illegal aliens who resided in the United States, and the imposition of an employer-sanctions regime to deter further illegal immigration to this nation.[15]

The White House Contacts Simpson to Discuss Immigration Policy

The purpose of Day's letter to Hodsoll was to emphasize the pivotal role Simpson was destined to play in the efforts to pass immigration reform legislation which Congress was certain to undertake in the wake of the release of SCIRP's final report. Simpson's importance in the politics of immigration reform derived from his chairmanship of the immigration subcommittee, which would have to approve any immigration reform bill before it could be considered by the Judiciary Committee, and ultimately the full Senate. Simpson's vocal dissent from SCIRP's recommendations, which supported the continuation of the high levels of legal immigration existing since 1965, allowed him to emerge as the leader of the immigration restrictionist forces in Congress.

The President's Task Force on Immigration and Refugee Policy had to take Simpson's views into account in developing its own recommendations on immigration reform, which it planned to make to Reagan in the coming months. This was true for the simple reason that those recommendations would require legislation. Such legislation could not be passed unless it was approved first by the immigration subcommittees of the Senate and House, respectively. As chairmen of the two subcommittees, Simpson, together with Mazzoli, would have a strong hand in determining whether such legislation was passed by both houses of Congress.

As the White House staff member on the President's Task Force on Immigration and Refugee Policy, Hodsoll wasted no time arranging a meeting between himself and Simpson, which occurred one day after he was apprised of the Senator's views on immigration in the letter he received from Day on March 18, 1981. Five days after he received the letter, Hodsoll sent a memo to Max Friedersdorf, Assistant to the President for Legislative Affairs, reporting on a meeting he had with Simpson. Attending the meeting was Kenneth Starr, Counselor to the Attorney General, who would later gain fame and notoriety as the independent counsel who played a prominent role in triggering the House's passage of two articles of impeachment against Clinton in 1998: "Last week, March 19, I joined Ken Starr, Counselor to the Attorney General, in meeting with Al Simpson in regard to immigration and refugee issues. Senator Simpson's subcommittee will be holding hearings during the month of April to obtain public response to the Selection Commission on Immigration and Refugees."[16]

When Reagan established the President's Task Force on Immigration and Refugee Policy on March 6, 1981, he was scheduled to travel to Tijuana to meet with President Jose Lopez Portillo. Immigration represented a major item on the agenda of the two presidents during their summit meeting. Mexico represents the single largest source of immigration to the United States, both legal and illegal, of any nation in the world. In 1996 Mexicans represented 27.2 percent of all immigrants who resided in the United States.[17] From 1989 to 1993, Mexico represented the single largest source of legal immigration to the United States, with Mexicans constituting 10.3 percent of all legal immigrants.[18] An overwhelming majority of illegal aliens who reside in the United States are Mexican. In 1996, 54 percent of all illegal aliens were Mexican.[19] The importance of immigration as an issue governing Mexican-American relations has been aptly noted by Kevin F. McCarthy and Georges Vernez: "Mexico provides almost half of all immigrants to California and is the primary source of illegal immigration [to the United States]. . . . The issue of Mexican immigration cannot be divorced from the broader context of U.S.–Mexico relations—much as the U.S. and Mexican governments might like it to be. Instead, both countries must realize the special role Mexican immigration plays in the lives of both countries."[20]

With immigration certain to represent a major topic of discussion between Reagan and Lopez Portillo, Simpson wanted to see the president before he held his summit meeting with his Mexican counterpart. By communicating his views on immigration directly to Reagan, Simpson hoped that the president would take the senator's opinions into account when he met Lopez Portillo to discuss this issue. In his memo to Friedersdorf, Hodsoll recommended that the White House arrange a meeting between Reagan and Simpson: "Simpson has very strong views about our immigration policy and would like very much to meet with President Reagan for about fifteen minutes before the President goes to Mexico. I recommend that this meeting be arranged. Would you like me to follow through on the arrangements or would you prefer to do so?''[21]

Reagan's planned trip to Tijuana to meet Lopez Portillo was eventually canceled. Instead, Reagan welcomed Lopez Portillo to the White House during the Mexican president's trip to Washington, which took place June 8–9, 1981. Pursuant to the recommendations made by Hodsoll in his memo to him on March 23, Friedersdorf arranged for a fifteen-minute meeting between Reagan and Simpson on June 1. The White House regarded this meeting as extremely important in assuring the success of the work of the President's Task Force on Immigration and Refugee Policy. To underscore the importance of this meeting, Reagan was joined in his conference with Simpson by the highest-ranking officials of his administration, including Vice President George Bush, Attorney General William French Smith, White House Chief of Staff James A. Baker III, Edwin Meese III, Counselor to the President, and Martin Anderson, Assistant to the President for Policy Development. Hodsoll and Friedersdorf also attended this meeting.

In his memo announcing the establishment of the President's Task Force on Immigration and Refugee Policy, Reagan had imposed a deadline of the first week of May for the group to issue its recommendations. However, the Task Force had failed to meet this deadline, and was still deliberating on its recommendations at the time Reagan met Simpson. The White House fully understood that Congress would need to pass legislation implementing those recommendations. No such legislation was likely to be passed without Simpson's support. That support would be necessary if Simpson's immigration subcommittee was to approve such legislation. Such approval would be needed before any immigration reform legislation could be passed by the Judiciary Committee, and ultimately the full Senate.

To assure Simpson's support for the recommendations of the President's Task Force on Immigration and Refugee Policy, the White House devoted considerable attention to Reagan's meeting with the senator. Indeed, on May 29, 1981, three days before the meeting between Reagan and Simpson took place, Friedersdorf sent the president a memo, which contained a detailed schedule of the conference. Friedersdorf noted that the purpose of the meeting was "To respond to a request from Senator Simpson to discuss his views on immigration policy with the President prior to the Lopez Portillo visit." Friedersdorf noted the critical role Simpson played in the development of immigration policy, both as a member of SCIRP and chairman of the Senate immigration subcommittee, pointing out that "If the administration proposes changes in current law regarding immigration and refugees, they will be considered by Simpson's subcommittee."

Friedersdorf devoted a substantial part of his memo to apprising Reagan of Simpson's views on immigration reform.

The Senator's own strategy for reform, which he describes as "a 3-legged stool," consists of: (a) increased enforcement [of federal immigration law]; (b) sanctions against employers who knowingly hire illegals; (c) some identification mechanism for legal workers. He opposes establishment of a new "guest worker" program, but might be willing to accept this approach, as well as amnesty for those already here, if his "3-legged stool" were in place. He supports the establishment of an absolute ceiling on legal immigration to establish control, and feels the INS is underfunded and understaffed.

In addition to Simpson's views on immigration reform, Friedersdorf apprised Reagan of the status of the work of the President's Task Force on Immigration and Refugee Policy: "The meeting with Senator Simpson will occur just as the report of the Attorney General's Task Force on Immigration and Refugee Policy is nearing completion. The report is in a holding pattern to allow discussion with Lopez Portillo before making administration decisions."

Friedersdorf noted that the President's Task Force on Immigration and Refugee Policy had yet to develop its key recommendations on immigration reform. Nevertheless, the Task Force was leaning toward endorsing SCIRP's recommendation for passage of legislation which would impose a moderate increase in levels of legal immigration, grant amnesty to illegal aliens who resided in the United States, and establish an employer-sanctions regime designed to deter further illegal immigration to this nation. SCIRP had recommended that the annual ceiling on the number of legal immigrants admitted to the United States be raised by 60,000, from 290,000, the level established under the Immigration Act of 1965, to 350,000. The President's Task Force on Immigration and Refugee Policy was considering recommending that this ceiling be raised by 40,000, two-thirds the level which SCIRP proposed.[22]

The President's Task Force on Immigration and Refugee Policy's tentative support for amnesty and employer sanctions was fully consistent with Simpson's views on illegal immigration. However, the Task Force's decision to lean in favor of a moderate increase in levels of legal immigration were inconsistent with Simpson's support for a substantial reduction in the annual number of legal immigrants admitted to the United States. As a result, a potential conflict between the White House and Simpson seemed to be looming.

Nevertheless, Friedersdorf still believed that the White House could work with Simpson in assuring passage of legislation which implemented the recommendations of the President's Task Force on Immigration and Refugee Policy. Attached to Friedersdorf's memo was a list of talking points, which Reagan was to have used in his meeting with Simpson, designed to foster cooperation between the senator and the White House in assuring passage of such legislation.

Welcome Senator Simpson. Acknowledge the great importance of the issue [immigration and refugee policy] which he has come to discuss with you. Let the Senator outline his recommendations. Since the Attorney General's report has not yet been completed, you should avoid making specific comments at this time. You might mention that several of the Senator's suggestions are being considered by the Attorney General's Task Force.

Senator Simpson has indicated his willingness to "carry the administration's water" on this issue in terms of guiding his subcommittee's action. Express appreciation for his cooperation, particularly in view of the fact that he is under pressure to move ahead on this issue. Simpson may ask how you intend to present your immigration program to Congress. Assure him that you want to work together on this issue.[23]

Despite the White House's desire to work with Simpson in passing immigration reform legislation, deep philosophical differences between the two sides remained on this issue. While the Reagan administration supported the high levels of legal immigration existing since 1965, Simpson favored a substantial reduction in the number of legal immigrants admitted to the United States. The White House needed to prevent those differences from provoking a confrontation with Simpson. Indeed, the White House needed Simpson's cooperation if Reagan was to have any hope of obtaining Senate passage of legislation containing the recommendations on immigration reform which he planned to make in the coming months.

Accordingly, the White House urged Reagan to avoid discussion with Simpson on the specific issues involved in immigration reform in order to avoid any confrontation between the two political leaders over the subject. Friedersdorf specifically requested that Reagan avoid such a discussion in his list of talking points, which he sent the president to prepare him for his June 1, 1981 meeting with Simpson. As a result, Reagan would finesse his differences with Simpson in all of the meetings he would hold with the senator over the issue of immigration during the six-year effort to pass immigration reform legislation in Congress, implementing SCIRP's recommendations, which culminated in the enactment of IRCA into federal law in 1986. That effort was led by Simpson and Mazzoli, who co-sponsored the various versions of IRCA passed by both houses of Congress during the 1980s, before enactment of the final version. In pursuing this effort, Simpson and Mazzoli received little support from the White House. As Peter H. Schuck notes,

Simpson and Mazzoli decided to use the commission's proposals . . . as a starting point for their own bill. Then, to the surprise of old immigration hands, William French Smith, Reagan's Attorney General and friend, endorsed the soundness of their general approach. Simpson sensed, however, that the White House staff did not share Smith's enthusiasm. In Simpson's meetings with the President in the Oval Office, Reagan would applaud Simpson's efforts and Reagan's aides would nod their assent. In practice, however, the White House failed to give Simpson any meaningful support on immigration legislation. This lack of significant presidential involvement in the legislative struggles over immigration would continue throughout the decade.[24]

FAIR LOBBIES THE WHITE HOUSE ON IMMIGRATION POLICY

Simpson was not the only restrictionist voice who attempted to influence the White House on the issue of immigration. Rather, Simpson was joined in this effort by the Federation for American Immigration Reform (FAIR), the leading interest group which supports the adoption of a restrictive immigration policy. FAIR was established in 1979 by a number of prominent population control activists and environmentalists concerned about the negative impact they believe mass immigration has had in fueling excessive and unsustainable population growth and environmental degradation in the United States.[25] FAIR currently has 70,000 members throughout the United States.

Since its establishment, FAIR has actively lobbied Congress to pass comprehensive reform legislation. FAIR supports the imposition of a moratorium on all legal immigration, with the exception of the spouses and nonadult children of American citizens and a limited number of refugees. FAIR estimates that adoption of its recommendations on immigration reform would limit the annual number of legal immigrants admitted to the United States to 300,000.[26] As we saw in the previous chapter, in fiscal 1994, 804,416 legal immigrants were admitted to the United States. Accordingly, FAIR's recommendations would result in a reduction in levels of legal immigration by over 60 percent. In addition, FAIR supports the imposition of effective measures "to stop illegal immigration."

FAIR bases its support for the imposition of severe restrictions on legal immigration on the following arguments: first, "immigration is fueling unprecedented population growth and overcrowding" by adding one million individuals annually to the population of the United States; second, "immigration fuels unemployment and depresses wages and working conditions," since most of the one million aliens immigrating to the United States annually are poorly educated and unskilled workers, who compete against native-born Americans with similar human-capital endowments, for a limited supply of jobs; third, "immigration is extremely costly," since the government must spend, by FAIR's estimate, $65 billion annually to provide social services to aliens who reside in the United States, both legally and illegally.[27]

On April 8, 1981, Roger Conner, the executive director of FAIR, wrote Hodsoll to urge the White House to develop an immigration policy which is "in the public interest as a whole, rather than what would serve the interest of a particular class, ethnic group, or institution." To assist the White House in the development of such an immigration policy, Conner attached a fact sheet from FAIR, issued in February 1981, to his letter, which summarized the findings of recent public opinion polls on immigration. Conner argued that "recent public opinion polls on immigration and refugee matters . . . [show] a surprising convergence of intense public support for a realistic policy."[28]

The fact sheet from FAIR was designed to illustrate that the public was intensely interested in the issue of immigration and strongly supported passage of comprehensive immigration reform legislation. The fact sheet began with a summary of the findings of an October 1980 Roper Poll, which showed that 44 percent of those surveyed wanted the issue of illegal immigration to be addressed in the presidential campaign. Illegal immigration ranked sixth among the issues the respondents wanted addressed in the campaign, behind five major problems which collectively are largely responsible for having determined the outcome of the 1980 presidential election: inflation, the Iranian hostage crisis, economic stagnation, the energy crisis, and the American military decline.

Another Roper Poll, released on June 18, 1980, found that 91 percent of those surveyed wanted the federal government to "make an all-out effort against illegal entry into the U.S." of undocumented individuals. As we have seen, SCIRP recommended the establishment of an employer-sanctions regime as a means to deter further illegal immigration to the United States. An overwhelming majority of those surveyed supported the imposition of an employer-sanctions regime.

A Gallup Poll, released on November 30, 1980, asked its respondents the following question: "Do you think it should or should not be against the law to employ a person who has come to the United States without proper papers?" Seventy-six percent of those surveyed expressed their belief that it should be illegal to employ an individual without proper documentation, 18 percent stated that it should not be, and 6 percent had no opinion.

Employer sanctions alone are insufficient to deny illegal aliens jobs. Indeed, experience has shown that illegal aliens may easily circumvent employer sanctions by presenting their employers fraudulent documents which falsely purport to verify their eligibility to work in the United States. To enable employers to detect and crack down upon document fraud, Congress needs to couple employer sanctions with the establishment of a fraud-resistant worker verification system which would enable firms to determine the authenticity of such documents.

As we will see, the worker verification proposal, which received the most serious consideration in 1981, involved the issuance of a national identity card to all individuals eligible to work in the United States. A national data bank, containing personal information on all individuals carrying a national identity card, would be established. Employers would use the information contained in the national data bank, both to verify the authenticity of the identity card presented to them and to validate that the card does indeed belong to the individual who is presenting it. As a result, a national identity card, supported by a data bank, would create the appropriate safeguards to enable employers to detect and crack down upon document fraud, thereby depriving illegal aliens of the ability to circumvent employer sanctions.

The 1980 Gallup Poll, cited earlier, found overwhelming public support for the creation of a national identity card. The poll asked its respondents the following question: "Do you believe everyone in the United States should be required to carry an identification card, such as a Social Security card, or not?" Sixty-two percent of those surveyed expressed their belief that everyone should be required to carry such a card, 33 percent stated that they should not be obliged to do so, and 5 percent had no opinion.

Employer sanctions represented only one element of the two-pronged approach which SCIRP recommended to address the problem of illegal immigration. The other major recommendation was the granting of amnesty to illegal aliens who resided in the United States since prior to January 1, 1980. However, a majority of the public opposed the establishment of an even more restrictive amnesty program, which would grant permanent legal residence to illegal aliens who had lived in the United States for at least seven years. The 1980 Gallup Poll, cited earlier, asked its respondents the following question: "It has been proposed that illegal aliens, who have been in the United States for seven years, be allowed to remain in the U.S. Do you favor or oppose this proposal?" Fifty-two percent of those surveyed opposed granting amnesty to illegal aliens who have resided in the United States for at least seven years, 37 percent supported it, and 11 percent had no opinion. In addition to supporting the imposition of punitive measures designed to deter further illegal immigration, an overwhelming majority of the public supported reducing levels of legal immigration to the United States. Eighty percent of those surveyed supported legislation to "reduce quotas on the number of legal immigrants who can enter the U.S. each year."[29]

Overall, the polling data which FAIR presented to the White House showed that an overwhelming majority of the public supported the imposition of severe restrictions on legal immigration, combined with a crackdown on illegal immigration. This was fully consistent with FAIR's restrictionist immigration policy agenda. By presenting polling data which illustrated the fact that an overwhelming majority of the public had restrictionist views on immigration, FAIR hoped to influence the White House to recommend measures both to reduce levels of legal immigration and stem the flow of illegal immigration to the United States.

In addition to the FAIR fact sheet summarizing the findings of recent public opinion polls on immigration, Conner attached a brochure to his letter explaining the aims of the interest group. Arguing that "immigration is out of control," FAIR, in its brochure, noted that "the pressure to migrate to the United States is increasing. In fact, the number of legal immigrants has risen steadily for the past decade, to its highest number in fifty years—reaching 800,000 in 1980. And the number of illegal immigrants may be greater. The Immigration and Naturalization Service (INS) made more than a million apprehensions last year—ten times the number in 1960." FAIR warned that mass immigration was driving population growth in the United States to excessive and unsustainable levels.

A presidential commission in 1972 concluded that the national interest would not be well served in any way by a larger population. Since then, Americans have voluntarily limited the number of children in each family, and U.S. growth has slowed. But immigration has negated that progress. With our present rate of immigration, population growth in the United States is the highest of all developed nations. Our option to rationally choose an optimum population size for the United States is being foreclosed.[30]

FAIR's argument that mass immigration was driving population growth in the United States to the highest levels of any industrial nation is confirmed by the data. From 1993 to 2025, the population growth of the United States is projected to rise by 22 percent, primarily as a result of mass immigration.[31] By contrast, other major industrial nations will experience a substantially lower rate of population growth, due to the severe restrictions they have placed upon immigration.[32] From 1993 to 2025, the population of France is projected to rise by 8 percent, Britain 7 percent, and Japan 2 percent. The populations of Germany and Italy are actually projected to decline during this period by 2 percent and 4 percent, respectively. Except for the United States, only Canada, among all the major industrial nations, will experience a high rate of population growth, which is projected to rise by 19 percent during this period.[33] This is due to the fact that Canada. like the United States, maintains an open and liberal immigration policy.[34]

Hodsoll responded positively to the polling data which he received from Conner. On April 27, 1981, Hodsoll wrote Conner to assure him that the information which FAIR provided the White House would assist the President's Task Force on Immigration and Refugee Policy in developing recommendations on immigration reform which it planned to make to Reagan in the coming months: ''Thank you for your letter of April 8 and its attachments which are extremely useful. Your group has clearly thought about the problem [of immigration]. Your ideas are very helpful to us. It is a very tough issue. We are now wrestling with our final report to the President. Again, many thanks for your help.''[35]

FAIR JOINS HUDDLESTON IN LOBBYING CONGRESS FOR PASSAGE OF COMPREHENSIVE IMMIGRATION LEGISLATION

FAIR's lobbying activities were aided by the existence of a powerful ally which it had in Congress—Senator Walter D. Huddleston of Kentucky. Huddleston was second only to Simpson as a leader of the immigration restrictionist forces in Congress. Huddleston represented a far more extreme restrictionist voice in Congress than Simpson. Indeed, Huddleston favored reducing levels of legal immigration by a substantially greater amount than Simpson.

In 1981, Huddleston joined Representatives Robin Beard of Tennessee and Tony Coelho of California in introducing the Immigration and National Security Act in Congress. The bill would have imposed an annual numerical ceiling which limited the total number of legal immigrants admitted to the United States to 350,000.[36] This number was substantially below the annual numerical ceiling, limiting the total number of legal immigrants admitted to the United States to a range of from 400,000 to 550,000, which Simpson had recommended in his statement commenting on the proposals contained in SCIRP's final report. As we saw in the previous chapter, in fiscal 1981, the year Huddleston, Beard, and Coelho introduced the Immigration and National Security Act in Congress, 596,600 legal immigrants were admitted to the United States. As a result, the bill would have reduced levels of legal immigration by over 40 percent.

The growing alliance between Huddleston and FAIR alarmed supporters of mass immigration. Immigration enthusiasts feared that Huddleston might convince other members of Congress to join him in his effort to drastically reduce levels of legal immigration. With thousands of members throughout the United States, FAIR could use its substantial grassroots organizational capabilities to support Huddleston's efforts to mobilize congressional support for substantial reductions in levels of legal immigration.

Immigration enthusiasts attempted to convince the White House to oppose the efforts of Huddleston and FAIR to pass legislation imposing severe restrictions upon legal immigration. Leading this effort was Robert H. McBride, who served as American ambassador to Mexico from 1969 to 1974. Following his retirement from the Foreign Service, McBride joined David R. Gregory, a professor at Dartmouth College, in establishing the Inter-American Council on Manpower and Development (ICMD).

The purpose of the ICMD was to recommend to Congress solutions to the problem of illegal immigration consistent with maintaining America's close and strong relationship with Mexico. As we have seen, over half of all illegal aliens residing in the United States were born in Mexico. As a result, illegal immigration had the potential to poison Mexican–American relations, if Congress attempted to impose harsh and punitive measures against undocumented individuals. By exacerbating the plight of Mexicans who reside in the United States illegally, such action was sure to inflame the Mexican government, which had an obvious interest in assuring that its citizens living in this nation are treated humanely.

As a former American ambassador to Mexico, McBride had an obvious interest in promoting good relations between the United States and Mexico. McBride was especially opposed to restrictionist immigration reform legislation, like the Immigration and National Security Act, because he believed that it would have an adverse impact upon Mexican–American relations. By imposing severe restrictions on legal immigration, the bill threatened to deprive Mexicans of the opportunity to immigrate to the United States legally in order to be reunited with their family members living in the United States. Such action would create severe personal hardship for Mexicans who reside on both sides of the border. Accordingly, such action was sure to poison relations between the United States and Mexico.

Responding to the suggestion of Bill Wilson, a close personal friend of Reagan, whom the president appointed as the American ambassador to the Vatican, on March 30, 1981, McBride and Gregory wrote Anderson to urge the White House to oppose efforts in Congress to pass restrictionist immigration reform legislation. McBride and Gregory noted that a recent conference of immigration policy experts had found SCIRP's recommendations on immigration reform insufficient because they failed to include provisions to regulate the flow of Mexican workers to the United States. Those experts supported the negotiation of a labor treaty between the United States and Mexico, which would allow a limited number of Mexican workers to immigrate to this nation on a temporary basis to fill shortages existing within the American labor market. In addition to its shortcomings, McBride and Gregory feared that SCIRP's final report would trigger passage of restrictionist immigration reform legislation sponsored by Huddleston and FAIR.

The commission's March 1, 1981 report to Congress was evaluated and analyzed for its practicability by a cross-section of migration experts at the Fourth National Legal Conference on March 26–27, 1981. In general it received little or no support from either advocates for a more open immigration policy or from those supporting greater restrictions. In particular, it failed to adequately address in-depth the issue of temporary Mexican immigration to the U.S. Nevertheless, it is our opinion that during the coming months the ''report'' will act as a catalyst to consolidate the position of the restrictionists who consider all types of immigration to the U.S. as being ''out of control.''

Restrictionist organizations like FAIR (Federation for American Immigration Reform) are increasingly active, gaining a wider support, and backing the Immigration and National Security Act introduced by Walter D. Huddleston and seven other Senators (S. 776) and by Representatives Robin Beard (R-Tenn) and Tony Coelho (D-CA) in the House (H.R. 2782). This highly restrictionist bill, and others to come, that fail to take into account the growing economic and social interdependence between the U.S. & Mexico will have a negative impact upon both governmental and business relations between our two countries. This could not come at a worse time as the importance of the relationship grows along with rapid Mexican economic development.[37]

A BIPARTISAN MAJORITY OF THE SENATE DEMANDS COMPREHENSIVE IMMIGRATION REFORM

McBride's and Gregory's fears that sentiment was growing in Congress to impose additional restrictions on immigration seemed to be realized on July 8, 1981, when a bipartisan group of fifty-one senators—including thirty-three Republicans and eighteen Democrats—wrote Reagan. The lead signatories of the letter were the primary immigration restrictionist members of Congress—Senators Huddleston and Simpson. Echoing Smith's declaration that the United States had lost control of its borders, Huddleston and Simpson charged that levels of immigration, both legal and illegal, had risen to excessive and unsustainable levels.

More immigrants and more refugees came to the United States last year than in any other year in history. However, they came not as a result of decisions made here in Washington, but because of decisions made in Hanoi, Havana, Port-au-Prince, and dozens of other foreign cities. Attorney General Smith characterized the problem most accurately when he stated, on June 27, that the United States ''has lost control of our own borders.''

Uncontrolled legal immigration is creating additional burdens for the American people and is kindling a growing resentment which threatens our historic generosity toward immigrants. At the same moment, illegal immigration is continuing to escalate and is creating what the Attorney General has called ''a fugitive class living outside society's laws and its protection.'' In response to these distressing facts, public opinion polls disclose that 91% of those polled want ''an all-out effort'' to end illegal immigration, and 80% want reductions in legal admissions. We in the Congress feel a strong sense of urgency in addressing these issues.

Huddleston and Simpson expressed confidence that Reagan would recommend legislation to assure that immigration policy serves the national interest.

The total immigration problem is extremely complex, emotionally charged, and has important foreign policy considerations; and we appreciate the tremendous effort you are making to prepare a comprehensive immigration policy. In the past, you have demonstrated repeatedly that you are willing to make the very difficult and painful decisions— and on the basis that they were in this country's best interests.

We sincerely urge you to continue this policy when you consider the recommendations made by the Cabinet and the Task Force on Immigration and Refugee Policy. The population and immigration pressures, which this country must deal with in the next few years, will not allow us the continued luxury of making easy short-term decisions, which merely delay needed solutions. We have seen the results of that in previous administrations.

Huddleston and Simpson concluded their letter by assuring Reagan that ''We in the Senate stand ready to work with you in a cooperative and bipartisan manner to develop a strong and fair immigration system, which can be effectively enforced.''[38]

Huddleston, Simpson, and the other forty-nine senators who signed the letter to Reagan on July 8, 1981, essentially urged the president to recommend comprehensive immigration reform legislation which would address the issues of both legal and illegal immigration. The senators suggested that Reagan recommend legislation reducing levels of legal immigration, while imposing measures to deter further illegal immigration to the United States. Such recommendations would fully address the concerns, which the senators raised, that immigration, both legal and illegal, had risen to excessive and unsustainable levels.

Since virtually every member of Congress strongly opposes illegal immigration, it is not surprising that the fifty-one senators would demand measures to stem the flow of illegal immigration to the United States. However, since most members of Congress strongly support legal immigration, it is surprising that a bipartisan majority of the Senate would regard the high levels of legal immigration existing since 1965 as being excessive and unsustainable, and suggest the need for a reduction in the number of legal immigrants admitted to the United States. The fact that a bipartisan majority of the Senate would express their opposition to the post-1965 levels of legal immigration, and suggest the need for the imposition of additional restrictions on legal immigration, reflected the fact that restrictionist sentiment in Congress was growing following the issuance of SCIRP's final report, which contained its recommendations on immigration reform, much as McBride and Gregory had feared.

BEARD ATTEMPTS TO INFLUENCE REAGAN TOWARD ADOPTION OF A RESTRICTIONIST IMMIGRATION POLICY

Huddleston and Simpson represented the leaders of the restrictionist forces in the Senate. Leading those forces in the House was Representative Robin Beard of Tennessee. As we have seen, in 1981, Beard joined Huddleston in introducing the Immigration and National Security Act in Congress, which imposed an annual ceiling limiting the total number of legal immigrants admitted to the United States to 350,000. The bill would also impose measures designed to deter further illegal immigration to the United States, including a beefing up of the Border Patrol, the imposition of an employer-sanctions regime which prohibited firms from knowingly hiring illegal aliens, and the establishment of a worker verification system, based upon the use of the Social Security card, as a secure and reliable means to determine the identity of individuals who seek employment.

On June 17, 1981, Beard wrote Reagan in anticipation of the recommendations of the Task Force on Immigration Reform, which were to be presented to the president two weeks later. Beard offered his own recommendations on immigration reform, which he asked Reagan to consider, as the president reviewed the proposals of the Task Force. Beard hoped that Reagan would take his recommendations into consideration in developing his administration's immigration policy, which would follow his review of the proposals on immigration reform of the Task Force. Beard's recommendations pertain to the three most important issues confronting the Reagan administration and Congress in their efforts to develop an immigration policy: amnesty, employer sanctions, and establishing appropriate limits on levels of legal immigration.

Beard recommended that Reagan oppose the granting of amnesty to illegal aliens who reside in the United States, which SCIRP had proposed in its final report. Beard argued that amnesty would only encourage further illegal immigration to the United States. Aliens would have additional incentives to immigrate to the United States illegally, in response to the granting of amnesty to undocumented individuals, in the hope they too might be able to obtain permanent legal residence once Congress established its next amnesty program. Accordingly, Beard warned that the establishment of an amnesty program would only increase the flow of illegal immigration to the United States.

A proposal for general amnesty, rewarding illegal immigrants for having broken the law in the past, would act as a powerful magnet for further illegal immigration undertaken in the hope of another future amnesty. It is now estimated that there are 5 to 10 million illegal immigrants living in America, many holding jobs. In the last several years the INS has apprehended over a million illegal aliens per year. Since those apprehended represent only a fraction of those actually entering, the enormity of the problem is easily discerned.

Beard argued that it would be inappropriate for Reagan and Congress to consider establishing an amnesty program until effective measures had been established to stem the flow of illegal immigration to the United States. To this end, Beard urged Reagan to recommend that Congress impose an employer-sanctions regime designed to deprive illegal aliens of jobs: "Before we consider amnesty, we must stem the massive flow of illegal immigrants to this country. My bill attacks illegal immigration in two basic ways: by making it illegal to hire persons not legally residing in this country, and by increasing the size of the Border Patrol. Enforcement of the prohibition against hiring illegal immigrants would be by verifiable Social Security number."

Beard believed that employer sanctions were essential to protect American workers from the competitive threat posed by the presence of a large illegal alien population in the United States. Indeed, Beard challenged the notion that illegal aliens served only as a source of cheap labor for the agricultural sector. Rather, Beard argued that illegal aliens threatened to displace American citizens from high-paying manufacturing and construction jobs: "Illegal immigrants do not just hold agricultural or entry-level jobs. They are increasingly found in highly-paid construction and manufacturing positions. Why should American workers have to compete with the world's poor millions for jobs in their own country?"

Beard's recommendations that Reagan oppose amnesty and support employer sanctions represented the congressman's two major proposals to address the problem of illegal immigration. Equally important to Beard was the issue of legal immigration. Beard believed that the Immigration Act of 1965 had driven legal immigration to excessive and unsustainable levels. Accordingly, Beard urged Reagan to recommend a substantial reduction in levels of legal immigration. To this end, Beard reminded Reagan that the immigration reform bill, which he had introduced in the House, would impose stringent limits upon legal immigration: "My bill sets an absolute ceiling of 350,000 for all legal immigrants, including refugees, coming into this country. This is more than the rest of the world's nations combined. This country can still be a land of immigrants, but there must still be a wise rationale for our future policy."

Beard concluded his letter by urging Reagan to "Please consider these recommendations. Ultimately our national sovereignty is defined by the security of our national borders. No other industrial country in the world allows its borders to be violated on such a massive scale as the United States."[39]

Beard essentially urged Reagan to adopt the restrictionist immigration policy agenda which he, Huddleston, and Simpson were attempting to implement through their own efforts to pass comprehensive immigration reform legislation in Congress. To some extent, Beard exaggerated the problem to the United States posed by mass immigration, especially as it pertained to illegal immigration. Beard's estimate that between 5 million and 10 million illegal aliens were residing in the United States is wildly exaggerated. As we saw in the previous chapter, the most authoritative estimate, which the Urban Institute provided, is that between 2.5 million and 3.5 million illegal aliens resided in the United States in 1980, the year before Beard wrote Reagan.

Beard's charge that illegal aliens threatened to displace Americans from high-paying manufacturing and construction jobs is not credible. Illegal aliens are generally confined to low-wage jobs; they tend to earn substantially lower incomes than native-born Americans and legal immigrants.[40] Moreover, as we have seen, the empirical evidence shows that the job displacement of American workers resulting from the mass immigration existing since 1965, both legal and illegal, has been minimal.

In his letter to Reagan, Beard clearly exaggerated both the number of illegal aliens who resided in the United States and the threat they posed to American workers. Nevertheless, Beard was reflecting the sentiments of the overwhelming majority of the public, and many members of Congress, when he argued that the United States had lost control of its borders as a result of the flood of immigration, both legal and illegal, which has poured into the United States since 1965. Beard's letter, together with the letter by Huddleston and Simpson several weeks later, only emphasized to Reagan the fact that restrictionist sentiment within Congress was growing, and that steps needed to be taken to address the mounting problems posed by mass immigration.

SWARTZ LOBBIES THE WHITE HOUSE AND CONGRESS AGAINST EMPLOYER SANCTIONS

The effort in Congress to pass restrictionist immigration reform legislation, which Huddleston, Simpson, and FAIR led, confronted fierce opposition from interest groups supporting the continuation of mass immigration. Pro-immigration forces have actively worked to prevent any attempt to impose new restrictions on immigration, both legal and illegal, since efforts to do so began in Congress in 1981. The political figure who has led pro-immigration forces in their efforts to prevent the passage of restrictionist immigration reform legislation since 1981 is Rick Swartz, the most successful and prominent pro-immigration lobbyist in Washington. During the 1970s, Swartz developed an interest in immigration policy while practicing as a civil rights attorney representing Haitian refugees seeking asylum in the United States. In 1981, Swartz, who by then had become the head of the Lawyers' Committee for Civil Rights Under Law, established the National Immigration Forum, America's leading interest group supporting mass immigration, which he directed during its first years.

During the 1990s, Swartz gained prominence as the lobbyist who stitched together a powerful coalition of interest groups representing the immigrant ethnic and business communities, which successfully defeated efforts in Congress to pass legislation reducing levels of legal immigration. As a testament to the power of the pro-immigration lobby, Swartz and his political allies succeeded in transforming the Kennedy-Simpson bill of 1988, which was designed to impose modest restrictions upon legal immigration, into the Immigration Act of 1990, one of the most expansionist immigration bills ever passed. The Immigration Act of 1990 actually raised levels of legal immigration by 40 percent. Immigration restrictionists renewed their efforts to pass legislation reducing levels of legal immigration following the Republican Party's takeover of both houses of Congress in 1994. However, those efforts were thwarted by Swartz and his pro-immigration lobby, which succeeded in building a bipartisan majority in the House to delete all reforms in legal immigration from the Illegal Immigrant Reform and Immigrant Responsibility Act (IIRIRA) of 1996.[41]

Swartz responded to the release of SCIRP's final report by actively lobbying the White House and Congress to reject the commission's recommendation for the imposition of an employer-sanctions regime designed to deprive illegal aliens of jobs. In a statement issued following release of the report, Swartz attacked employer sanctions as a costly, cumbersome, and unworkable means to deter further illegal immigration to the United States.

The Select Commission's recommendations fail to address the critical questions about the likely cost and the likely effectiveness of a scheme which emphasizes regulation of individual hiring transactions . . . With respect to costs, we believe that the commission's recommendations pose serious dangers to social order, community health, civil rights, and civil liberties. They will also result in a cumbersome and all-pervasive regulatory scheme, which will cost billions of dollars and impose substantial regulatory burdens on employers. With respect to effectiveness, there is no assurance that the commission's proposals will actually provide the results sought.

Swartz charged that employer sanctions would be costly, since they could not be effectively enforced unless firms had a means to verify the eligibility of individuals whom they wish to hire to work in the United States. One worker verification proposal under serious consideration in 1981 was the establishment of a national data bank, which would contain personal information on every individual eligible to work in the United States. Each individual, whose identity is recorded in the data bank, would be issued a card containing an identification number.

Each individual hired for a job would present his or her identity card to the employer. The employer would contact the national data bank in order to verify that the identification number listed on the card is valid, and that it belongs to the individual presenting it. The issuance of an identity card to every individual eligible to work in the United States, linked to a national data bank, would enable employers to verify the authenticity of the identification number presented to them by individuals. This would assure that firms comply with the legal obligations under employer-sanctions legislation.

Swartz charged that a fraud-resistant worker verification system would be costly. He noted that, by SCIRP's own estimates, it would cost the federal government $100 million to issue an identity card to every individual eligible to work in the Unitd States, and from $180 million to $230 million annually to administer the provision and maintenance of those cards. He noted that the estimated cost of establishing a national data bank containing personal information on every individual eligible to work in the United States was $87 million.

In addition, the federal government would have to spend $500 million to administer the national data bank during its first year of operation. This cost would gradually decline to $203 million annually after the national data bank had been in operation for six years. The cost would stabilize at that level after the initial six-year period that the national data bank was in operation. This would be in addition to the costs employers would have to incur to comply with the worker verification system, which would be organized around a national identity card.

In addition to its financial costs, Swartz charged that employer-sanctions legislation would result in ethnic discrimination against legal immigrant workers. SCIRP recommended that Congress pass legislation which imposed civil and criminal sanctions upon employers who knowingly hire illegal aliens. In order to escape those sanctions, employers would have incentives to avoid hiring immigrant workers, including those eligible to work in the United States. This would assure that firms comply with their legal obligations under employer-sanctions legislation. Swartz emphasized the potential for ethnic discrimination against legal immigrant workers which employer sanctions would create: "An employer may attempt to protect himself from . . . liability [for knowingly hiring an illegal alien] by refusing to hire anyone who 'might be foreign.' This will result in widespread discrimination against minority citizens and permanent legal residents of 'foreign' (e.g., Hispanic or Asian) appearance."

Swartz acknowledged that the potential for ethnic discrimination arising from employer sanctions could be mitigated through a fraud-resistant worker verification system. Such a system would enable employers to verify the eligibility of individuals whom they wish to hire to work in the United States. Under such a system, firms need not fear that they might be in violation of employer-sanctions legislation. Rather, such a system would enable employers to verify the eligibility of those immigrants. This would assure employers that the immigrants they hire are indeed eligible to work in the United States, without fear that they might be residing in this nation illegally. This assurance would eliminate the incentive for firms to avoid hiring immigrant workers in order to guarantee that they are in compliance with their legal obligations under employer-sanctions legislation. However, Swartz warned that such a system would create new problems pertaining to civil liberties. Specifically, Swartz warned that such a system would result in an invasion of individual privacy.

It is unfortunately true that the more effective and less discriminatory any system of identification is, the more of a threat it poses to civil liberties. The storage and retrieval of information in a national data bank raises concerns, particularly since its function is to regulate the employer relationship. Since work is essential to the enjoyment of any substantial social goods, one must be wary of allowing the government to determine who may and may not work. If the universal identifier is to be a card, then one must fear harassment by local police officers, who will selectively demand that it be produced, much as they demand alien registration cards from Hispanic citizens in many localities today.

Swartz concluded his statement by reiterating that the employer-sanctions legislation, which SCIRP recommended, would represent a costly, cumbersome, and unworkable means to deter further illegal immigration to the United States: "The package recommended by the commission is not cost-effective. It is clear that it will entail a substantial expenditure of government funds for enforcement efforts and the creation of a bureaucracy to administer an identification system, will impose economic costs on employers, and will pose dangers to fundamental social values. [Moreover], there is no indication that the recommendations will provide the results sought. We propose that the recommendations be rejected."[42]

Swartz continued his attacks against employer sanctions in another statement, which he issued following the release of SCIRP's final report. He argued that employer sanctions are unworkable because illegal aliens represent a vital source of cheap labor for many industries. Indeed, many industries often employ illegal aliens because they are willing to work for less than the minimum wage, and in unsafe and unhealthful working conditions. This makes the employment of illegal aliens very profitable for many industries. With the employment of illegal aliens, industries can save substantial sums in avoiding compliance with federal minimum wage and occupational safety and health regulations. As a result, many industries have financial incentives to continue hiring illegal aliens, even if Congress passed legislation prohibiting such an employment practice.

Employer sanctions legislation will not be very effective. . . . Employers who employ undocumented workers because they will work for less than the minimum wage or under less than legally-adequate working conditions have a financial incentive to violate employer sanctions legislation. [Indeed], since these employers have already made the choice to violate existing labor laws, it is reasonable to believe that they will also be willing to violate employer sanctions legislation. Enforcement of employer sanctions legislation against these employers will be extremely difficult.[43]

Swartz's charge that many employers knowingly hire illegal aliens, because they represent a vital source of cheap labor, is correct. In order to obtain employment, illegal aliens are often willing to work for less than the minimum wage, and in unsafe and unhealthful working conditions. As Juan F. Perea puts it, "For a chance at a better life, the undocumented are willing to work hard for much less than they deserve, and often for less than they would be entitled to under United States law. Because it is in the financial interest of those hiring undocumented persons to pay less, there is substantial demand for their underpaid services. . . . Employers ignore immigration laws and hire undocumented workers in order to lower their labor costs and increase profits."[44]

Employers prefer hiring illegal aliens over American citizens and permanent legal residents because undocumented workers can be easily exploited. American citizens and permanent legal residents may report any violations of federal labor law to the government. As a result, employers must pay American citizens and permanent legal residents at least the minimum wage and assure safe and healthful working conditions for them. Failure to do so would result in those Americans reporting violations of federal labor law to the government. Violators of federal labor law would face stiff fines, and possible imprisonment.

By contrast, illegal aliens are in no position to report any violations of federal labor law to the government. Indeed, illegal aliens who do so face a high likelihood that they would be identified and turned over to the INS for deportation to their native nations. Accordingly, illegal aliens have no choice but to accept less than the minimum wage, and employment under unsafe and unhealthful working conditions. Employers of illegal aliens save substantial sums in paying their workers less than the minimum wage and in failing to bring their workplaces into compliance with federal occupational safety and health regulations. As Perea puts it, "The undocumented . . . are extraordinarily vulnerable to exploitation. They dare not assert any rights they have publicly out of fear that identification will result in their deportation from the country."[45]

Swartz noted once again the substantial financial costs to the federal government which a fraud-resistant worker verification system, based upon the use of a national identity card and supported by a data bank, would incur. He also repeated his charge that such a system would represent a threat to both the civil liberties of all American citizens and the civil rights of legal immigrant workers.

Employer sanctions legislation . . . would involve much more serious costs than the mere monetary expense. Both the identity card and the data bank verification systems would endanger important civil liberties values. The identity card has the potential for becoming a type of internal passport, and a data bank system could be used to store confidential information about individuals far in excess of that necessary to determine whether they are legally entitled to work. Moreover, employer sanctions legislation will create discrimination against members of minority groups. Employers will be afraid of being prosecuted for hiring undocumented workers. They may, therefore, refuse to hire members of minority groups, who are likely to be undocumented.[46]

Swartz's argument that employer sanctions represented a costly, cumbersome, and ineffective means to deter further illegal immigration defined the case against employer sanctions which the pro-immigration lobby has made since 1981. Congress defied the pro-immigration lobby when it passed IRCA, which established an employer-sanctions regime. However, the pro-immigration lobby has effectively thwarted efforts in Congress to establish a fraud-resistant worker verification system, which would enable employers to comply with their legal obligations under the employer-sanctions provisions of IRCA. The worker verification proposals under congressional consideration have been variations on the creation of some form of national identity card, linked to a national computerized registry containing information on all individuals eligible to work in the United States, which Swartz bitterly attacked in 1981.

In the absence of a credible and effective worker verification system, illegal aliens have been able to easily obtain jobs by engaging in document fraud, and employers have been powerless to detect and crack down on such document fraud. With jobs readily available to illegal aliens, employer sanctions have had no discernible effect in stemming the flow of illegal immigration to the United States. The pro-immigration lobby has succeeded in preventing the establishment of a fraud-resistant worker verification system by making the same arguments against it, which Swartz first voiced in 1981.[47] Swartz represents an important figure in the politics of immigration reform, not only because he organized the pro-immigration lobby, which has succeeded in preventing passage of comprehensive immigration reform legislation since 1981; he is also important for having defined the case against a fraud-resistant worker verification system, which the pro-immigration lobby has effectively used since 1981 to prevent Congress from establishing such a system.

MALDEF LOBBIES THE WHITE HOUSE AND CONGRESS TO INFLUENCE THE DEVELOPMENT OF IMMIGRATION POLICY

In his lobbying campaign against employer sanctions, Swartz received invaluable support from the Mexican American Legal Defense and Education Fund (MALDEF). As the largest interest group representing the Mexican-American community, MALDEF has an obvious interest in immigration policy. As we have seen, Mexicans represent the largest single immigrant group, consisting of over one-quarter of all foreign-born individuals who reside in the United States. Mexicans represent a disproportionately large share of illegal aliens. Over half of all illegal aliens who reside in the United States were born in Mexico.

MALDEF Opposes Employer-Sanctions Legislation

On May 6, 1981, Vilma S. Martinez, president of MALDEF, appeared before a joint hearing of the immigration subcommittees of the Senate and House, respectively, to respond to SCIRP's final report. Martinez was especially concerned about SCIRP's recommendation for passage of employer-sanctions legislation designed to deter further illegal immigration to the United States. Latinos in general, and Mexicans in particular, represent the overwhelming majority of illegal aliens who reside in the United States. Echoing the argument of Swartz, MALDEF feared that employers would avoid hiring legal immigrant Latino workers, fearing that they might be residing in the United States illegally. This would assure firms that they are in compliance with their legal obligations under employer-sanctions legislation.

MALDEF had every reason to fear that employer-sanctions legislation would result in ethnic discrimination against legal Latino immigrant workers. In 1996, 73 percent of all illegal aliens were born in Latin America.[48] As we have seen, 54 percent of all illegal aliens were born in a single Latin American nation—Mexico. The fact that nearly three-quarters of all illegal aliens are Latin Americans, and over half Mexican, has created the false, but popular, stereotype that most, if not all Latino, especially Mexican, immigrants are undocumented. As Juan F. Perea puts it, ''The public identification of 'illegal aliens' with persons of Mexican ancestry is so strong that many Mexican Americans and other Latino citizens are presumed to be foreign and illegal.''[49]

Given the stereotypical assumption that most, if not all, Latino immigrants reside in the United States illegally, many employers will automatically suspect that foreign-born Hispanics who seek employment lack authentic documentation. By refusing to hire Latino immigrants, including those lawfully authorized to work in the United States, firms would reduce the likelihood that they might be employing illegal aliens in violation of their legal obligations under employer-sanctions legislation.

Congress would couple legislation prohibiting employers from knowingly hiring illegal aliens with punitive measures involving stiff fines and possible jail sentences. Firms would not want to take any chances on hiring illegal aliens, since such an employment practice could expose them to civil litigation and possible criminal prosecution.

In her statement issued before the joint hearing of the immigration subcommittees, Martinez announced MALDEF's opposition to employer sanctions, charging that they would represent a threat to the civil rights of legal immigrant Latino workers.

For Mexican Americans and other Americans, who share the physical characteristics of persons thought to constitute the bulk of the undocumented population, employer sanctions will undoubtedly exacerbate existing patterns of employment discrimination. Well-meaning employers, fearful of government sanctions, will shy away from persons who appear ''foreign.'' Racist or biased employers will simply use the ''fear'' of sanctions as an excuse to avoid hiring qualified minorities. At the very least, employers untrained and inexperienced in the intricate immigration laws are likely to err in their assessment of who is undocumented.

Like Swartz, Martinez acknowledged that the potential for ethnic discrimination arising from employer sanctions would be mitigated by the establishment of a fraud-resistant worker verification system. By enabling employers to verify the eligibility of individuals, such a system would assure firms that the immigrants they employ are in fact lawfully authorized to work in this nation, and are not residing here illegally. As we have seen, the worker verification proposal which received the most serious consideration in 1981 was the creation of a national identity card. Martinez repeated the warning, which Swartz made, that a national identity card would represent a threat to the civil liberties of all American citizens, especially Latinos.

We have serious civil liberties objections to a national identity card. Such an identification system is likely to be used for purposes other than work-status identification, rendering it a ready vehicle for abuse of confidential information. Financial, medical, and a host of other records, which might be keyed to a national identification number, would be readily available to anyone with access to that number and appropriate computer technology. Illegal activity of police officers in attempting to enforce federal immigration laws will be facilitated by the national identity card system; such police officers could then require Hispanic-looking citizens to produce the card to prove the legality of their presence in the U.S.

Martinez charged that employer sanctions would be unworkable for two reasons.

First, employers of illegal aliens are highly unlikely to be caught. The federal government simply lacks the resources to investigate the employment practices of every firm which might be employing illegal aliens. Given the fact that they are unenforceable, employer sanctions would have little, if any, effect in deterring employers wishing to hire illegal aliens from doing so. Since illegal aliens would continue to have ready access to jobs, employer sanctions would do little, if anything, to deprive foreign-born individuals of incentives to reside in the United States illegally. As a result, employer sanctions would have no discernible effect in curtailing the flow of illegal immigration to the United States.

Second, like Swartz, Martinez noted that illegal aliens represent a vital source of cheap labor for many industries. They save substantial sums employing illegal aliens. They would continue to hire illegal aliens, even if Congress were to pass legislation which prohibited them from doing so.

In the unlikely event that a firm were to be caught employing an illegal alien, it would have to pay nothing more than a token fine. This would represent a minimal financial loss when balanced against the substantial losses many industries would incur if they were forced to refrain from hiring low-wage, low-cost illegal aliens, and instead employ American citizens and permanent legal residents. Industries which employ American citizens and permanent legal residents would have to pay them substantially higher wages than illegal aliens. In addition, industries would have to spend substantial sums to maintain safe and healthful working conditions for their American laborers.

Martinez made clear her belief that employer sanctions would be completely unworkable.

Employer sanctions could not be adequately enforced. Such enforcement would require a massive commitment of federal resources, particularly since most undocumented workers are employed in relatively small industrial firms and service companies. The traditional low priority accorded immigration enforcement within the Department of Justice and the more recent emphasis upon frugality, which has characterized the federal sector, militate against any such commitment. To the contrary, the resources devoted to the enforcement of employer sanctions are likely to be minimal, as are the resources devoted to other federal labor regulation activities.

Employer sanctions would not effectively curtail illegal immigration. The minimal legal and financial risk to employers, who desire to exploit undocumented labor, is insufficient to overcome the powerful human and economic forces which underlie undocumented worker migration. The small fine proposed for an employer, who knowingly hires undocumented workers, does not seriously undermine the economic advantage of undocumented workers, since a more competitive market wage rate would be necessary to attract domestic workers. Moreover, given the lack of an extensive enforcement effort, an employer runs negligible risk of being caught. . . . Rather than forego the benefits of hiring undocumented workers, employers who seek this type of workforce will, in all likelihood, successfully evade the law.

Martinez concluded that "while there is no reason to believe that employer sanctions would accomplish any valid policy end, it is clear that they would result in creation of an additional regulatory burden to employers and would result in discrimination against Mexican-American citizens and legal residents."[50]

MALDEF Supports the Establishment of an Amnesty Program

Employer sanctions represented only one of the two major recommendations which SCIRP recommended to address the problem of illegal immigration. The other recommendation was to grant amnesty to illegal aliens who resided in the United States. Martinez announced MALDEF's support for amnesty. Martinez's announcement came as no surprise. As we will see in Chapter 5, nearly three-quarters of all illegal aliens who received amnesty under IRCA were born in Mexico.

With Mexicans representing the overwhelming majority of illegal aliens eligible for amnesty, the Mexican-American community had a strong interest in the establishment of a legalization program. It would enable a substantial segment of the Mexican-American community who resided in the United States illegally to obtain permanent legal residence, and eventual American citizenship. Accordingly, amnesty was vital to enabling Mexican illegal aliens to obtain the legal and political rights—the right to reside in the United States permanently, qualify for entitlement programs, and vote—which they lack as undocumented individuals. As the leading interest group representing the Mexican-American community, MALDEF had a strong interest in assuring passage of amnesty legislation.

However, Martinez made clear that MALDEF opposed SCIRP's recommendation that "legalization begin when appropriate enforcement mechanisms have been instituted" to deter further illegal immigration to the United States. As we will see in Chapter 5, one prominent member of SCIRP, Senator Simpson, interpreted this recommendation to mean that the amnesty program could not go into effect until employer sanctions had proved successful in curtailing the flow of illegal immigration to the United States. To be sure, this interpretation was rejected by another prominent member of SCIRP, Senator Edward M. Kennedy of Massachusetts, who insisted that amnesty could proceed, even in the absence of the successful implementation of employer sanctions. However, SCIRP's recommendations on amnesty were subject to differing interpretations, as the disagreement between Simpson and Kennedy shows. Suffice it to say that one may reasonably interpret those recommendations to mean that amnesty would not go into effect until employer sanctions had proven successful in stemming the flow of illegal immigration to the United States—the view which Simpson held.

However, employer sanctions are unworkable unless they are coupled with the establishment of a fraud-resistant worker verification system, which would enable firms to comply with their legal obligations under employer-sanctions legislation. The pro-immigration lobby was determined to prevent Congress from establishing such a system, guaranteeing that employer sanctions would have no discernible effect in stemming the flow of illegal immigration to the United States. Immigration reform legislation which established an employer-sanctions regime without a fraud-resistant worker verification system would be designed to fail. If such legislation tied the implementation of amnesty to the success of employer sanctions in stemming the flow of illegal immigration, then the amnesty program would never go into effect, given the certainty that employer sanctions would fail. To assure that the amnesty program would go into effect, the pro-immigration lobby needed to guarantee that Congress would grant permanent legal residence to illegal aliens who lived in the United States on an unconditional basis, and that legalization not be linked to the successful enforcement of employer sanctions. Accordingly, Martinez urged that Congress establish an amnesty program which would be implemented on an unconditional basis, even if employer sanctions failed to have any discernible effect in curtailing the flow of illegal immigration to the United States.[51]

MALDEF Supports Raising Levels of Legal Immigration

In addition to voicing MALDEF's position on SCIRP's recommendations to address the problem of illegal immigration, Martinez outlined the interest group's position on reforms in legal immigration. Martinez endorsed SCIRP's recommendation for a moderate increase in levels of legal immigration. However, Martinez attacked SCIRP for having failed to address the special problem of Mexicans seeking to immigrate to the United States legally.

Until 1965, the United States maintained an open border with the rest of the nations of the Western Hemisphere, including Mexico. The Immigration Act of 1965, for the first time in American history, imposed an annual ceiling, which limited the number of legal immigrants admitted to the United States from the rest of the Western Hemisphere, to 120,000. However, the ceiling applied to the rest of the Western Hemisphere as a whole. Legal immigrants born in each nation of the Western Hemisphere would be admitted to the United States in unlimited numbers until the hemispheric ceiling of 120,000 had been reached.

The Immigration Act of 1965 imposed an annual ceiling which limited the total number of legal immigrants admitted to the United States from any single foreign nation of the Eastern Hemisphere to 20,000.[52] In 1976, Congress extended this ceiling on legal immigration to the rest of the nations of the Western Hemisphere.[53] This resulted in extreme hardship for Mexicans who wished to immigrate to the United States legally.

In the years before the imposition of an annual numerical ceiling on total legal immigration from any single foreign nation of the Western Hemisphere, 40,000 to 50,000 Mexicans immigrated legally to the United States annually. As a result, the annual ceiling, which limited the total number of Mexicans admitted to the United States to 20,000, satisfied less than half the annual number of Mexicans who wished to immigrate to the United States legally.[54] Those Mexicans unable to immigrate to the United States legally, because the annual ceiling on immigration from Mexico had already been reached, had to wait their turn before being granted permission to do so.

As the backlog of Mexicans waiting to immigrate to the United States legally grew in the years since imposition of the annual numerical ceiling on total legal immigration from any single foreign nation of the Western Hemisphere, so did the amount of time Mexicans had to wait before being granted permission to obtain permanent legal residence in this nation. Unable or unwilling to wait the many numbers of years necessary before receiving permission to immigrate legally, many Mexicans found themselves with no alternative but to do so illegally. As a result, the imposition of an annual numerical ceiling, limiting total legal immigration from Mexico, has represented a major factor in the substantial flow of illegal immigration from that nation, which has occurred since the imposition of the ceiling in 1976. Martinez urged that Mexico either be exempted from the annual ceiling, which limited the total number of legal immigrants admitted to the United States from any single foreign nation to 20,000, or be granted more visas to relieve the massive backlog of Mexicans waiting to immigrate to the United States legally.

As recently as 1976, there was no fixed limitation on the number of immigrant visas issued to nationals of the Western Hemisphere countries, and Mexican citizens obtained 40,000–50,000 such visas each year. The existing per-country limitation of 20,000 visas creates a hardship on Mexicans attempting to enter the U.S. legally. There is currently a five-year backlog for spouses and adult children of permanent legal residents from Mexico, and long waits for siblings and other close relatives. This is unfair, since there are many countries . . . whose citizens are not desirous of entering the U.S., where there is no waiting period for visas. Legal backlogs, which are perceived as hopelessly long, encourage illegal immigration outside the waiting-list visa system. . . . An alternative approach, which has gained considerable support in recent years, would recognize our special relationship with our neighbors by exempting Mexico and Canada from per-country limitations or granting them a separate, enlarged allotment of visas.[55]

A MEXICAN GUEST WORKER PROGRAM EMERGES AS A POSSIBLE "SOLUTION" TO THE PROBLEM OF ILLEGAL IMMIGRATION

As we have seen, over half of all illegal aliens who reside in the United States were born in Mexico. Since fiscal 1983, over one million illegal aliens annually have been apprehended by the INS, with the single exception of fiscal 1989.[56] As we saw in the previous chapter, 90 percent to 95 percent of those illegal aliens are Mexicans caught either crossing, or in close proximity to, the American border.

One major proposal to stem the flow of illegal immigration across Mexican border, which received serious consideration in 1981, was the establishment of a guest worker program. A limited number of Mexicans would be admitted each year as guest workers to take jobs in the United States where domestic labor shortages exist. Mexican guest workers would remain in the United States for a limited period of time, after which they would be expected to return to Mexico.

A guest worker program would be expected to curtail the flow of illegal immigration across the Mexican border, since there are millions of Mexicans who wish to work in the United States, for two reasons: first, wages in the United States are many times higher than they are in Mexico; and second, jobs are substantially more plentiful in the United States than they are in Mexico. Mexicans wishing to work in the United States on a temporary basis, who are not granted visas to do so, would have no alternative but to illegally cross the American border in search of jobs in the United States. By granting Mexicans a legal avenue to find work in the United States, a guest worker program is designed to substantially reduce incentives for Mexicans to immigrate to the United States illegally. Since Mexico serves as the single largest source of illegal immigration, a substantial reduction in illegal immigration from Mexico would result in a sharp overall drop in the flow of illegal immigration to the United States.

The United States has had extensive experience with a Mexican guest worker program. In 1942, Congress established the Mexican Labor Program, popularly known as the "bracero" program.[57] The mass recruitment of men to fight in World War II created a severe labor shortage in the agricultural sector. The bracero program was designed to relieve this labor shortage by allowing Mexicans to work in American agriculture on a temporary basis.

Mexicans were willing to work for substantially lower wages and under more harsh labor conditions than their American counterparts. As a result, agribusiness quickly became addicted to cheap Mexican farm labor. As Kitty Calavita, an expert on the bracero program, puts it,

The bracero program became synonomous with substandard wages and living conditions. Although guarantees regarding wages, duration of employment, housing, health insurance, and other specifics were written into bracero contracts, these protections were poorly enforced and routinely circumvented.

Also well-documented was the downward pressure on local farm workers' wages. Although bracero contracts required employers to pay "prevailing wages," and growers had to demonstrate that a shortage of labor existed before being certified to contract braceros, study after study found that in regions where braceros were concentrated, workers' bargaining power declined and wages fell.[58]

Agribusiness quickly became addicted to cheap Mexican farm labor. To accommodate the needs of agribusiness, Congress extended the bracero program after the end of World War II. However, the American Federation of Labor–Congress of Industrial Organizations (AFL–CIO) actively lobbied the White House to terminate the bracero program. The AFL–CIO complained that Mexicans were displacing American farm workers from their jobs and depressing wages. In response to the demands of the AFL–CIO, the Johnson administration terminated the bracero program in 1964.

The termination of the bracero program is widely cited as a major factor for the sharp increase in illegal immigration from Mexico since 1964. Mexicans who had immigrated to the United States legally under the bracero program now had no alternative but to do so illegally, in order to continue working in American agriculture. Given this fact, it is not surprising that policymakers in Washington were actively considering reestablishment of a Mexican guest worker program as a major means to reduce the flow of illegal immigration from Mexico.

To be sure, the United States has maintained a guest worker program for unskilled laborers under Section H-2 of the Immigration and Nationality Act of 1952.[59] However, the H-2 program is very restrictive; guest workers may only enter the United States to fill jobs where no Americans can be found. Since there are very few jobs where no American workers can be found, only a limited number of guest workers have been allowed to enter the United States under the H-2 program. In fiscal 1994 only 28,872 unskilled foreign-born workers were admitted to the United States under the H-2 program.[60] The proposals under active consideration in 1981 involved the establishment of a new, substantially enlarged guest worker program in place of the much smaller H-2 program.

On March 3, 1981, Reagan announced that he was granting serious consideration to recommending the establishment of a guest worker program as a major means to reduce the flow of illegal immigration from Mexico. Reagan's announcement came in a television interview with Walter Cronkite, anchorman of the CBS Evening News. Reagan told Cronkite that he was "very intrigued" by a proposal which the governors of the border states of the United States and Mexico made to establish a guest worker program. By granting temporary employment to Mexicans who wished to work in the United States, the program would be designed to reduce incentives for them to immigrate to the United States illegally in search of jobs. Reagan revealed that he intended to take up the issue of a guest worker program during his summit meeting with Lopez Portillo, which, at that time, was scheduled to take place in Tijuana on April 26–28, 1981.[61]

OPPOSITION DEVELOPS TO THE ESTABLISHMENT OF A MEXICAN GUEST WORKER PROGRAM

Reagan's announcement that he was granting serious consideration to recommending the establishment of a Mexican guest worker program provoked opposition from the National Committee for Full Employment, an interest group composed of many important civil rights, labor, and religious organizations.[62] In December 1980, the committee established a Task Force on Undocumented Workers to develop a consensus among the interest groups that formed the committee on the issue of illegal immigration. The Task Force responded to Reagan's announcement that he was actively considering recommending the establishment of a Mexican guest worker program by issuing a statement strongly opposing such a proposal. The Task Force charged that such a program would subject Mexican workers to exploitation from American employers, and displace American workers by enabling firms to hire low-wage Mexicans as an alternative to high-wage Americans. To effectively compete against Mexicans, Americans would have to accept lower wages than would otherwise be the case. Job displacement and wage depression occurred among American farm workers during the period when the bracero program was in effect.

We are concerned about the statement made by President Reagan indicating that he was "intrigued" by a proposal regarding a large-scale temporary workers program which had been advocated by some border state Governors.

The United States and Mexico experimented with several variations of temporary workers programs for a generation, and they were disasters. Let's not make the same mistake twice. The bracero program, which operated from 1942 to 1964, brought ill-paid Mexican campesinos to work for U.S. agribusiness by the hundreds of thousands. While it served as a windfall (in the form of cheap, docile labor) it depressed wages and working conditions for competing U.S. workers, postponed rationalization of the agricultural labor market, exploited Mexican farm workers, and caused endless, needless grief in U.S.– Mexican relations. Even if the administration devises a somewhat less exploitative program than the old bracero program, temporary foreign worker programs worldwide tend to provide less than equal rights for workers. Furthermore, their stay in the host nation is often more than temporary. That certainly has been the European experience with "guest workers." It makes no sense to bring additional workers to the U.S. at a time when there are eight million unemployed U.S. residents.

The Task Force on Undocumented Workers concluded that "the administration should not be seeking a quick and simplistic fix" to the problem of illegal immigration from Mexico by recommending the establishment of a guest worker program.[63]

On March 20, 1981, David S. North, a consultant to the National Committee for Full Employment, sent Hodsoll a copy of the statement issued by its Task Force on Undocumented Workers opposing establishment of a Mexican guest worker program. Attached to the copy of the statement was a letter from North, who announced that the the Task Force "respectfully submits the enclosed statement to the President regarding the proposed temporary workers program. The Task Force feels that such programs have failed in the past and are unlikely to be useful in the future."[64]

On March 31, 1981, Hodsoll wrote North, "Thank you for your letter of March 20 regarding temporary workers programs. I fully understand the points you make. Guest worker programs, unless properly framed, can pose problems. The inter-Cabinet Task Force on Immigration and Refugee Policy, which has been established by the President, will take into account your views and those of the National Committee for Full Employment as we proceed with trying to synchronize U.S. immigration and refugee law with reality."[65]

Joining the National Committee for Full Employment in its opposition to a Mexican guest worker program was MALDEF. In her statement issued to a joint hearing of the immigration subcommittees of the Senate and House, respectively, on May 6, 1981, Martinez announced MALDEF's opposition to the establishment of such a program. Martinez argued that all guest worker programs under active consideration would subject Mexican laborers to exploitation by American employers, while denying them important legal rights and protections.

We have fundamental objections to all of the proposed "guest" worker programs. . . . For the United States to take full advantage of the opportunity to revitalize our workforce, full rights and access to permanent legal residence status should be accorded to immigrant workers. None of the proposals adequately safeguards the right of foreign workers to fair treatment or prevents the erosion of civil rights of Mexican Americans which a large-scale guest worker program would trigger.

Martinez argued that past and current experience with guest worker programs demonstrated that they were unfair to Mexican laborers.

Historical experience with guest worker programs, as well as current practice, indicates that such programs are designed or used in ways that are inherently unfair to the workers. Before such programs were institutionalized, Mexican workers were imported and summarily expelled as dictated by labor needs, often with attendant hardship to the workers and their families. In the bracero program of the 1940s to the early 1960s, Mexican workers were abused by employers, who held by contract, entire control over the workers' ability to remain and work in the United States. Although the Mexican government had negotiated labor rights for the workers, there was virtually no attempt to enforce these assurances; grossly substandard pay and working conditions resulted. Growers also manipulated the bracero program to keep unions from organizing agricultural workers.

In addition to subjecting Mexican laborers to exploitation by American employers, Martinez argued that a guest worker program would not reduce incentives for Mexicans to immigrate to the United States illegally. Rather, many Mexican workers admitted to the United States on a temporary basis would be sure to overstay their visas in order to retain their jobs in this nation. Many guest workers would not return to Mexico, where they faced a high likelihood of unemployment. At best, former guest workers would only be able to find jobs in Mexico paying a fraction of the wages they earned in the United States.

A guest worker program would not stem the flow of undocumented workers into the country. While such a program might temporarily legalize and identify a segment of the important immigrant population, it would ultimately increase the number of workers who enter and remain in the country illegally. Historically, guest worker programs in both the United States and Europe have had this effect, as guest workers overstay their temporary visas, return to places and jobs with which they became acquainted while temporarily admitted, and opt for freer, albeit riskier, status of uncontrolled entry, employment, and residence.

Martinez concluded that a guest worker program represented neither a fair nor effective means to meet the labor needs of the American economy; nor would it reduce the flow of illegal immigration from Mexico. Rather, to accomplish those objectives, Martinez recommended that Mexican workers who entered the United States to fill existing domestic labor shortages be allowed to obtain permanent legal residence in this nation. This would assure that Mexican workers would received the legal protections and political rights which they would not have if they were admitted to the United States only on a temporary basis.

The expedient adoption of a massive temporary worker program would create many problems and would not resolve the "problem" it purports to address—that of eliminating undocumented workers, while providing necessary foreign labor in our workforce. A more effective and fairer program would seek to incorporate those persons, whose energy and skill we need, into our society. . . . Workers, who over a period of time staff our industries, pay taxes, and contribute to our economic welfare, should receive the social and economic benefits accorded to U.S. residents. They should be given an opportunity to remain here and to become permanent legal residents, and eventually, citizens.[66]

On May 1, 1981, Martinez sent Meese a copy of the statement outlining MALDEF's position on immigration policy, which she delivered to a joint hearing of the immigration subcommittees of the Senate and House, respectively, five days later. Attached to the copy of the statement was a letter from Martinez requesting that Meese pay close attention to that portion of the text which pertained to MALDEF's opposition to the establishment of a Mexican guest worker program.

On April 28 I sent you a mailgram stating our opposition to proposed guest worker programs and promising to forward a more complete position paper by May 4. Enclosed herewith is a copy of the testimony, which I will deliver before a joint congressional committee hearing on immigration issues. The part of my written testimony that treats guest worker programs is at pages 10–14. I invite your attention to the full statement of MALDEF's position on immigration policy, but especially to that portion on guest worker programs.[67]

Meese sent Martinez's letter to Hodsoll, who in turn transmitted it to Anderson. Attached to the letter was a memo from Hodsoll to Anderson: "Attached is a letter to Ed Meese on the subject of guest worker programs from Vilma Martinez of MALDEF. I thought you should be aware of her perception of the Hispanic community's views."[68]

MALDEF was not the only interest group representing the Latino community which voiced its opposition to the establishment of a Mexican guest worker program. Another such group was the League of United Latin American Citizens (LULAC). In June 1981 LULAC held its national convention in New Mexico, which Vice President George Bush attended. On June 22, Bush sent a memo to Attorney General William French Smith, who served as chairman of the President's Task Force on Immigration and Refugee Policy. In his memo, Bush conveyed the views expressed by LULAC leaders at their national convention regarding the establishment of a Mexican guest worker program directly to Smith.

I attended the LULAC National Convenion in New Mexico last week. There was much talk there on the guest worker program. The national LULAC leaders opposed it, but several LULAC members suggested that if there was to be a guest worker program, certain key ingredients should be as follows: 1. freedom of movement; 2. freedom of selection of job; 3. that the guest worker have the same rights as the permanent alien; 4. entitled to equal protection under the law; 5. given full access to public services; 6. that they pay taxes; and 7. that the public school systems provide free education to children of Mexican guest workers in those states where the program is implemented.

Bush concluded his memo to Smith by expressing his hope that the views which LULAC leaders expressed on the establishment of a Mexican guest worker program would be taken into account in any recommendations the President's Task Force on Immigration and Refugee Policy might make concerning this issue: "I pass this information along for consideration by your Task Force."[69]

The concerns raised by organized labor and interest groups representing the Latino community over the establishment of a Mexican guest worker program were shared by members of SCIRP. In the final report, containing its recommendations on immigration reform, SCIRP announced its opposition to the establishment of a guest worker program. As an alternative to a guest worker program, SCIRP recommended that Congress expand and liberalize the H-2 program to assure the United States a sufficient supply of foreign workers to fill shortages existing within the domestic labor market.

In his comments on SCIRP's final report, one of its members, Joaquin Otero, made it clear that the commission unequivocally rejected the establishment of a Mexican guest worker program: "The commission made it crystal clear that the overwhelming majority [of its members] had rejected consideration of any new large-scale, temporary, or guest worker program now or in the future. This decision should be reported in unmistakable terms, leaving no room for conjecture or misinterpretation."[70]

CONCERNS ARE RAISED WITHIN THE REAGAN ADMINISTRATION OVER A GUEST WORKER PROGRAM

In considering whether to recommend the establishment of a Mexican guest worker program, the White House not only had to contend with opposition from liberal labor groups and immigrant ethnic groups such as the National Committee for Full Employment and MALDEF, respectively. The White House also had to address concerns raised over such a program from within the Reagan administration. As we have seen, previous Mexican guest worker programs, especially the bracero program, had resulted in the subjection of Mexican laborers to exploitation by American employers. As a result, the reestablishment of such a program was sure to raise concerns within the Mexican government, which had an obvious interest in assuring that its citizens who resided in the United States were treated fairly and humanely. Accordingly, any guest worker program which Reagan might recommend could have an adverse effect upon Mexican–American relations.

Concerns within the Reagan administration over this issue were especially strong within the Labor Department. On March 30, 1981, Marion F. Houstoun, an immigration policy specialist within the department sent an issue paper to David Hiller, Special Assistant to the Attorney General, who served as chairman of the Task Force on Immigration and Refugee Policy. The purpose of Houstoun's paper was to recommend how Reagan should treat the sensitive issue of a Mexican guest worker program during his summit meeting with Lopez Portillo, which, at the time, was scheduled to take place in Tijuana April 26–28.

In his issue paper, Houstoun noted that a Mexican guest worker program would represent a top priority on the agenda of the upcoming summit meeting between Reagan and Lopez Portillo. This was the result of the remarks Reagan made in his interview with Cronkite on March 3, 1981, when the President announced that he was "very intrigued" with a proposal, which the governors of the border states of the United States and Mexico made, to establish a guest worker program as a means to reduce incentives for Mexicans to immigrate to the United States illegally in search of employment: "During his March 3 interview with Walter Cronkite, the President expressed his interest in the U.S.-Mexico visiting worker program proposed by several U.S. and [Government of

Mexico] GOM border state Governors, and announced his intention to discuss this proposal with the GOM President in April. Should the President elaborate on those remarks? If so, how?''

Given the fact that a guest worker program represented a very sensitive issue in Mexico, Houstoun predicted that the Mexican government would want to discuss this issue with the Reagan administration before Congress proceeded with the establishment of any such program.

The recent release of the final report of the Select Commission on Immigration and Refugee Policy, in the context of . . . continued large-scale illegal immigration, has generated considerable public and congressional interest in federal action [on this issue]. Since at least half of the estimated 3.5 to 6 million illegals currently in the U.S. are thought to be Mexican nationals, migration is one of the most sensitive of all U.S.-Mexico issues. Mexico closely follows U.S. immigration policy developments. The GOM will therefore be interested in an elaboration of the President's remarks to Cronkite. At a minimum, Lopez Portillo can be expected to want assurances that consultations with Mexico would precede U.S. government action in this area.

Houstoun recommended two options for Reagan to consider in determining how to address the issue of a guest worker program during his summit meeting with Lopez Portillo.

(1) Maintain reactive posture regarding worker proposal. Deal with this sensitive U.S.-Mexico issue by not initiating any discussion of the illegal immigration problem or the [United States Government] USG-GOM border Governors' visiting worker proposal. Should the subject be raised, assure the GOM President that consultations with the GOM would precede USG action in this area.

(2) Raise issue but maintain open all future options. Express concern regarding adverse effects of continued illegal immigration, on the U.S., sending nations, and the undocumented workers themselves. State interest in USG-GOM visiting worker proposal. Signal administration's interest in USG action—while holding all options open—by stating that the complexity and sensitivity of this issue mandate a thorough review by the administration. That this led the President to create a Cabinet-level Interagency Task Force and to charge it with the responsibility for a comprehensive review of U.S. immigration and refugee policies, including of the recently-submitted recommendations of the Select Commission. Assure the GOM President that consultations would precede USG action in this area.[71]

Attached to Houstoun's issue paper was a memo from him to Hiller, which reaffirmed the fact that a guest worker program is an issue that straddles the political boundaries between domestic immigration policy and foreign relations between the United States and Mexico: "Attached, as requested, is the migration issue paper, drafted along the lines we discussed on the phone, for the upcoming meeting of the President with GOM President Lopez Portillo. . . . Immigration is a paradigm of the proverbial seamless web: It's impossible to sort out domestic from foreign policy implications.''[72]

On May 4, 1981, representatives from the White House and State, Justice, and Labor Departments traveled to Mexico City to meet officials of the Mexican Foreign Relations and Labor Ministries in order to discuss the issue of Mexican immigration to the United States. A major item on the agenda of the meeting between representatives of the Mexican and American governments concerned the establishment of a guest worker program, which the President's Task Force on Immigration and Refugee Policy was considering including in its recommendations on immigration reform that it planned to present to Reagan in the coming months. On May 6, 1981, Kate Moore, Special Assistant to the White House Chief of Staff, who participated in the meeting, sent Hodsoll a memo which summarized the results of the conference. Moore noted that Mexican representatives to the meeting had asked their American counterparts "Two questions (which) probed our willingness to protect Mexican workers. These questions may or may not have been raised with the backdrop of the temporary worker program in mind."[73]

Attached to Moore's memo was a list of questions, which representatives of the Mexican Foreign Relations and Labor Ministries had asked members of the White House and State, Justice, and Labor Departments. Included in that list were the following two questions Moore had referred to in her memo regarding the treatment of Mexican workers in the United States: first, "Will the U.S. enforce laws relating to the human rights of workers as well as laws regarding labor standards and immigration?"; and second, "How much authority does the President have to place behind enforcing the labor laws? Will he make a strong attempt to enforce those laws?"[74]

Moore noted that representatives of the Mexican Foreign Relations and Labor Ministries were concerned about the possible establishment of a guest worker program in the United States, given the potential that it created for the exploitation of Mexican workers by American employers, and the possibility that it would fail to achieve its objective of stemming the flow of illegal immigration from Mexico: "The Mexicans wanted to know how large a temporary worker program might be. In the after-dinner discussions, however, it should be noted that Ambassador Luis Wybo, Director of Protection Affairs in the Foreign Secretariat, indicated that he felt a temporary worker program might prove a problem and provoke more illegal immigration. I think we should be careful not to overrate the Mexican enthusiasm for a temporary worker program."[75]

As the memos from Houstoun and Moore suggest, a guest worker program is a politically explosive issue, having important implications for both domestic American politics and Mexican–American relations. Organized labor, which maintained a stong presence within the National Committee for Full Employment, has long opposed guest worker programs, believing that they result in job displacement and wage depression among American workers, as employers use low-wage Mexican laborers as an alternative to high-wage Americans. The Mexican-American community, represented by MALDEF, also opposed a guest worker program, believing that it would result in the exploitation of Mexican workers by American employers. The Mexican government shared those concerns, as Moore's memo clearly shows. Houstoun's memo reveals that the Reagan administration was troubled about the potential adverse impact the establishment of a guest worker program would have on America's traditionally close relationship with Mexico. For reasons of both domestic and international politics, the White House needed to tread very carefully as it considered the politically explosive issue of a Mexican guest worker program.

BRIGGS PRESENTS THE ECONOMIC CASE AGAINST THE ESTABLISHMENT OF A GUEST WORKER PROGRAM

Organized labor and the Mexican-American community were politically motivated in their opposition to the establishment of a guest worker program. In addition to the political arguments against the establishment of the program, a strong economic case against it existed. That case was best made by Vernon M. Briggs, Jr., who would emerge as one of the preeminent experts on the economics of immigration during the 1990s. Briggs presented his case against the establishment of a guest worker program directly to the White House in a meeting he had with Hodsoll on May 7, 1981. The day following their meeting, Briggs sent a paper he had written to Hodsoll arguing against such a program. Briggs's paper essentially repeated the two central arguments, which organized labor and the Mexican-American community made against such a program: first, that it would result in substantial job displacement of American workers; and second, that it would do nothing to stem the flow of illegal immigration to the United States.

Briggs argued that a guest worker program would result in job displacement because employers prefer to hire immigrants as an alternative to Americans. This is not just because immigrants are generally willing to work for lower wages than Americans. Rather, immigrants represent docile workers, who are less likely than Americans to insist upon enforcement of their legal rights. Employers can easily take advantage of immigrant workers in order to exploit them for financial advantage.

Foreign workers can be expected to be docile workers. Citizen workers know that they have job entitlements. These entitlements include minimum wage protection but also extend into a number of other areas, such as overtime pay provisions, safety requirements, equal employment opportunity protection, and collective bargaining rights. It is these additional employee entitlements that an employer can often escape if foreign workers are available. For even though foreign workers (and illegal immigrants for that matter) may technically be covered by these work standards, their presence creates a situation in which these safeguards cannot be guaranteed in practice. For the enforcement mechanisms for most of these laws are based upon employee complaints and actions. It is highly unlikely that foreign workers will know their rights. Even if they are so knowledgeable, they will probably be reluctant to do anything about abuses for fear of losing their jobs, and, relative to the job alternatives available in their native lands, they may not even perceive the violations as being exploitative. . . .

Thus even if the wage rates an employer must pay are identical for foreign workers and for citizen workers, the foreign workers will be preferred. It is the knowlege that foreign workers will be less likely to make demands for job rights or to join unions that will make them highly prized. Thus, these will be the critical considerations that will provide, as they now do, the crucial advantages for employers in hiring illegal immigrants.

In order to effectively compete against immigrants, Americans will have to accept the same low wages and poor working conditions which foreign-born workers are willing to tolerate in order to obtain jobs. As a result, Briggs argues that ''Citizen workers who compete with foreign workers will find, as in the past, that their existing work conditions usually either become frozen or decline. Under few circumstances will they improve.'' Many Americans will, of course, reject the low wages and poor working conditions which immigrants are willing to accept, thereby resulting in foreign-born workers displacing natives from their jobs.

The purpose of a guest worker program is to provide a legal means for Mexicans who wish to work in the United States to do so. In the absence of such a program, Mexicans wishing to work in the United States would have no alternative but to enter this nation illegally in search of jobs. However, Briggs argued that, to serve as an effective means to deter further illegal immigration, a guest worker program would have to be very large in order to accommodate the demands of the millions of Mexicans who wish to work in the United States. Yet, by allowing substantial numbers of Mexicans to compete with Americans for a limited supply of jobs, a large guest worker program would result in substantial job displacement of American workers.

Accordingly, policymakers faced the following dilemma: the only kind of guest worker program which was likely to have any discernible effect in reducing the flow of illegal immigration to the United States would be a large one; but a large program would result in substantial job displacement of American workers. As a result, Briggs concluded that ''A foreign worker program is no answer to the complex problem of illegal immigration. To be effective, it would have to be substantial in size; but if it were substantial in size, it would clearly have an adverse impact upon certain segments of the domestic labor force.''

Briggs's arguments against the establishment of a large guest worker program are based upon the assumption that mass immigration results in substantial job displacement of American workers. The empirical evidence presented earlier clearly shows this widely held assumption to be false. Immigrants generally take low-wage menial jobs, which native-born Americans tend to shun. As a result, immigrants and native-born Americans rarely compete for the same jobs, resulting in little job displacement of natives, as the empirical evidence contained in a RAND study (presesented earlier) shows. This would be especially true for

Mexican guest workers, who are generally employed in the agricultural sector of the western United States. Few Americans wish to engage in the backbreaking work of picking strawberries, lettuce, and other fruits and vegetables in the fields of California and other western states. As a result, Briggs's argument that a large guest worker program would result in substantial job displacement of American workers is not credible.

In addition to allegedly fostering job displacement, Briggs argued that a guest worker program will have no effect in stemming the flow of illegal immigration to the United States. Once in the United States, guest workers are unlikely to return to their native nations, where they face either unemployment, or, at best, employment in a job paying them only a fraction of the wage which they earned in this country.

The proposals for a foreign worker program simply neglect all of the experience that the United States has had (as well as many cases in Europe) with foreign worker programs. Specifically, when workers come from economically less developed countries to a country like the United States, they are made aware of the opportunities that for many were beyond their wildest imagination. The relatively higher wages and broader array of job opportunities will create, as they have in the past, a tendency for many to remain. A situation is also set up in which children are born and marriages occur. Both of these actions involve potential claims for citizenship. In the United States, with its multiracial and multiethnic group population, it is more likely that these pressures will occur than would ever be true in Europe. Rather than reduce the costs of uncontrolled immigration to American society, a foreign worker program will only add to the problem.[76]

Briggs's argument that a guest worker program would increase, rather than reduce, incentives for aliens to immigrate to the United States illegally was supported by Beard. As we saw, on June 17, 1981, Beard wrote Reagan to present his recommendations on immigration reform. Beard asked Reagan to consider his recommendations before defining his administration's immigration policy following his review of the proposals of the President's Task Force on Immigration and Refugee Policy. Beard urged that Reagan not include a guest worker program among the recommendations on immigration reform he planned to make to Congress in the coming weeks.

I would personally recommend against a guest worker program. Guest worker programs have never worked in the past, and it is unlikely that a guest worker program would now succeed. All European foreign labor programs have been ended or severely limited, and residual social problems are evident in, for example, France and Germany. Even the inital Task Force memorandum states that "Rather than curtailing illegal immigration, a large temporary worker program may stimulate further illegal immigration, as was the case following the bracero program."[77]

Briggs's argument that a guest worker program would not curtail the flow of illegal immigration to the United States, since many guest workers would be likely to remain in this nation rather than return to their native countries follow-ing the expiration of their temporary visas, is credible. A guest worker program would be especially ineffective as a means to deter further illegal immigration from Mexico. Many Mexican guest workers would not return to their native nation once their temporary visas expired.

Once in Mexico, former guest workers would face the high likelihood that they would be unable to find work, given the high unemployment rate existing in that nation. At best, former guest workers would be likely to find work paying only a fraction of the wages they had earned in the United States. To escape the poverty and unemployment of Mexico, many guest workers would remain in the United States after their temporary visas had expired.

As a result, a guest worker program would have no discernible effect in reducing the flow of illegal immigration from Mexico, much as Briggs argues. To be sure, such a program would reduce the number of Mexicans who illegally cross the American border. Those Mexicans would enter the United States le-gally as guest workers instead.

However, since many Mexicans would remain in the United States beyond the expiration of their temporary visas, in order to retain the jobs they have in this nation, a guest worker program would increase the number of Mexicans who enter the United States legally but subsequently remain in this nation il-legally. As a result, such a program would only alter the balance between Mex-icans who enter without inspection and those who overstay their visas, without having any discernible effect in actually reducing the aggregate flow of illegal immigration from Mexico.

Given the powerful political opposition to the establishment of a guest worker program (which organized labor and the Mexican-American community mounted), the possibility that it could damage America's traditionally close re-lationship with Mexico, and the partially persuasive economic case against it, as articulated by Briggs, one would assume that the Reagan administration would have quickly abandoned any serious consideration of recommending es-tablishment of such a program, once the political obtacles and economic argu-ments against it became clear. However, this was not the case. As we will see in the following chapter, the President's Task Force on Immigration and Refugee Policy recommended the establishment of a Mexican guest worker program, albeit a modest one, in the final report, which it presented to Reagan on July 1, 1981. The Reagan administration remained undaunted by the political opposition to a guest worker program, and unpersuaded by the economic case against it made by Briggs.

CONCLUSION

Reagan entered the White House determined to focus his attention on the issues of the economy and defense—the two most important concerns which had dictated the outcome of the 1980 presidential election. However, the release of SCIRP's final report on immigration reform, which came just five weeks after Reagan's inauguration, quickly propelled immigration policy to the top of the national agenda. Recognizing that immigration was now an issue which he would have to address, Reagan established the President's Task Force on Immigration and Refugee Policy, which he charged with the responsibility of presenting recommendations on immigration reform which he would consider proposing to Congress.

Reagan's announcement of his decision to establish the President's Task Force on Immigration and Refugee Policy provoked an intense lobbying campaign directed at the White House by members of Congress and interest groups representing opposing sides of the immigration debate. Restrictionist forces, led by Simpson, Huddleston, and FAIR, urged the White House to recommend reductions in levels of legal immigration, coupled with effective measures to deter further illegal immigration to the United States. The pro-immigration lobby, led by Swartz and MALDEF, urged the continuation of the mass immigration existing since 1965, and opposed the imposition of punitive measures, especially employer sanctions, designed to stem the flow of illegal immigration to the United States.

However, the number of members of Congress and interest groups lobbying the White House on immigration policy remained relatively small. There are substantially more members of Congress and interest groups currently lobbying the White House on immigration policy than was the case in 1981. When Reagan entered the White House, immigration was just emerging as an important issue, and the subject had yet to attract the interest of many members of Congress and organized constituencies.

There were substantially fewer immigrants in 1981 than there are today. With a substantially smaller immigrant population to draw support from, ethnic groups were not as well organized to lobby on immigration policy in 1981 as they are today. Indeed, MALDEF remained the only major immigrant ethnic group which actively lobbied the White House and Congress on immigration policy in 1981.

The lack of interest-group pressure gave the White House substantial latitude to design an immigration policy which the Reagan administration believed was in the national economic interest. Reagan had the luxury of not having to answer to powerful special interests on the issue of immigration, as would later be the case with Bush and Clinton. The White House took advantage of that luxury to develop an immigration policy which could serve the national economic interest rather than satisfy the desire of organized constituencies with a vital stake in this issue. However, while the lack of interest-group pressure was a definite asset to the White House in its efforts to develop an immigration policy, the Reagan administration was crippled in its ability to effectively address this issue by the lack of accurate and reliable information, as we saw in the previous chapter. This lack of information was the single strongest impediment to the development of a viable immigration policy, which Reagan hoped to present to Congress once he received the recommendations of the President's Task Force on Immigration and Refugee Policy, as we will now see.

Chapter 3

The Reagan Administration Announces Its Immigration Policy

When the Reagan Administration assumed office in 1981 . . . [the] stirrings seemed especially auspicious for [immigration] reform. . . . With illegal migration now certified as a national issue, a new President determined (in the words of his Attorney General, William French Smith) to "regain control of our borders" . . . reformers on Main Street and Pennsylavania Avenue geared up to do battle.[1]

—Peter H. Schuck, professor, Yale Law School

Following its establishment by Reagan on March 6, 1981, the President's Task Force on Immigration and Refugee Policy undertook an intense four-month review of immigration policy, which resulted in the issuance of a report containing its recommendations on immigration reform, presented to Reagan on July 1. Those recommendations served as the basis for statements which the Justice Department, Reagan, and Smith, respectively, issued on July 30 announcing the administration's immigration policy. The key elements of the Reagan administration's newly developed immigration policy pertained to the problem of illegal immigration. The administration essentially endorsed SCIRP's two-pronged agenda to address this problem, which recommended the granting of amnesty to undocumented individuals who resided in the United States, coupled with the imposition of an employer-sanctions regime, designed to deter further illegal immigration to this nation. Following the issuance of the administration's statements defining its immigration policy, Simpson and Mazzoli introduced immigration reform legislation designed to implement the recommendations of SCIRP and the Reagan administration. Consistent with those recommendations, amnesty and employer sanctions represented the key elements of the Simpson-Mazzoli bill, which became known as the Immigration Reform and Control Act (IRCA).

However, a number of important interest groups, especially the Latino community and agribusiness, had a vital stake in the issue of immigration reform. Those interest groups had many allies in Congress on both sides of the aisle. Placating those interest groups, and their allies in Congress, turned out to be an exceedingly difficult and time-consuming task which required a number of political compromises. Indeed, it was not until October 1986 (five and a half years after the release of SCIRP's final report, which contained its recommendations on immigration reform) that the political compromises necessary to build the bipartisan majorities in both houses of Congress, needed to pass IRCA, were finally made. The extraordinary length of time required to pass IRCA illustrates the difficulty and complexity of immigration—both in terms of the web of conflicting interests, which have to be placated on this issue, and the enormous amount of information, much of it unavailable, policymakers need to have in order to develop an immigration policy which serves the national economic interest.

HODSOLL APPRISES BAKER AND ANDERSON ON THE WORK OF THE PRESIDENT'S TASK FORCE ON IMMIGRATION AND REFUGEE POLICY

As the sole White House staff member serving on the President's Task Force on Immigration and Refugee Policy, Hodsoll took care to keep senior White House officials apprised of the status of the group's review of immigration policy, from the time it was established by Reagan on March 6, 1981 until it formally presented the final report to him on July 1. Hodsoll was particularly concerned about making the White House sensitive to the politics of immigration reform. As we saw in the previous chapter, Conner had presented to Hodsoll a fact sheet from FAIR which summarized the findings of public opinion polls on immigration taken in 1980. Those polls clearly showed that the public was hostile to mass immigration, both legal and illegal, and supported comprehensive immigration reform. Those polls were largely responsible for triggering efforts to pass comprehensive immigration reform legislation in Congress, spearheaded by Simpson, leader of the restrictionist forces on Capitol Hill. Hodsoll believed that the White House had to take the public hostility to mass immigration, and the congressional efforts to pass comprehensive immigration reform legislation, into account when the Reagan administration defined its immigration policy, once the Task Force on Immigration and Refugee Policy presented the report to the president on July 1.

On April 30, 1981, Hodsoll sent a memo to Baker which contained his own analysis of the politics of immigration reform. In his memo, Hodsoll concentrated on public unease about the revolutionary demographic changes which mass immigration was having upon American society.

You should be aware of the fact that half the current immigrants are estimated to be illegal; 80% of this is Hispanic. . . .

Assuming current trends (based on the past 5 years) continue with an average net inflow of a million immigrants (500,000 legal and 500,000 illegal), by 2030 one out of four Americans will either be immigrants or descended from immigrants arriving in this country after 1980. Of these, the average net inflow of Hispanics will be 500,000, half of total immigration. 400,000 of these are expected to be illegal (80% of total illegals); 100,000 are expected to be legal (20% of total legals). In 50 years, the proportion of Hispanics to others in the country would grow from a present of 1 in 18 to 1 in 6, and even 1 in 5.

In heavily impacted states like California, Texas, and Florida, Hispanics could grow to account for up to 1 in 3 during the same period. Many communities in Southern California, South Florida, and the southern parts of Texas, New Mexico, and Arizona would have Hispanic majorities. Even today, El Paso and San Antonio have Hispanic majorities. Los Angeles is 27.5% Hispanic. New Mexico is 36.6% Hispanic, and Texas is 21% Hispanic.[2]

In his memo to Baker, Hodsoll greatly exaggerated the number of aliens who immigrate to the United States illegally. Rather than representing half of the number of aliens who immigrate to the United States annually, undocumented individuals constitute less than a third of the total.[3] This is still a large number, but substantially less than the figure Hodsoll quoted. As Hodsoll's memo shows, this figure represented an erroneous estimate, which the Central Intelligence Agency (CIA) provided. Hodsoll's estimate that 80 percent of all aliens who immigrate to the United States illegally each year are Latino is essentially accurate, as we saw in the previous chapter.

Hodsoll provided accurate figures on the projected future growth of the Latino community. As a result of the mass immigration from Latin America existing since 1965, the share of the population which is Hispanic has risen from 3.5 percent in 1960 to 9 percent in 1990.[4] Hodsoll's projection that Hispanics could represent a fifth of the population by 2030, if current levels of immigration from Latin America continue, is essentially accurate. Assuming this immigration continues, the share of the population which is Hispanic is projected to rise to 22.5 percent by 2050.[5]

Hodsoll also provided accurate projections on the contribution which mass immigration is making to the population growth of the United States. Hodsoll predicted that, if current levels of immigration continue, by 2030 a quarter of all Americans will either be immigrants or descendants of those who have immigrated to the United States since 1980. As we saw in the previous chapter, Bouvier estimates that, if current levels of immigration continue, 36 percent of all Americans will either be immigrants or descendants of those who have immigrated to the United States since 1970.

Attached to Hodsoll's memo to Baker was a copy of a Gallup Poll, released on November 30, 1980, whose contents were summarized in the FAIR fact sheet which Conner sent to Hodsoll on April 8, 1981.[6] As we saw in the previous chapter, the Gallup Poll found that an overwhelming majority of the public supported the establishment of both an employer-sanctions regime and a national identity card. A smaller, though still decisive, majority of the public opposed the establishment of an amnesty program. The Gallup Poll provided clear evidence of public support for a crackdown on illegal immigration.

The people are concerned about this. A November 1980 Gallup poll (attached) shows that large majorities would make it against the law to hire illegal aliens and require everyone to carry an ID card. Even conservatives like Thurmond and Simpson (Chairmen of the relevant Senate committees) are for employer sanctions and some form of ID card. Democrats on the House side (Mazzoli) are in the same ballpark. Conservative Republicans in Los Angeles (like Schabarum) are equally for employer sanctions.[7]

On May 4, 1981, Hodsoll sent a memo to Anderson.[8] Attached to his memo was a paper Hodsoll had prepared on the meeting between representatives of the Mexican and American governments, held that very day in Mexico City to discuss the issue of Mexican immigration to the United States (mentioned in the previous chapter). Hodsoll noted that a public backlash against immigration was developing in the United States as a result of the massive exodus of Cubans to South Florida during the Mariel boatlift of 1980, the continued influx of Haitian boat people to the shores of South Florida, and the enormous flow of illegal immigration across the Mexican border. Hodsoll expressed his belief that the White House must reconcile Reagan's own support for the high levels of legal immigration existing since 1965 with the growing public and congressional opposition to mass immigration. The reconciliation of the growing divergence between the White House on the one hand, and the public and Congress on the other, on the issue of immigration would have to be made by the President's Task Force on Immigration and Refugee Policy when it presented its report to Reagan in the coming months.

The President is himself a firm believer in a high degree of freedom in immigration. Part of the greatness of the Western Hemisphere countries results from immigration—particularly true of Mexico, Canada, and U.S. BUT:

Heavy influx of Cubans last year, and continuing influx of Haitians and others from the Caribbean, are resulting in nearly intolerable problems in Florida and the Gulf states.

State and local officials and people in the Southwestern states are increasingly expressing their concerns to the White House and the Congress about illegal immigration across the border.

Recent Gallup Polls show a high degree of unwillingness to tolerate a continuation of the status quo.

The Select Commission (which began under President Carter and includes a wide spectrum of opinion) proposes a program which would include significant new measures to enforce immigration laws, not provide for any new temporary workers program, but permit a one-time legalization of persons already in the U.S.

The Congress is likely to move in this area. The mood of the Congress is restrictive—

both Democrats and Republicans. Conservatives (such as Strom Thurmond and Al Simpson) are thinking in terms of new enforcement measures (including employer sanctions and identity cards).

Hodsoll informed Anderson that the recommendations of the President's Task Force on Immigration and Refugee Policy would be intended to strike a balance between Reagan's own support for the high levels of legal immigration existing since 1965 and the growing public and congressional opposition to the massive flood of illegal immigration experienced during the last three decades. Hodsoll appealed to Anderson for his cooperation and support in this effort.

We have been considering a variety of new elements which would balance needs for additional immigration and temporary workers with better controls of the rates of flow and impacts. We need to bring the law and reality closer together.

But we want to do this with your cooperation and help. We want as much as possible jointly to develop common approaches to these problems. We fully recognize you also have a problem.

We would welcome perceptions of your problem and your ideas and suggestions.[9]

BAKER AND MEESE APPRISE REAGAN ON THE WORK OF THE PRESIDENT'S TASK FORCE ON IMMIGRATION AND REFUGEE POLICY

On June 3, 1981, Baker and Meese sent Reagan a memo apprising him of the status of the President's Task Force on Immigration and Refugee Policy's review of immigration policy. In their memo, Baker and Meese analyzed the challenges the White House faced as it grappled with the problem of defining its immigration policy, especially as it pertained to immigration from Mexico.

Pressures to immigrate to the United States continue to increase at a time in the U.S. of inflation, unemployment, and cuts in social programs. Pressures are particularly great from Mexico—one-sixth of its population is unemployed or underemployed; there is a tradition of illegal immigration and a very large open border. Poverty and unemployment push Mexican migration; higher wages (seven times), availability of employment, and ease of entry pull it [to the United States].

Given our relatively restrictive immigration laws, illegal immigration probably equals legal immigration (not counting refugees)—250,000 to 500,000 per year in flows; 3 to 6 million residing in this country (80% Latin American; 60% Mexican). This is changing our population, particularly in the Southwest, where many communities will likely have Hispanic majorities in the next decades.

Baker and Meese noted that a public and congressional backlash against mass immigration had developed. For the public and Congress, the mass exodus of Cuban refugees to the shores of South Florida during the Mariel boatlift of

1980, had crystalized the need for the imposition of additional restrictions on immigration.

Americans perceive [immigration] as a major national problem. The spring 1980 mass influx of Cubans to South Florida. Liberals like Governor Lamm (Colorado) join conservatives like Pete Schabarum (Los Angeles) in wanting greater restriction. The relevant congressional committees (Thurmond, Simpson, Mazzoli) are similarly inclined. Governor Graham and Senator Hawkins of Florida feel politically threatened. . . . A bipartisan select commission (created by Congress under Carter) reported this spring; it emphasized enforcement.

Baker and Meese argued that the rising restrictionist sentiment, both within Congress and among the public, was the result of changes in the racial composition of the United States and job displacement of American workers which mass immigration threatened to create.

The [anti-immigrant] perception has two elements:
1. Fear of community change. While not representing America's best instincts, these are political facts that cannot be ignored.
2. Potential American [job] displacement and adverse labor conditions. Most illegals are now in blue collar and service occupations (vs. agriculture). This is perceived as more threatening. But we could, in the decades ahead, have shortages in unskilled occupations. The number of U.S. youths who normally perform these lower-skilled jobs will be smaller; the number of similar Mexican youths, larger. Unemployed American youths are not likely to move in great numbers to the growth areas of the Sunbelt (where most of the illegals come). Americans should be able to compete if they wish; Mexican illegals average four years of schooling or less and lack English language capability. Still there could be some [job] displacement.

Baker and Meese argued that the Mexican government has an interest in having its citizens immigrate to the United States, both legally and illegally. Mexico suffers from high rates of poverty and unemployment. The existence of large masses of poor and unemployed citizens poses a direct threat to the stablity of the Mexican government.

Unable to provide decent-paying jobs to its millions of poor and unemployed citizens, the Mexican government has an interest in having those individuals immigrate to the United States, even if this is done illegally. Once in the United States, poor and unemployed Mexicans are likely to find jobs paying several times greater wages than the employment they are capable of obtaining in their native nation, assuming they can find any work there at all. By reducing the labor surplus in Mexico, immigration to the United States serves to prevent the abysmally low wages in Mexico from falling even further, thereby alleviating poverty in that nation. Mexicans working in the United States often send remittances to their families who remain behind in Mexico, which represents an important source of revenue for that nation. As a result, the United States serves as a safety value where millions of poor and unemployed Mexicans can go to raise their standard of living, both for themselves and their families who remain behind in Mexico.

As we saw in the previous chapter, immigration is governed under a preference system. Practically all visas are reserved for aliens, who either have family members residing in the United States legally or possess skills in critical demand. Aliens who do not meet either of those two criteria are generally prohibited from immigrating to the United States legally; their only alternative is to do so illegally. Most such aliens who find themselves forced to immigrate to the United States illegally are Mexicans seeking employment in this nation. By reducing the number of poor and unemployed Mexicans, illegal immigration serves to defuse the potential for political instability arising from the harsh economic conditions existing in Mexico.

In their memo to Reagan, Baker and Meese emphasized the importance of the United States as a safety valve for Mexico: "The Mexican government has little interest in changing the status quo [on illegal immigration] which allows a population and employment 'safety valve.' Illegals are viewed as a U.S. problem."[10] Consistent with the argument of Baker and Meese, Kevin F. McCarthy and Georges Vernez have emphasized the critical role which immigration to the United States plays in relieving political and economic tensions in Mexico: "Mexico . . . has a high economic and social stake in seeing emigration flows continue. Emigration has reduced unemployment rates and raised wage levels for those who remained behind. . . . In addition, remittances sent to family members by immigrants are one of the major sources of foreign exchange for Mexico. . . . Any reduction in the flows of both people and money between Mexico and the United States would affect the former disproportionately."[11]

Baker and Meese argued that immigration has become a polarizing issue, with the two opposing sides of this question having made conflicting and irreconcilable demands upon Congress: Restrictionists demanded sharp reductions in existing levels of legal immigration, coupled with the imposition of effective measures to deter further illegal immigration; immigration enthusiasts opposed both the imposition of any additional restrictions upon legal immigration, and punitive measures, especially employer sanctions, designed to deprive foreign-born individuals of incentives to reside in the United States without authentic documentation. In addition, the Mexican government has an interest in using the United States as a safety valve, where poor and unemployed Mexicans can go to find jobs paying substantially higher than they are capable of obtaining in their own native nation. As a result, the Mexican government did not desire any measures Congress might adopt to crack down on illegal immigration.

Accordingly, Baker and Meese concluded that "Immigration is 'no win.' Improved policies cannot solve the problem, and will most certainly be criticized from one quarter or another. Some restrictionists will push to keep all immigration down, even though the Mexicans, and some here, might like to sweep this problem once again under the rug."

Baker and Meese informed Reagan that the President's Task Force on Immigration and Refugee Policy intended to stake out a middle ground between the opposing extremes in the immigration debate. The Task Force would reject both restrictionist demands for sharp reductions in existing levels of legal immigration and the recommendation of immigration enthusiasts against the imposition of punitive measures, especially employer sanctions, designed to deter further illegal immigration to the United States. Rather, the Task Force would develop an immigration policy which combined support for the high levels of legal immigration existing since 1965 with the imposition of punitive measures designed to deprive aliens of incentives to immigrate to the United States illegally.

Your Task Force has rejected the status quo [on immigration]. It would constitute acquiescence in lack of border control, acknowledgment of unwillingness to enforce the law. A great nation should be able to enforce its borders; immigration law is not like parking tickets. Illegals fear coming into hospitals for basic inoculations; tension exists between blacks and Cubans in Miami; Southern California and Texas are closing hospitals and schools to illegals. While we may not stop illegal immigration, we need a policy which deals with the realities of Mexico, and politically permits assimilation over time of new immigrants within a legal framework more respected than breached. The Task Force also rejects new limits on legal immigration. The U.S. has today one of the lowest rates of immigration in relation to its population of any developed country. Long backlogs of persons waiting in line to immigrate generate pressures for illegal immigration; they also work hardships within families.[12]

AN ANALYSIS OF THE BAKER-MEESE MEMO TO REAGAN

In their memo to Reagan, Baker and Meese provided inaccurate figures on both legal and illegal immigration. They estimated that between 3 million and 6 million illegal aliens were residing in the United States, and that their number was growing at an annual rate of from 250,000 to 500,000. However, the best estimate, which the Urban Institute provided, is that 2.5 million to 3.5 million illegal aliens resided in the United States in 1980, the year before Baker and Meese sent their memo to Reagan, with their number growing at an annual rate of 200,000.[13] Baker's and Meese's claim that the United States has the lowest per capita rate of legal immigration of any industrial nation is completely false. Rather, with the exception of Canada, the United States has the highest per capita rate of immigration of any nation in the world. Over half of all the world's immigrants enter the United States annually.[14]

Baker's and Meese's provision of inaccurate figures on immigration was designed to justify the recommendations on immigration reform which the President's Task Force on Immigration and Refugee Policy intended to present to Reagan in the coming weeks. Those recommendations called for a continuation of the high levels of legal immigration existing since 1965, combined with the imposition of an employer-sanctions regime designed to deter further illegal immigration to the United States. To justify those recommendations, Baker and Meese needed to argue that, while levels of legal immigration were not so high as they may seem, the United States was being engulfed by a wave of illegal immigration. Accordingly, Baker and Meese provided inaccurate figures, which exaggerated the number of illegal aliens while minimizing the high levels of legal immigration existing since 1965. This was necessary in order to justify the White House's development of an immigration policy which recommended a continuation of existing levels of legal immigration, while proposing punitive measures designed to stem the flow of illegal immigration to the United States.

Despite their inaccurate figures on immigration, Baker and Meese dispelled the false, but widely held, notion that illegal aliens displace Americans from their jobs. In their memo to Reagan, Baker and Meese noted that illegal aliens generally hold low-wage, menial jobs, which native-born Americans generally will not take. Accordingly, illegal immigration poses no real threat to the jobs of American workers.

The claim that immigrants, both legal and illegal, displace Americans from their jobs is often used by immigration restrictionists to justify their call for comprehensive immigration reform. However, as we saw in the previous chapter, the empirical evidence shows that job displacement of American workers resulting from the mass immigration existing since 1965 has been minimal. Baker and Meese had strong political motivations to challenge the assumption that illegal aliens displace Americans from their jobs. They revealed in their memo to Reagan that the President's Task Force on Immigration and Refugee Policy was granting serious consideration to recommending the establishment of a large new guest worker program, which would allow up to 600,000 Mexicans to enter the United States to work at any given time.[15] The hundreds of thousands of Mexicans who illegally cross the American border annually in search of jobs would no longer have to do so, since they would be able to enter the United States legally as guest workers under the Task Force's recommendations. By allowing such a large number of Mexicans to immigrate to the United States legally as guest workers, the Task Force hoped that such a program would reduce the flow of illegal immigration from Mexico.

To be sure, "only" 600,000 Mexicans would be allowed to reside in the United States as guest workers at any given time. Since millions of Mexicans wish to work in the United States, there would still not be enough guest worker visas to satisfy the enormous demand among Mexicans to work in the United States. Once all the guest worker visas had been allotted, Mexicans would have no alternative but to illegally cross the American border in order to find jobs in this nation. Nevertheless, under the guest worker program a sufficient number of guest worker visas would be allotted to substantially reduce the flow of illegal immigration from Mexico.

Baker and Meese recognized that a guest worker program would provoke vociferous political opposition, not just from MALDEF, but from immigration restrictionists and organized labor, who, in addition to arguing that such a program would have no discernible effect in stemming the flow of illegal immigration from Mexico, also claimed that it would result in substantial job displacement and wage depression among American workers. One prominent immigration restrictionist, Vernon M. Briggs, Jr., made this argument in the paper on guest worker programs he sent to Hodsoll on May 8, 1981, which was discussed in the previous chapter.

Baker and Meese had reason to be concerned about the opposition to a Mexican guest program which was sure to come from immigration restrictionists. Indeed, the leader of immigration restrictionist forces in the House, Robin Beard of Tennessee, sent a letter to Reagan two weeks after the president received the memo from Baker and Meese, proclaiming his opposition to such a program, as we saw in the previous chapter. Beard argued that such a program would have no effect in stemming the flow of illegal immigration, since many Mexican guest workers could be expected to remain in the United States once their visas expired.

Organized labor maintains a strong presence within the Democratic Party, while immigration restrictionists do the same within the Republican Party. Accordingly, organized labor and immigration restrictionists could have joined forces in constructing a bipartisan majority in both houses of Congress to prevent inclusion of a guest worker program in any immigration reform legislation which lawmakers might pass. To confront the powerful opposition to a guest worker program which was sure to arise in Congress, the White House needed to deny that such a program would result in substantial job displacement of American workers. Baker and Meese did just that in their memo to Reagan.

By challenging the widely held assumption that illegal immigration results in substantial job displacement of American workers, Baker and Meese provided a rationale for the President's Task Force on Immigration and Refugee Policy's expected recommendation of the establishment of a large new guest worker program. Since Mexican guest workers would be taking jobs Americans generally shun, the White House could persuasively argue that Americans need not fear substantial job displacement and wage depression resulting from establishment of such a program. The White House intended to use this argument to counter the expected opposition to a Mexican guest worker program from immigration restrictionists and organized labor, who would repeat their claim that such a program would threaten the jobs and wages of American workers.

BAKER AND MEESE PREPARE REAGAN FOR HIS UPCOMING SUMMIT MEETING WITH LOPEZ PORTILLO

Baker's and Meese's memo to Reagan came just five days before the president was to meet with Lopez Portillo at the White House. In their memo, Baker and Meese gave Reagan a sense of the direction the President's Task Force on

Immigration and Refugee Policy wanted the White House to follow in its development of an immigration policy. However, the Task Force wanted to withhold making specific recommendations to Reagan until after he met with Lopez Portillo. In the meantime, Baker and Meese attached talking points to prepare Reagan for this meeting: "To allow discussion with Lopez Portillo before making administration decisions, your [Attorney General] A.G. Task Force on Immigration and Refugee Policy is in a holding pattern. They have largely completed their work, but deferred a final Cabinet-level decision meeting. This memorandum is to apprise you privately of where the Task Force is coming out and propose talking points with Lopez Portillo."[16]

Based upon the talking points which Baker and Meese prepared for Reagan, the president was to have made the following statements on immigration to Lopez Portillo during their summit meeting.

Both our countries have benefited over the years from the extensive flows of Mexican and U.S. citizens back and forth across the border.

At the same time, we both have a problem. Last year's mass exodus from Cuba, the continuing influx from Haiti, and the visibility of the South Florida mess sparked many to advocate increased restrictions [on immigration] and enforcement [of federal immigration law]. Congress is pushing in this direction.

Cuba's refusal to take back criminals, misfits, and the mentally ill makes this worse. Another Mariel [boatlift] would cause a real backlash [against immigration].

A major clamp down [on illegal immigration] would also be difficult for you.

We thus need to work together to bring the law and reality together in a mutually equitable way.

Following the discussion on immigration laid out in Baker's and Meese's talking points, Reagan was to have apprised Lopez Portillo of the major recommendations on immigration reform which the Task Force on Immigration and Refugee Policy was considering presenting to the president in the coming weeks.

As you know, I established a Task Force on [immigration] matters in March. It has nearly completed its work. Before deciding, I want to discuss with you personally the approaches we are considering. I understand our experts have recently consulted.

We are considering:

Increasing the permanent resident quotas for Canada and Mexico: It seems appropriate to consider such an increase for our closest neighbors.

Legalization for those here a long time: Either a small legalization or a large one with perhaps permanent resident and temporary worker components.

A new temporary worker program: Either one for major new flows, or an experimental program based on state needs.

Enforcement: We will want to increase enforcement of fair labor standards and a more effective strategy at the border (where we will need your help). We are also considering making it illegal for U.S. employers to knowingly employ those here illegally. This will require some kind of U.S. identity card system.

Concluding the discussion on immigration sketched out in Baker's and Meese's talking points, Reagan was to have invited Lopez Portillo to offer any suggestions which his administration could use as it prepared to announce its immigration policy.

I would like any views you might have as my administration must testify before Congress later this month. There are also several measures that would help us both.

We could set up a joint working group (perhaps meeting periodically at alternate cities). Such a group could focus on making U.S.–Mexican consular relations a model. We could also ease documentation requirements for citizens of both countries frequently crossing the border.

You could help us by taking stronger measures to eliminate illegal transit through Mexico of Central Americans seeking to enter the U.S. illegally. We could jointly implement more effective border controls. And we would like you to consider greater enforcement of your own worker documentation requirements.[17]

In their memo, Baker and Meese informed Reagan that his administration would move quickly to announce its newly developed immigration policy after the president held his summit meeting with Lopez Portillo, which was scheduled to take place at the White House during June 8–9, 1981: "Following the visit [of Lopez Portillo], we would complete informal consultations with Congress, affected states and localities, and concerned private organizations. We would plan a Cabinet meeting for final decision about June 18. Senate hearings begin June 23. The Attorney General agrees with this process."

Baker and Meese informed Reagan that the President's Task Force on Immigration and Refugee Policy would conclude its review of immigration policy by presenting him with a report containing its recommendations: "The Task Force's report will contain decision packages on (i) the Cuban-Haitian problem, (ii) legal immigration, (iii), illegal immigration, (iv) refugee benefits and services. The packages are politically and legally interconnected. A separate decision is being prepared on USG management and organization."[18]

ALLEN COMMENTS ON THE BAKER-MEESE MEMO TO REAGAN

Because Baker's and Meese's memo to Reagan touched heavily upon the issue of Mexican–American relations, the White House sent the document to be reviewed by Richard V. Allen, Assistant to the President for National Security Affairs and director of the National Security Council (NSC), before transmitting it to the Chief Executive. After reviewing the memo, Allen sent a memo of his own to Hodsoll informing him that "I have no objection to the draft memo insofar as it describes immigration issues on the Task Force report. A memo could give the President a useful and more detailed preview of these issues, their political implications, and agency and staff positions prior to apprising Lopez Portillo generally of the issues under consideration."

Allen informed Hodsoll that the NSC was undertaking its own review of immigration policy, which was being conducted simultaneously with that of the President's Task Force on Immigration and Refugee Policy: "Our current review has focused on these issues dealt with in the memo; namely the legal and illegal immigration issues. We are still looking at other issues in the Task Force report, such as the Cuban-Haitian problem. The issues in your memo are primarily domestic, but they have some significant foreign policy implications, particularly for Mexico."[19]

Allen devoted the remainder of his memo to reviewing the recommendations the President's Task Force on Immigration and Refugee Policy was considering presenting to Reagan. Those recommendations, pertaining to both legal and illegal immigration, were summarized by Baker and Meese in their memo to Reagan.

To address the issue of legal immigration, Baker and Meese informed Reagan that the President's Task Force on Immigration and Refugee Policy was considering endorsing SCIRP's own recommendation to raise the annual number of legal immigrants admitted to the United States by 100,000 during the next five years. This would be designed to clear out the massive backlogs of aliens waiting to be admitted to the United States which had developed over the years. This backlog was the result of the Immigration Act of 1965, which imposed an annual ceiling limiting the number of legal immigrants admitted to the United States from any single foreign nation to 20,000. This ceiling was originally limited to the nations of the Eastern Hemipshere. However, in 1976, Congress extended this ceiling to the other nations of the Western Hemisphere.

As we saw in the previous chapter, the annual number of Mexicans admitted to the United States was over twice the annual ceiling of 20,000 when it was imposed upon Mexico and the other foreign nations of the Western Hemisphere in 1976. As a result, a massive backlog of Mexicans waiting for permission to immigrate to the United States has developed. Many Mexicans have had to wait years before being granted such permission. Either unwilling or unable to wait the long periods necessary before being granted permission to immigrate to the United States legally, many Mexicans have had no alternative but to do so illegally. To relieve this backlog, MALDEF recommended that extra visas, in excess of the 20,000 allotted to Mexico annually, be reserved for America's southern neighbor. The President's Task Force on Immigration and Refugee Policy was considering increasing the annual ceiling on the number of Mexicans admitted to the United States to 50,000.

By increasing levels of legal immigration during the following five years, and more than doubling the annual number of visas to be allotted to Mexicans, the President's Task Force on Immigration and Refugee Policy intended to reduce the backlog of Mexicans waiting for permission to immigrate to the United States. As Baker and Meese noted in their memo to Reagan, "The increases in legal immigration are to reduce pressures for illegal immigration, particularly from Mexico.''

In addition to its recommendations on legal immigration, Baker and Meese informed Reagan that the President's Task Force on Immigration and Refugee Policy was considering endorsing the three major proposals, which SCIRP made, to address the problem of illegal immigration: the imposition of an employer-sanctions regime designed to deter further illegal immigration, beefing up the Border Patrol in order to enhance the capability of agents to interdict aliens who attempted to illegally cross America's southern border, and granting amnesty to undocumented individuals residing in the United States.

The President's Task Force on Immigration and Refugee Policy was especially interested in forging greater cooperation between the United States and Mexico in confronting the problem of illegal immigration by third-country nationals. Many individuals who illegally cross the American border are not Mexicans but third-country nationals, especially Central Americans, who use Mexico as a jumping-off point.

The Mexican government has an interest in allowing its poorest citizens to illegally cross the American border in search of a better life in the United States. However, the Mexican government has no interest in allowing third-country nationals to use its territory to do the same, since the poverty and unemployment existing outside Mexico are obviously not its problem. Accordingly, in their memo to Reagan, Baker and Meese informed the president that his Task Force on Immigration and Refugee Policy believed that the United States should attempt to elicit Mexican cooperation in preventing third-country nationals from using its territory to illegally cross the American border.[20]

Commenting on the recommendations the Task Force was considering presenting to Reagan, as summarized in the Baker-Meese memo to the president, Allen remarked that ''The recommendation to increase legal immigration levels temporarily, with some increased cooperation in preventing and enforcing [federal law] against illegal immigration, appears reasonable to me.'' However, Allen warned Hodsoll that the Task Force needed to justify its recommendation to increase existing levels of legal immigration, in light of the rising restrictionist sentiment against mass immigration, both within Congress and among the public, which Baker and Meese acknowleged in their memo: ''The memo could usefully include a few reasons why the Task Force is recommending increases, rather than the status quo or decreases on entry levels, during times of 'restrictionist' moods. Also, we could adversely affect our foreign policy if efforts to increase these levels failed to receive the necessary congressional support and resulted in increased 'restrictionist' measures.''

However, Allen expressed his belief that Congress might go along with a White House recommendation to increase levels of legal immigration, if it were coupled with measures to address the problem of illegal immigration, including amnesty and employer sanctions: ''Some attempted legalization and employer sanctions . . . might offer a more balanced approach [to immigration reform] politically and thus have a better chance of success.'' Allen concluded that an immigration policy which balanced increases in levels of legal immigration with measures to address the problem of illegal immigration "could come closer to meeting my concerns" over the political difficulty the White House faced in its attempts to raise levels of legal immigration, at a time of rising restrictionist sentiment in Congress against mass immigration.[21]

IMMIGRATION AND PUBLIC OPINION

As we have seen, the White House was extremely sensitive to public opinion polls on the issue of immigration. In his letter of April 8, 1981 to Hodsoll, Conner had presented the White House aide with polling data, from the Gallup and Roper organizations, demonstrating public support for reductions in existing levels of legal immigration, combined with the imposition of an employer-sanctions regime designed to deter further illegal immigration to the United States. Hodsoll had used this data to argue in memos to Baker and Anderson that a public backlash against mass immigration had developed, and that strong popular support existed for a restrictionist immigration policy agenda. In their memo to Reagan on June 3, 1981, Baker and Meese argued that the White House must take the public support for additional restrictions on immigration into account in the administration's development of its immigration policy.

The Reagan administration's commitment to immigration reform was largely driven by polls showing a strong public demand for congressional action on this issue. In a document drafted on March 14, 1986, Charles P. Smith, a White House aide, argued that "The public and media are concerned over immigration and believe that some control and reform is needed." Smith summarized the findings of two recent polls which showed strong public support for a restrictionist immigration policy: "An October 1984 Gallup poll of 1,500 showed that 75 percent of the national sample thought it should be against the law to hire an illegal alien. . . . A December 1985 survey by *U.S. News & World Report* that included responses from 36,000 of its readers showed that 75 percent believed immigration should be restricted further, while only 17 percent believed that amnesty should be granted to illegal aliens already here.''[22]

WIRTHLIN PRESENTS THE WHITE HOUSE WITH
POLLING DATA ON ILLEGAL IMMIGRATION

However, the White House was not content to rely upon public opinion polls such as Gallup and Roper, which had no political connection to the Reagan administration in developing its immigration policy. Rather, the White House wanted to conduct its own polling on immigration. To this end, the White House commissioned its own pollster, Richard B. Wirthlin, to survey public opinion on illegal immigration. Wirthlin headed his own polling firm, Decision Making Information (DMI), based in Washington. On June 18, 1981, Wirthlin sent Dick

Richards, an aide to the White House Chief of Staff, a memo which reported the results of his poll on illegal immigration.

Wirthlin conducted his poll on illegal immigration in early June 1981, the same week Reagan held his summit meeting with Lopez Portillo at the White House. In his poll, Wirthlin asked his respondents the following question: "President Reagan had been meeting this week with President Lopez Portillo of Mexico. One of the big things on their agenda is the issue of Mexican immigration into the U.S. Many ideas have been suggested as ways to control more effectively the influx of illegal immigrants from Mexico. Again, please tell me whether you agree or disagree with each of the following proposals."

Wirthlin asked his respondents to express their opinions on three statements on illegal immigration. After reporting the polling results on the three statements, Wirthlin provided an ideological, socioeconomic, and demographic breakdown on public opinion on each statement. In summarizing the contents of Wirthlin's memo, his polling results on each of the three statements are presented, followed by his analysis of the data taken from the public response to each statement.

The first statement which Wirthlin asked his respondents to express their opinions on was the following: "Illegal aliens who can prove they have been living in the United States for at least ten years should be granted official resident status and the right to apply for citizenship." Thirty-eight percent of those surveyed strongly agreed with this statement, 32 percent agreed somewhat, 8 percent disagreed somewhat, 21 percent strongly disagreed, and 2 percent had no opinion: "Support for the issuance of resident status to 10-year aliens is highest among liberals, older Americans, and people in the $10,000–$30,000 income range. Interestingly enough, geographic distinctions appear to make very little difference as support runs approximately 70%/30% for the idea regardless of location. Whites tend to be less disposed to the issue than blacks or Hispanics, but nevertheless favor the idea by over two-to-one."

The second statement Wirthlin asked his respondents to express their opinions on was the following: "We need some kind of work permit system so that Mexican workers may enter the U.S. legally, but temporarily, to boost the number of available agricultural workers on a seasonal basis." Thirty-five percent of those surveyed strongly agreed with this statement, 33 percent agreed somewhat, 11 percent disagreed somewhat, 19 percent strongly disagreed, and 2 percent expressed no opinion.

The temporary work permit system . . . derives its support from the more conservative end of the political spectrum. Labor families, as to be expected, are less willing to accept the proposal, but still give it a 62% positive rating. The idea receives greatest support from the West (72%), followed by the South (69%), Midwest (67%), and Northeast (65%). Blacks disagree most strongly with the idea (44%), compared to negative readings for whites and Hispanics of 28% and 30%, respectively.

The third statement Wirthlin asked his respondents to express their opinions on was the following: "In order to control the number of alien workers in this country, we should set up a system to admit a certain number of guest workers and then penalize heavily those businessmen who hire aliens who have entered the U.S. without such a permit." Sixty-six percent of those surveyed strongly agreed with this statement, 17 percent agreed somewhat, 8 percent disagreed somewhat, 7 percent strongly disagreed, and 2 percent expressed no opinion.

The proposal to put the onus on business is so overwhelmingly supported overall—83% agree, 15% disagree—that demographic or political distinctions are relatively insignificant. An interesting finding is that the highest level of disagreement lies with the "very liberals," responding with 22%. By political identification "strong Republicans" resemble "strong Democrats," each with disapproval scores of 18%. Similarly surprising is the finding that support for the plan increases with increases in the income level of the respondents. On racial dimensions, whites gave the highest support (86%) followed by blacks and Hispanics (76% each).[23]

The results of Wirthlin's poll conflict with those of the Gallup Poll, released on November 30, 1980, on the issue of granting amnesty to illegal aliens. As we saw in the previous chapter, Hodsoll had attached a copy of the Gallup Poll to the memo he sent Baker on April 30, 1981 in order to demonstrate that restrictionist sentiment against mass immigration among the public was on the rise. The Gallup Poll showed a majority of the public was opposed to granting amnesty to illegal aliens who had resided in the United States for a long period of time. Wirthlin came to the opposite conclusion, finding the existence of overwhelming public support for the granting of such amnesty.

Why did the Wirthlin and Gallup polls produce diametrically opposing results on the issue of amnesty? The most likely answer is that Wirthlin provided his respondents an opinion—that illegal aliens who had resided in the United States for at least ten years should be granted amnesty. This opinion, on the surface, appeared to be a reasonable one, resulting in an overwhelming majority of Wirthlin's respondents agreeing with it. However, the Gallup Poll asked its respondents whether illegal aliens who have resided in the United States for at least seven years should be allowed to remain in this nation, and presumably be granted amnesty. When asked to express an opinion, rather than respond to one, a majority of those surveyed by the Gallup Poll opposed amnesty.

The Wirthlin and Gallup polls reveal public ambivalence about amnesty. When polled, the public either supported amnesty or opposed it, depending upon how the question was phrased. This gave the White House an enormous amount of latitude in determining whether to recommend the establishment of an amnesty program. The White House was free to either support or oppose an amnesty program, without any fear that the position which Reagan eventually staked out on this issue would provoke strong public opposition.

As we saw in Chapter 1, SCIRP recommended that Congress grant amnesty to illegal aliens who had resided in the United States since prior to January 1, 1980. The Reagan administration was inclined to accept this recommendation. Indeed, in their memo to Reagan on June 3, 1981, Baker and Meese made it clear that the President's Task Force would recommend that Congress grant amnesty to illegal aliens who had resided in the United States continuously for at least three years.[24] This recommendation would be among the proposals on immigration reform which the Task Force intended to present to Reagan in the coming weeks. The Reagan administration was determined to recommend the establishment of an amnesty program, regardless of what public opinion on this issue might be.

Amnesty represented only one of the two major issues under active consideration in 1981 to address the problem of illegal immigration. The other issue concerned employer sanctions. While diverging on the issue of amnesty, the Wirthlin and Gallup polls came to the same result on the question of employer sanctions, finding that the overwhelming majority of the public supported the imposition of an employer-sanctions regime designed to deprive illegal aliens of jobs. Both polls found that over three-quarters of the public supported employer sanctions.

One important finding from Wirthlin's poll is the existence of a wide divergence between interest groups representing the Latino community, and the Hispanic population as a whole, on the issue of employer sanctions. Interest groups representing the Latino community, led by MALDEF, opposed employer sanctions, believing that they would result in ethnic discrimination against legal Hispanic immigrant workers, as we saw in the previous chapter. However, Wirthlin's poll clearly shows that over three-quarters of Latinos surveyed supported employer sanctions. Accordingly, interest groups representing the Latino community, especially MALDEF, were at odds with the Hispanic population as a whole in the opposition of the former to employer sanctions. This served to undermine the credibility of those interest groups in their efforts to prevent Congress from imposing an employer-sanctions regime, since their opposition to such action was not shared by the Latino community which they represented.

WIRTHLIN PRESENTS THE WHITE HOUSE WITH POLLING DATA ON THE CREATION OF A NATIONAL IDENTITY CARD

In addition to his poll on illegal immigration, Wirthlin took another survey on whether the public supported or opposed the creation of a national identity card. As we have seen, employer sanctions alone cannot serve as an effective means of depriving illegal aliens of jobs. Illegal aliens have the ability to circumvent employer sanctions in illegally obtaining jobs through document fraud.

By presenting their employers with fraudulent documents, which falsely purport to verify their eligibility to work in the United States, illegal aliens may easily obtain jobs, in violation of employer-sanctions legislation. To enable firms to detect and crack down on document fraud, Congress needed to couple the imposition of an employer-sanctions regime with a fraud-resistant worker verification system. Such a system would enable firms to verify the authenticity of the documents presented to them by individuals. This would assure employers that the individuals they hire are eligible to work in the United States and are not residing in this nation illegally.

As we saw in the previous chapter, the worker verification proposal which received the most serious consideration was the creation of a national identity card. The federal government would issue such a card to every individual eligible to work in the United States. Individuals would present their identity cards to employers who wished to hire them. A national data bank would be established, which employers would use to verify that the card was authentic and belonged to the individual presenting it.

Wirthlin took a poll to measure public opinion on the creation of a national identity card. On June 18, 1981—the same day he sent his memo to Richards reporting on the results of his poll on illegal immigration—Wirthlin sent another memo to Baker, Meese, and Michael Deaver, Deputy Chief of Staff and Assistant to the President. In the latter memo, Wirthlin reported the results of his poll on the creation of a national identity card.

To measure public opinion on the creation of a national identity card, Wirthlin produced a hypothetical Mr. Smith and Mr. Jones. Wirthlin stated the opinions of Mr. Smith and Mr. Jones on the issue of a national identity card. Wirthlin then asked his respondents, with whom—either Mr. Smith or Mr. Jones—they agreed on this issue. Wirthlin's question to his respondents read as follows:

Mr. Smith says it is essential, if we really want to control the influx of illegal aliens, that the federal government require all U.S. citizens to carry some type of national, forge-proof identification.

Mr. Jones says that instituting some stringent national identification system would very seriously threaten individual freedom and probably not be very effective in controlling illegal aliens anyway, since there is no such thing as "forge proof."

Wirthlin asked his respondents the following question: "Do you feel exactly like Smith, more like Smith than Jones, more like Jones than Smith, or exactly like Jones?" Forty-six percent of those surveyed stated that they felt exactly like Jones, 22 percent more like Jones than Smith, 16 percent more like Smith than Jones, and 13 percent exactly like Smith. Overall, Wirthlin's poll showed that 68 percent of those surveyed opposed the creation of a national identity card, and 29 percent supported it. In his memo to Baker, Meese, and Deaver, Wirthlin noted his polling results.

The results show definitively that there is very little support for a national identification system, even if the issue is carefully raised in the context of a way to deal with the problem of illegal aliens.

Support instead weighs heavily on Jones' side of the argument, with fully 68% agreeing with Jones' stance against a national I.D. card. This opposition to the card is consistent regardless of any demographic classification, including political affiliation and ethnic background. Opposition levels increase with increase in income and education levels of the respondents. What support there is for the idea exists most notably among older Americans, and as to be expected, residents of Southern states, where the illegal alien problem is most severe. Yet, even in these categories, the idea does not receive much support.

Wirthlin noted that liberals and conservatives were united in their opposition to the creation of a national identity card, considering it to represent an invasion of individual privacy.

What makes the national identification system such a disastrous idea is the way that it unites both ends of the ideological spectrum in opposition to the idea. Liberals oppose the plan as an abridgement of civil liberties, while conservatives oppose the plan on the grounds that it is yet another intrusion by "big brother" government into the lives of its citizens. In addition, no one believes very strongly the notion that any system could in fact be "forge proof."

Wirthlin concluded that should the White House launch an effort to establish a national identity card, public concerns over individual privacy would overshadow those pertaining to illegal immigration on this issue. This would result in the rapid dissolution of what little public support existed for such a card during the course of a public debate over its establishment: "If we should launch the idea of such an identification card program, I believe that the suggestion would be quickly yanked out from under the 'favorable' setting of the issue as a way to control 'illegal' aliens, and standing alone, be even less supported than this question reflects."[25]

Attached to Wirthlin's memo to Baker, Meese, and Deaver was an ideological breakdown of public opinion on the issue of a national identity card. Wirthlin's poll revealed that the strong public opposition to such a card spanned the entire ideological spectrum from far Right to far Left. Those surveyed who identified themselves as very conservative opposed the creation of such a card by a margin of 63 percent to 33 percent, those somewhat conservative did so by a margin of 70 percent to 27 percent, moderates did so by a margin of 65 percent to 34 percent, those somewhat liberal did so by a margin of 71 percent to 28 percent, and those very liberal did so by a margin of 71 percent to 27 percent.[26]

As we saw in the previous chapter, the pro-immigration lobby strongly opposed the creation of a national identity card, arguing that it represented a costly, cumbersome, and ineffective means to deter further illegal immigration, which would result in an invasion of individual privacy. The results of Wirthlin's poll showed that an overwhelming majority of the public agreed with this sentiment. However, Wirthlin's poll is in direct conflict with the Gallup Poll released on

November 30, 1980, which showed that an overwhelming majority of the public supported the creation of a national identity card.

Wirthlin made no effort to reconcile the conflict between his poll and that of the Gallup organization. Instead, Wirthlin assumed that his poll was correct, and used the results of the survey to lobby the White House against recommending the creation of a national identity card. Rather than acting as an objective poll-ster, who was attempting to provide the White House the accurate and reliable information it needed in order to decide whether to recommend the creation of a national identity card, Wirthlin turned out to be an advocate for those opposed to such a proposal.

Why did the polls reach diametrically opposing results on the issue of a national identity card? The most likely answer is that the Gallup Poll asked its respondents a straightforward question: Did they believe that every individual should be required to carry an identity card? An overwhelming majority of those surveyed believed that this was a reasonable requirement.

Indeed, the public understood that Congress would only create a national identity card if it were tied to an employer-sanctions regime, designed to deprive illegal aliens of jobs. An overwhelming majority of the respondents in the Gallup Poll believed that the requirement that the public carry identity cards was an appropriate sacrifice to make in order to enable firms to comply with their legal obligations under employer-sanctions legislation.

However, Wirthlin's poll provided its respondents with the two primary ar-guments against the creation of a national identity card: that it would serve as an ineffective means to deter further illegal immigration to the United States, and result in an invasion of individual privacy. The public found those argu-ments to be persuasive. Wirthlin's poll shows that, when informed of those arguments, the public tended to reverse themselves, and oppose the creation of a national identity card. Any effort by the White House to create such a card would provoke opposition, which would span the ideological spectrum. Oppo-nents of such a card would argue that it would serve as an ineffective means to deter further illegal immigration and result in an invasion of individual privacy. Wirthlin's poll shows that the two arguments would strike a responsive chord with the public, and that opponents of a national identity card would have the capability to turn popular opinion against it based upon those claims which the people tended to find persuasive.

The results of Wirthlin's poll made it clear that the White House would find it very difficult to prevail politically in any effort which it might launch to create a national identity card. Given the concerns the public had about a national identity card, it is unlikely that Congress would have been willing to include the creation of such a card in employer-sanctions legislation. Accordingly, the results of Wirthlin's poll essentially eliminated whatever chance existed that the Reagan administration would include the creation of a national identity card among the recommendations on immigration reform which it planned to make to Congress.

HILLER REPORTS TO SMITH ON THE RESULTS OF THE JUSTICE DEPARTMENT'S CONSULTATIONS ON IMMIGRATION POLICY

The President's Task Force was committed to presenting recommendations to Reagan which had broad public and congressional support. To this end, the Justice Department undertook extensive consultations with parties interested in immigration policy, including members of Congress, state and local government public officials, and interest groups representing organized labor, the Latino community, and immigration reform activists.[27] On June 30, 1981, David D. Hiller, Special Assistant to the Attorney General, sent a memo to Smith reporting on the results of the department's consultations which touched on the major issues pertaining to both legal and illegal immigration, including beefing up the Border Patrol, employer sanctions, amnesty, the creation of a national identity card, the establishment of a guest worker program, and increasing levels of legal immigration. As chairman of the President's Task Force on Immigration and Refugee Policy, Smith intended to use this information in order to assure that the final recommendations on immigration reform were fully capable of commanding broad support within Congress and among the organized groups with an interest in immigration.

Hiller Reports on Issues Pertaining to Illegal Immigration

Hiller began his memo to Smith reporting on the results of the Justice Department's consultations on issues pertaining to illegal immigration. Hiller reported that widespread agreement existed among all individuals and interest groups which the department consulted that Congress should appropriate funds to beef up the Border Patrol in order to enhance the capability of agents to apprehend and return to Mexico aliens who attempt to illegally cross the American border.

This is the one element of the [immigration reform] program to which no one has taken exception. It is generally agreed that the INS is understaffed and substantial additional resources may be necessary in order to more effectively control the border. The Congress, including both Simpson and Mazzoli, are prepared to vote additional monies.

Local governments agree (e.g., Pete Schabarum), as does labor. Hispanic groups and other minorities do not disagree, at least with regard to border enforcement, which does not pose risks of discrimination believed to accompany investigations in the interior. In sum, it is fair to say that a consensus exists to increase enforcement of existing [immigration] laws, including operations of INS along the border.

While a consensus existed on beefing up the Border Patrol, Hiller noted that there was widespread disagreement on the issue of employer sanctions among the individuals and interest groups the Justice Department consulted. To be sure,

Hiller reported the existence of strong support for employer sanctions in Congress, especially among its Republican members.

There seems to be a consensus among those, who favor strong enforcement of the immigration laws that a rule against hiring illegals is indispensible. This view cuts across political views. . . .

In the Congress, the relevant committee chairmen favor employer sanctions (Thurmond, Simpson, and Mazzoli). Other Republican Congressmen do so as well (McClory, Fish, Burgener, Lowery, Hunter, Rhodes, Pashayan). As Ham Fish states the views of this group, "employer sanctions are the key to enforcement [of federal immigration law]; they address the magnet effect [drawing illegal immigration to the United States] of employment in the U.S." On the other side, Senator East favors employer sanctions as well.

However, Hiller noted that strong opposition to employer sanctions also existed in Congress, including many of its Republican members: "Some Republican Congressmen do oppose employer sanctions. Jack Schmidt opposes them on antiregulatory grounds and because of the risk of discrimination against Hispanics, who are strongly represented in New Mexico. Congressman Tom Loeffler (Texas) opposes them on ideological grounds and because of the risk of economic disruption in Texas."

Hiller noted that the strongest opposition to employer sanctions came from interest groups representing the Latino community: "Hispanic groups indicate strong opposition to employer sanctions, on account of the risk that employer sanctions will discriminate against persons, who look or sound foreign, in order to avoid liability for hiring an illegal."

The potential for employer sanctions to result in ethnic discrimination against legal immigrant workers would be mitigated by the establishment of a fraud-resistant worker verification system. It would enable employers to determine the autenticity of the documents presented to them by individuals. This would eliminate the need for employers to refuse to hire immigrant workers, including those eligible to work in the United States, for fear they might be residing in this nation illegally.

Hiller reported that interest groups representing the Latino community would be willing to accept employer sanctions if they were coupled with a worker verification system which contained "safeguards against discrimination." In addition, those interest groups would be willing to accept employer sanctions if they were coupled with the granting of amnesty to illegal aliens who resided in the United States. Hiller expressed his view that legislation which combined employer sanctions with amnesty "may present enough balance to be acceptable to Hispanics."

As we have seen, the major worker verification proposal under consideration in 1981 was the creation of a national identity card designed to establish the identity of individuals who seek employment. Hiller reported that there was widespread disagreement among the individuals whom the Justice Department consulted over the issue of a national identity card. However, supporters of employer sanctions agreed that the Social Security card should be used by firms as a means to verify the eligibility of individuals to work in the United States. Moreover, steps should be taken to make the card tamper-proof.

With regard to worker identification, the reactions were somewhat mixed. . . . Most, who favor employer sanctions, recognize that it is necessary to provide the employer some simple way of satisfying his legal obligations, and that existing IDs are no good for this purpose (e.g., Simpson, Mazzoli, Fish, Rhodes). Typical of reactions on this question was Pete Schabarum's: "The American people will not support a national worker identification card. But the Social Security card should be considered as a basic document for worker identification purposes. Steps should be taken to make the cards more difficult to forge and greater effort should be made to issue them only to citizens." Some, however, would go further. Senator Simpson favors a new worker identification card. Congressman Rhodes supports a computerized call-in data bank system, as is used for the verification of credit card sales.

As with employer sanctions, Hiller reported that widespread disagreement on the issue of amnesty existed among the individuals and interest groups the Justice Department consulted. Not suprisingly, amnesty received its strongest support from interest groups representing the Latino community. Hiller noted that amnesty "is the element of the [immigration reform] program most strongly favored by Hispanic groups." This is understandable, given the fact that the overwhelming majority of illegal aliens were born in Latin America. By granting permanent legal residence to many of its members, the Latino community stood to gain the most from the establishment of an amnesty program.

The President's Task Force was considering recommending two proposals which interest groups representing the Latino community opposed—the imposition of an employer-sanctions regime and the establishment of a guest worker program. Immigration reform legislation providing for employer sanctions and a guest worker program might have been acceptable to those interest groups if it were coupled with amnesty. Indeed, Hiller noted that interest groups representing the Latino community believed that amnesty was essential in "providing some balance for them to the cost they feel imposed by employer sanctions and a guest worker program."

In addition to interest groups representing the Latino community, Hiller found strong support for amnesty among "a majority of the Congressmen and other officials we have consulted." However, Hiller also reported strong opposition to amnesty among some Republican members of Congress: "There exists some disagreement on this point from Republicans. Senator East opposes legalization as do Congressmen Rhodes and Loeffler. Their objections are based upon an unwillingness to appear to be rewarding wrongdoers and the fear that legalization will encourage further illegal immigration. Senator Hayakawa indicated that he could agree with a limited legalization, say, for persons who were here five or more years.''

However, many members of Congress believed that amnesty represented the only practical and humane solution to addressing the problem of the millions of illegal aliens who resided in the United States. In addition, immigration reform legislation, which contained employer-sanctions provisions, would never be passed by Congress unless it were coupled with the establishment of an amnesty program. Liberal Democratic members of Congress, representing the interests of the Latino community, remained adamantly opposed to legislation which contained employer-sanctions provisions, and could only accept such a bill if it also established an amnesty program. Liberals represent the dominant ideological wing of the Democratic Party, which controlled the House throughout the Reagan administration. The Democratic majority in the House was in a position to kill immigration reform legislation which contained employer-sanctions provisions.

To elicit the necessary support for immigration reform legislation which contained employer-sanctions provisions, among the Democratic majority in the House, the Reagan administration needed to include amnesty amendments to such a bill. Support for amnesty was the political price the administration and conservative Republican members of Congress would have to pay in order to assure passage of employer-sanctions legislation. However, some conservative Republican members of Congress supported deferred amnesty, which would only be implemented once employer sanctions had succeeded in curtailing the flow of illegal immigration to the United States: "Others in Congress . . . believe legalization to be a regrettable necessity, particularly if employer sanctions are enacted, in order to avoid disrupting existing employment relations (Senators Thurmond and Simpson; Congressmen Mazzoli, McClory, Fish, Paul). Thurmond and Simpson would, like the Select Commission, defer legalization until enforcement measures were in place.''

As we have seen, the White House was considering the establishment of a guest worker program as a means to reduce the flow of illegal immigration from Mexico. Mexicans wishing to work in the United States would be granted temporary visas to enter this nation in order to obtain employment. Mexicans cross the American border illegally in search of employment. By granting Mexicans who wish to work in the United States a legal means to enter this nation, a guest worker program was designed to reduce incentives for such illegal crossings.

In their memo to Reagan on June 3, 1981, Baker and Meese informed the president that his Task Force on Immigration and Refugee Policy was considering recommending the establishment of a large guest worker program, which would allow up to 600,000 Mexicans to enter the United States on a temporary basis to work in this nation. However, interest groups representing the Latino community strongly opposed the establishment of such a program, charging that it would subject Mexican workers to exploitation by American employers. Organized labor also opposed the establishment of such a program, charging that it would allow employers to replace Americans with Mexican workers.

Employers would profit from the employment of Mexicans, both because they are willing to work for substantially lower wages than Americans, and in unsafe and unhealthful labor conditions, which natives generally find unacceptable. As a result, employers would be eager to replace American with Mexican workers. By providing employers with a sufficient number of Mexican workers to meet their labor needs, a large guest worker program would result in substantial job displacement of Americans.

To placate interest groups representing the Latino community and organized labor, the President's Task Force on Immigration and Refugee Policy decided to substantially scale back the guest worker program, which it was considering recommending to Reagan. In his memo to Smith, Hiller revealed that the Task Force was considering a small guest worker program, which would permit from 20,000 to 50,000 Mexicans to enter the United States at any given time, to work in this nation. However, Hiller reported that interest groups representing the Latino community and organized labor found even this substantially scaled-back guest worker program to be unacceptable, in part because they feared that it would serve as a precursor to a much larger program which Congress might attempt to establish in the future.

A temporary foreign worker program is opposed in principle by organized labor, minority groups, including Hispanics, and certain church groups and voluntary agencies. Opposition is based on the fear that additional foreign workers will adversely affect competing resident workers, particularly low-skilled and low-wage minority labor. These groups say they are as opposed to a small program, as they are to a large one, partly on a camel's nose theory, but plainly opposition will be moderated if the proposal is confined to an experimental basis.

Hiller reported that widespread disagreement existed among the public officials whom the Justice Department consulted over the establishment of a guest worker program.

The small program will be viewed as too little by some in Congress (e.g., Senators Hayakawa and Schmidtt; Congressman Lungren; Pete Schabarum). Senator Thurmond appears also to favor a substantial program. These believe that we need the labor of the foreign workers, and [since] we cannot stop the flow [of illegal immigration], we should regularize it. Governor Clements has proposed a large program, but says he is satisfied with a pilot.

Simpson and Mazzoli disfavor a large program, but would agree to one on an experimental basis.[28]

Hiller Reports on Issues Pertaining to Legal Immigration

In addition to measures to address the problem of illegal immigration, the President's Task Force on Immigration and Refugee Policy was considering recommendations to reform legal immigration. To relieve the massive backlog of Mexicans waiting for permission to immigrate to the United States, and reduce the amount of time they must wait before being granted such permission, the Task Force was considering recommending that the number of visas allotted to Mexico, as well as Canada, be doubled from 20,000 to 40,000, respectively. Hiller reported that the strongest support for this recommendation came from interest groups representing the Latino community, especially MALDEF: "Hispanic groups (e.g., MALDEF) strongly favor increasing permanent immigration from Mexico. Thus, together with legalization, this is one of the elements most attractive to Hispanics."

However, Hiller also reported that sharp division existed within Congress over granting preferential treatment to Mexico and Canada in the allotment of visas: "Some members of Congress have reacted favorably, recognizing the practical situation posed by our two closest neighbors (e.g., Congressmen Rhodes, Burgener, Lowery, Hunter, Loeffler, McCollum). Ham Fish opposes preferential Canadian and Mexican ceilings, believing them a discriminatory reversion to national quotas."

In addition to doubling the number of visas allotted to Mexico and Canada, the President's Task Force on Immigration and Refugee Policy was considering endorsing SCIRP's recommendation to raise the annual number of legal immigrants admitted to the United States by 100,000 during the next five years in order to relieve the massive backlog of aliens waiting to obtain permanent legal residence in the United States. As in the case of granting preferential treatment to Mexico and Canada in the allotment of visas, Hiller reported that sharp division existed within Congress over this recommendation: "There is some support for temporary visa increases in the worldwide ceiling on legal immigration, but reactions again are mixed (e.g., Congressmen Fish and Loeffler approve; McCollum and Lungren would approve as part of phase-out of the existing fifth preference for brothers and sisters of U.S. citizens; but others disagree (e.g., Senator Hawkins, Congressman Rhodes)."

As we saw in Chapter 1, the Immigration Act of 1965 imposed an annual ceiling which limited the number of legal immigrants admitted to the United States to 290,000. However, the immediate family members of American citizens were excluded from this ceiling, and admitted to the United States in unlimited numbers. As a result, annual levels of legal immigration have substantially exceeded this ceiling.

Immigration restrictionists in Congress supported the imposition of a total numerical ceiling on all legal immigration, which would include the immediate family members of American citizens. By closing the loophole, under existing federal law, which admits the immediate family of American citizens to the United States in unlimited numbers, the purpose of such a ceiling would be to substantially reduce levels of legal immigration. The Justice Department consulted with members of Congress and representatives of organized groups, with an interest in immigration, about their views concerning the imposition of such a ceiling. Hiller reported the existence of general opposition to such a ceiling, with the exception of some conservative Republican members of Congress: "A substantial sentiment [exists] among Republicans for an overall cap on legal immigration (e.g., Senators Thurmond, Simpson, Hawkins; Congressman McCollum). Others are opposed (e.g., Congressman Lungren). Congressman Rhodes could place a cap on legal immigration, but not on refugee admissions. Labor, ethnic groups, and church groups, including voluntary agencies, do not favor a cap on legal immigration."[29]

With the exception of beefing up the Border Patrol, Hiller reported that no consensus existed on any of the major issues pertaining to immigration reform among the individuals and interest groups which the Justice Department consulted. Indeed, widespread disagreement existed over the issues of employer sanctions, amnesty, a guest worker program, and increasing levels of legal immigration. The lack of a consensus over those issues greatly complicated the work of the President's Task Force. The Task Force needed such a consensus in order to develop recommendations on immigration reform which could gain broad support within Congress and among the organized groups with an interest in immigration. In the absence of such a consensus, any recommendations which the Task Force made were certain to provoke powerful opposition from some influential quarter.

As we will see, the recommendations which the President's Task Force finally made did provoke intense opposition from various members of Congress and organized groups with an interest in immigration policy. Such opposition substantially complicated the ability of Congress to implement those recommendations through legislation. Indeed, it would take five years, after the President's Task Force issued its recommendations on July 1, 1981, before Congress was finally able to pass legislation which addressed all the major issues pertaining to immigration policy touched upon in Hiller's memo to Smith.

THE PRESIDENT'S TASK FORCE ON IMMIGRATION AND REFUGEE POLICY PRESENTS ITS REPORT TO REAGAN

After nearly four months of deliberations, on July 1, 1981, Francis S. M. Hodsoll, who served as the White House staff member on the President's Task Force on Immigration and Refugee Policy, presented the report, containing its recommendations on immigration reform, to Reagan. Upon receiving the report, Reagan convened a Cabinet meeting to consider the document. Attached to the report was a memo from Hodsoll to Reagan apprising him of the contents of the document.

The Task Force report contains fourteen decision items. These items are contained in four decision packages: (i) the Cuban/Haitian problem, (ii) legal immigration and refugee admission, (iii) illegal immigration, and (iv) refugee benefits and services. . . . The four packages are interconnected, and can most appropriately be considered only as component parts of an overall policy.

With minor exceptions, all but two of the fourteen decision items are agreed among your advisors. The Cabinet meeting should therefore focus on: 1. Cuban/Haitian issues; 2. Illegal immigration.

The remainder of Hodsoll's memo elaborated upon the disagreement among members of the Task Force concerning the following two issues: first, what should be done about the 135,000 Cuban and Haitian refugees who fled to the United States during the Mariel boatlift of 1980; and second, what steps should be taken to address the problem of illegal immigration.

On the issue of the Cuban and Haitian refugees, Hodsoll reported that "All agencies agree that we should seek legislation (i) to authorize Cubans and Haitians, who arrived before October 1980, to apply for permanent resident status after residing here two years, (ii) to prevent the transport of illegal aliens to the U.S., particularly during mass exodus, (iii) to reform and expedite exclusion proceedings, and (iv) to provide for holding stations and emergency budgetary authority for future mass exoduses." Hodsoll noted that the major disagreement among members of the President's Task Force pertaining to the issue of the Cuban and Haitian refugees is "whether we should detain undocumented aliens upon arrival pending exclusion or granting of asylum." Hodsoll informed Reagan that "State, Justice, Trasury, Labor, and HHS recommend detention. The problem is that we lack adequate camps for this purpose. . . . If you decide in principle to approve a detention policy, it is recommended that you ask the Attorney General to lead an effort (including DOD, Interior, GSA) to review all federal facilities with a view to identifying sites of least political and operational costs."

Turning to the issue of illegal immigration, Hodsoll reported that members of the President's Task Force had reached substantial areas of agreement.

All agree that there should be additional international cooperation, border enforcement, and enforcement of the Fair Labor Standards Act. All agree that there should be some new temporary worker program: The majority believe that we should grant temporary worker status to a large number of those here illegally and create a pilot temporary worker program for Mexicans (50,000/yearly maximum) based on state labor needs. OMB and others would support a pilot program of 100,000.

Finally all agree that illegal aliens here a considerable period of time (and who demonstrate minimal English language capability and show interest in continuing as part of the community in which they are working) should be able to apply for permanent resident status.

Hodsoll noted that the major areas of disagreement among members of the Task Force on illegal immigration pertained to employer sanctions.

The principle issue [of disagreement] involves whether we should propose legislation that would establish employer sanctions (of four or more employees). Employers would be prohibited from "knowingly and wilfully" hiring illegal aliens. Employee eligibility [to work] would be determined by a requirement that new hires would have to show a Social Security card. The Social Security card itself would have to be "more secure" from fraud, and many of your advisers are very concerned that this would lead inexorably to a national identity card, while others feel that employer sanctions and an identity system are necessary to enforce our immigration laws. The employer sanctions and identity card issues are the most controversial ones.[30]

In his memo, Hodsoll reported that members of the President's Task Force had reached agreement on all issues on their agenda with exception of the problem of Cuban and Haitian refugees and the question of employer sanctions. However, a review of the Task Force's twenty-six-page report finds that its members made recommendations to Reagan on only two minor issues pertaining to immigration policy: the problem of Cuban and Haitian refugees and the provision of social welfare benefits to refugees and asylees. The Task Force failed to make recommendations to Reagan on either of the two major items on its agenda, which pertained to reforms in legal immigration and measures to address the problem of illegal immigration. Instead, the report of the Task Force presented Reagan with a confusing array of options to consider, which only served to complicate, rather than facilitate, his ability to make final decisions in defining his administration's immigration policy.[31] Accordingly, Reagan convened three Cabinet meetings on July 1, 13, and 16, 1981, respectively, to clarify what final recommendations on immigration reform his administration should make to Congress.

THE JUSTICE DEPARTMENT ANNOUNCES THE REAGAN ADMINISTRATION'S IMMIGRATION POLICY

The recommendations on immigration reform, which the Reagan administration finally made, were announced by the Justice Department in a statement it issued on the morning of July 30, 1981. The department began its statement by expressing its belief that "The time for a clear U.S. immigration and refugee policy is long overdue." The focus of the department's recommendations on immigration reform was to address the problem of illegal immigration. The department regarded the massive influx of illegal immigration experienced since 1965 as the most urgent and pressing problem in immigration policy which Congress should address. The department believed that the problem of illegal immigration was especially alarming, given the fact that the federal government lacked effective measures to deter further illegal immigration to the United States.

Current laws and enforcement procedures are inadequate—particularly with regard to illegal aliens and mass requests for asylum.

The Immigration and Nationality Act of 1965 and its 1976 amendments do not provide effective means for controlling illegal immigration.

The magnitude of illegal immigration seriously handicaps the Immigration and Naturalization Service's ability to enforce the law.

Current procedures regarding deportation are often too lengthy and complicated, thereby inhibiting effective and timely enforcement of our immigration laws. The laws do not provide for enforcement against those who knowingly hire illegal aliens.

There are inadequate guidelines and legislative authority for dealing with mass immigration (e.g., the Cuban influx of 1980).

There is a great need for cooperation between the U.S. and other countries regarding immigration policies.

The Justice Department argued that immigration, both legal and illegal, had risen to levels not seen since the great immigration wave, which occurred during the late nineteenth and early twentieth centuries.

Immigrants—both legal and illegal—are entering the U.S. in greater numbers than at any time since the early 1900s.

Largely because of the Cuban and Haitian influx and a large refugee admissions program, more than 800,000 persons were allowed to enter the U.S. in 1980—about a 300,000 increase from the previous year.

The Census Bureau has estimated that 3.5 million to 6 million people are in the U.S. illegally—at least 50% from Mexico. About 1–1.5 million entered illegally in 1980.

The Justice Department charged that the massive influx of illegal immigration to the United States posed a direct threat to the national economic interest: "Immigrants who enter the U.S. illegally are creating problems for themselves, as well as for the country. Since they are afraid to seek the protection of U.S. labor laws, many work in 'sweatshop' conditions for less than the legal minimum wage. An uncontrolled influx of illegal aliens can strain community services and create potential problems for some American job seekers."

The Justice Department recommended a number of measures to address the problem of illegal immigration, including beefing up the Border Patrol; strengthening enforcement of federal labor laws; imposing federal civil fines upon employers of four or more workers (who knowingly hire illegal aliens) of between $500 and $1,000 for each undocumented individual hired; authorizing the Justice Department to seek injunctions in federal court against employers who pursue "a pattern or practice" of hiring illegal aliens; requiring employers to verify and attest to the fact that individuals whom they wish to hire are eligible to work in the United States; establishing an experimental guest worker program, lasting two years, which would allow up to 50,000 Mexicans to enter the United States to work for up to nine to twelve months; and granting amnesty to illegal aliens in general, and Cubans and Haitians in particular, who had resided in the United States since prior to January 1, 1980 and January 1, 1981, respectively. In addition, the Justice Department announced that the Reagan administration would open discussions with the Mexican government designed to negotiate an agreement to prevent both illegal crossings along the American border by third-country nationals and the smuggling of undocumented individuals across the border.[32]

THE REAGAN ADMINISTRATION ADDRESSES THE ISSUE OF EMPLOYER SANCTIONS

Employer sanctions represented the cornerstone of the Reagan administration's policy to deter further illegal immigration to the United States. Aliens immigrate to the United States illegally primarily in search of employment. Accordingly, the incentives aliens have to immigrate to the United States illegally can only be eliminated by depriving them of employment. Passage of employer-sanctions legislation was essential to achieving this objective.

However, employer sanctions alone are insufficient to deprive illegal aliens of jobs. To assure that they comply with employer-sanctions legislation, firms must have some means to verify that individuals are indeed eligible to work in the United States.

Accordingly, the imposition of a fraud-resistant worker verification system is essential to assure that firms comply with their legal obligations under employer-sanctions legislation. As we have seen, the major worker verification proposal under consideration in 1981 was the creation of a national identity card, which would be issued to all individuals eligible to work in the United States. Employers would use a national data bank to verify that the card was indeed authentic, and belonged to the individual presenting it.

As we have seen, on June 17, 1981 Wirthlin sent a memo to Baker, Meese, and Deaver which summarized the results of a public opinion poll he had taken on the issue of a national identity card. The poll showed that an overwhelming majority of those surveyed opposed the creation of a national identity card, based upon the popular fear that it would result in an invasion of individual privacy. In his memo to Reagan on July 1, Hodsoll reported that the administration was divided over whether to recommend that Congress pass legislation which imposed an employer-sanctions regime. Moreover, in the event that the administration decided to recommend such legislation, its members remained divided over whether they should be coupled with the creation of a national identity card: While some administration officials agreed with the public that the creation of such a card would represent an invasion of individual privacy, others believed that it was essential to enforce employer-sanctions legislation.

However, it is safe to assume that Baker, Meese, and Deaver shared the results of Wirthlin's poll on a national identity card with interested members of the Reagan administration. This resulted in the development of a consensus within the administration against the creation of such a card. On July 24, 1981, Baker sent Reagan a memo informing him that "The administration is explicitly opposed to the creation of a national identity card."

However, Baker also reported to Reagan that the administration had decided to recommend that Congress pass legislation which imposed an employer-sanctions regime. Baker noted that "given employer-sanctions, the administration recognizes the need for a means of compliance with the law that would provide an employer with a good-faith defense" should he be caught having hired an illegal alien. To comply with employer sanctions and defend themselves against possible federal prosecution, firms would be required to solicit from individuals an INS document which certified their eligibility to work in the United States. If those individuals lacked such documents, then firms would be required to solicit any two among the following documents: a birth certificate, drivers' license, Social Security card, or registration certificate issued by the Selective Service system.

In his memo to Reagan, Baker informed the president that the administration remained divided over what additional steps Congress should require employers to take in order to verify the eligibility of individuals. Some members of the Reagan administration believed that Congress should require employers, and those whom they hire, to sign a form attesting, under penalty of perjury, that the newly hired individual is either an American citizen, a noncitizen legal resident, or a foreign-born worker, authorized to work in the United States on a temporary basis. The employer would further attest to the fact that he or she has examined the necessary documents, prescribed by federal law, in verifying the eligibility of the newly hired individual to work in the United States, and the employer has no reason to believe that the person in question is not lawfully authorized to work in this nation.

Baker noted that some members of the Reagan administration opposed requiring employers to fill out a form attesting to the fact that they had verified the eligibility of individuals. Those officials believed that "in an administration dedicated to reducing regulatory burdens, additional government forms and procedures should be avoided." However, other administration officials disagreed with this position. They pointed out that employers who hire illegal aliens, even through inadvertent means, would be subject to federal prosecution under employer-sanctions legislation.

To defend themselves against federal prosecution, employers would need to maintain records which attested to the fact that they acted in good faith in having attempted to verify the eligibility of individuals whom they wish to hire to work in the United States. Baker noted that the maintenance of such records would provide those employers with "a good-faith defense against unwittingly hiring an illegal alien." In his memo to Reagan, Baker informed the president that the administration would have to decide whether to recommend that Congress require employers and those whom they have hired to sign a form attesting to the eligibility of newly hired individuals to work in the United States, and to the fact that the employer had solicited the documents prescribed by federal law in verifying this eligibility.[33]

The Reagan administration's decisions on the issue of employer sanctions were announced by the Justice Department, in the statement it issued on July 30, 1981, which contained its recommendations on immigration reform to Congress. In its statement, the department reiterated that "The administration is explicitly opposed to the creation of a national identity card. But, given employer sanctions, the administration recognizes the need for a means of compliance with the law that would provide an employer with a good-faith defense" should he or she be caught having hired an illegal alien. To provide themselves with such a defense, employers would be required to solicit specific documents from individuals whom they wish to hire which verify their eligibility to work in the United States. The documents, which the Justice Department listed in the statement outlining its recommendations on immigration reform, were the same as those contained in Baker's memo to Reagan on July 24.

Employers and individuals whom they hire would also have to sign a form, which Baker had mentioned in his memo to Reagan, verifying that each newly hired individual is eligible to work in the United States, and that the employer had solicited the necessary documents affirming this fact.[34] By examining those documents, employers would show that they made a good-faith effort to verify this eligibility. If those employers were ever caught having employed an illegal alien, they would be able to show that they did so unknowingly. Employers cannot be held liable for accepting as authentic documents which turn out to be fraudulent. Accordingly, employers would not be subject to federal prosecution if they unwittingly hired an illegal alien who presented them with phony documents.

The employer-sanctions legislation which the Reagan administration recommended would have prohibited firms from knowingly hiring illegal aliens. Firms which inadvertently hire illegal aliens would not be subject to federal sanctions. Accordingly, by maintaining a form showing that they had made a good-faith effort to determine the eligibility of a newly hired individual, firms would be able to absolve themselves of any charges which the Justice Department might want to bring against them. This would assure that only firms which knowingly hire illegal aliens would be subject to federal prosecution. Employer sanctions represented the primary means which the Reagan administration recommended to deter further illegal immigration to the United States.

THE REAGAN ADMINISTRATION ADDRESSES THE PROBLEM OF ILLEGAL IMMIGRATION FROM MEXICO

However, while jobs represent the primary magnet drawing illegal immigration to the United States, the problem of illegal immigration is largely the result of Congress's decision to impose an annual ceiling, which limits the number of legal immigrants admitted to the United States from any single foreign nation of the Western Hemisphere to 20,000. As we have seen, the annual number of Mexicans admitted to the United States was over double this ceiling at the time it was imposed in 1976. This has resulted in a massive backlog of Mexicans waiting for permission to immigrate to the United States. Many Mexicans have had to wait several years before being granted such permission.

Either unable or unwilling to endure the long waiting periods before being granted permission to immigrate to the United States legally, many Mexicans have had no alternative but to do so illegally. The Reagan administration was committed to relieving the massive backlog of Mexicans waiting for permission to immigrate to the United States, and reducing the amount of time they would have to wait before doing so, in order to diminish incentives for them to immigrate to this nation illegally. To this end, the Justice Department recommended legislation doubling the number of visas allotted to Mexico, as well as Canada, from 20,000 to 40,000, respectively.[35]

REAGAN ISSUES A STATEMENT DEFINING HIS ADMINISTRATION'S IMMIGRATION POLICY

At the very moment that the Justice Department's statement outlining the Reagan administration's recommendations to Congress on immigration reform was being released, the president issued a statement of his own on the issue. Reagan's statement essentially reiterated the recommendations contained in the department's statement. Reagan began his statement by noting that "Our nation is a nation of immigrants. More than any other country, our strength comes from our own immigrant heritage and our capacity to welcome those from other lands."

However, Reagan also pointed out that there was a limit to how many immigrants the United States could accept: "No free and prosperous nation can by itself accommodate all those who seek a better life or flee persecution. We must share this responsibility with other countries." Reagan noted that

The bipartisan select commission, which reported this spring, concluded that the Cuban influx to Florida made the United States sharply aware of the need for more effective immigration policies and the need for legislation to support those policies.

For these reasons, I asked the Attorney General last March to chair a Task Force on Immigration and Refugee Policy. We discussed the matter when President Lopez Portillo visited me last month, and we have carefully considered the views of our Mexican friends. In addition, the Attorney General has consulted with those concerned in Congress and in affected states and localities and with interested members of the public.

Reagan announced his support for a continuation of the high levels of legal immigration existing since 1965: "We shall continue America's tradition as a land that welcomes peoples from other countries. We shall also, with other countries, continue to share in the responsibility of welcoming and resettling those who flee oppression." While supporting the maintenance of an open and liberal immigration policy, Reagan also stressed the need to "ensure adequate legal authority to establish control over immigration." To this end, Reagan repeated the recommendations on immigration reform which the Justice Department had made in the statement on immigration policy it issued simultaneously to that of the President, including measures "to enable us, when sudden influxes of foreigners occur, to decide to whom we grant the status of refugee or asylee; to improve our border control; to expedite (consistent with fair procedures and the Constitution) return of those coming here illegally; to strengthen enforcement of our fair labor standards and laws, and penalize those who would knowingly encourage violation of our laws" by hiring illegal aliens. Reagan also repeated other recommendations on immigration reform, which the Justice Department made, including measures granting preferential treatment to Mexico and Canada in the allotment of visas, establishing a Mexican guest worker program, and providing amnesty to illegal aliens who resided in the United States.

As we have seen, the Reagan administration remained adamantly opposed to the creation of a national identity card designed to enable employers to comply with their legal obligations under employer-sanctions legislation. The administration shared the widespread public view that such a card would result in an invasion of individual privacy. In his statement, Reagan endorsed this view, expressing his belief that any measures designed to deter further illegal immigration to the United States must "be consistent with our values of individual privacy and freedom."

Reagan concluded his statement by pledging to pursue an immigration policy which was fully consistent with the national interest: "Immigration and refugee policy is an important part of our past and fundamental to our national interest. With the help of the Congress and the American people, we will work toward a new and realistic immigration policy, a policy that will be fair to our own citizens, while it opens the door of opportunity to those who seek a new life in America."[36]

SMITH ELABORATES ON THE REAGAN ADMINISTRATION'S IMMIGRATION POLICY

At the precise moment that the statements which the Justice Department and Reagan issued were being released to the public, Attorney General William French Smith, who was responsible for enforcement of federal immigration law, and had served as chairman of the President's Task Force on Immigration Refugee Policy, appeared before a joint hearing of the immigration subcommittees of the Senate and House, respectively. The purpose of Smith's appearance before the subcommittees was to elaborate on the recommendations on immigration reform contained in the statements issued by the Justice Department and Reagan. Smith began his appearance by issuing a statement of his own in which he noted that "The history of America has been in large part the history of immigrants. Our nation has been overwhelmingly enriched by the fifty million immigrants, who have come here since the first colonists. For nearly our first century and one half as a nation, the Congress recognized our need for new arrivals by imposing no quantitative restrictions on immigration.''

However, Smith noted that since passage of the Immigration Act of 1921, ''the government and our people have recognized the need to control the numbers of immigrants and the process by which they enter our country.'' Smith charged that

In recent years our policies intended to affect that necesary control of our borders have failed. Last year, the number of immigrants legally and illegally entering the United States reached a total possibly greater number than any year in our history, including the era of unrestricted immigration.

We have lost control of our borders. We have pursued unrealistic policies. We have failed to enforce our laws effectively.

No great nation—especially a democratic nation—can long countenance ineffective and unenforced laws. That is especially true when the unsettling results are so apparent to our people.

Smith's argument that the United States had lost control of its own borders was the result of the federal government's failure to stem the massive flow of illegal immigration existing since 1965. Accordingly, Smith noted that the key to America's ability to regain control of its borders lies in the imposition of effective measures to deter further illegal immigration to the United States.

We must more effectively deter illegal immigration to the United States—whether across our expansive borders or by sea. The proposals announced this morning by the President would have that result. They represent a comprehensive and integrated approach. They reconize the realities we face and the fact that no policy will be enforceable if it ignores the true facts. Those basic facts are:

The presence of three to six million illegal aliens in this country; and the continuing growth of their numbers by from one-quarter to one-half million each year.

Smith summarized the Reagan administration's newly defined immigration policy as entailing three goals: the establishment of a guest worker program to provide a legal means for immigrants to obtain employment in the United States on a temporary basis, the granting of amnesty to illegal aliens who resided in the United States, and the imposition of effective measures to deter further illegal immigration to this nation.

The overriding purpose of the President's proposals is to make our laws and policies more realistic—and then to enforce those laws effectively. He believes that we must modestly expand opportunities for legal immigration to reflect America's attractiveness to the rest of the world. He believes that we must squarely recognize the existence of a hidden class of illegal aliens, who work and live within our society, but are beyond its sanctions and protections. And he believes we must develop new enforcement techniques that would allow us to enforce fully laws and policies which reflect those realities.

Smith noted that "The proposals announced today are the result of wide consultations, both within this country and internationally. They are the result of many months' work by the President's Task Force on Immigration and Refugee Policy, which I had the privilege of chairing. They represent the administration's best ideas on how to regain control of our national borders, without closing the door to this unique land of opportunity. . . . The administration's policy proposals will fulfill these purposes."[37]

Smith Addresses the Problem of Illegal Immigration

The major focus of the Reagan administration's newly defined immigration policy was in addressing the problem of illegal immigration. Accordingly, illegal immigration represented the central and overriding issue which Smith addressed in his statement before a joint hearing of the immigration subcommittees of the Senate and House on July 30, 1981. In his statement, Smith noted that there had been an exponential increase in illegal immigration since 1965.

Illegal immigration to the United States has increased drastically in recent years, to a point where it likely equals or exceeds legal admissions. In 1964 approximately 50,000 illegal aliens were apprehended in the United States. By 1979, the number of apprehensions had risen to more than 1 million. Although estimates vary considerably, most fix the illegal alien population of the U.S. at between three and six million, perhaps one-half of whom are Mexican nationals; and the illegal population grows by 250,000 to 500,000 persons each year.

Smith's estimates that between 3 million and 6 million illegal aliens resided in the United States, and that the net number of undocumented individuals living in this nation was growing at an annual rate of from 250,000 to 500,000, are the same as those that Baker and Meese cited in their memo to Reagan on June 3, 1981. However, as we have seen, those figures represent an exaggeration of the actual number of illegal aliens who resided in the United States, and the net growth in their numbers. In 1980, the year before the administration issued those figures, the best estimate, which the Urban Institute provided, was that between 2.5 million and 3.5 million illegal aliens resided in the United States, and that the net number of undocumented individuals was growing at an annual rate of 200,000.

To be sure, the illegal alien population of the United States in 1980 remained very large. Moreover, the net number of illegal aliens residing in the United States was growing at a very rapid rate. Accordingly, even though the Reagan administration had exaggerated the number of illegal aliens who resided in the United States, and the net annual growth in their numbers, illegal immigration remained a severe problem, which Congress had to address.

Smith noted that in the past illegal aliens used to work primarily in American agriculture. However, the illegal alien population had grown so large that undocumented workers were now employed in every sector of the American economy: "While illegal immigrants once were concentrated in agricultural employment in the Southwestern states, they now reside in all regions of the country. Only 15% of the illegals are estimated to work in agriculture; 50% are employed in service industries; and 30% are in blue collar jobs."

As we saw in the previous chapter, public opinion polls taken in 1980 show that illegal immigration represented among the most important problems the public wanted the federal government to address. A Roper Poll found that 91 percent of those surveyed wanted the federal government to launch "an all-out effort" to deter further illegal immigration to the United States. Alluding to other results of public opinion polls taken on illegal immigration, Smith noted that "The American people correctly perceive [illegal immigration] as a major problem. In a recent poll, nine of ten Americans said they favored 'an all-out effort' to stop illegal immigration. Americans justifiably want their government to take steps to bring immigration within effective regulation."

Smith announced that the Reagan administration was recommending legislation containing four specific measures to address the problem of illegal immigration, including a beefing up of the Border Patrol; the imposition of federal sanctions upon employers who knowingly hire illegal aliens; an experimental guest worker program, which would allow up to 50,000 Mexicans to work in the United States annually; and the granting of amnesty to undocumented individuals who resided in the United States. In addition, the administration pledged to seek international cooperation throughout the Western Hemisphere to deter further illegal immigration to the United States. Smith argued that "The five elements of the President's strategy should reduce substantially illegal immigration by expanding opportunities to work lawfully in the United States— through the experimental temporary worker program and legalization—and by prohibiting employment of those outside these programs."[38]

Smith Elaborates on the Reagan Administration's Measures to Address the Problem of Illegal Immigration

Smith elaborated on the Reagan administration's recommendation for legislation, imposing four specific measures to address the problem of illegal immigration. Turning to the first measure, Smith announced that the administration was requesting the appropriation of an additional $40 million for the INS to enable the agency to improve its enforcement of federal immigration law, both at the Mexican border and in the interior of the United States. The administration was also requesting the appropriation of an additional $35 million to the INS to detain illegal aliens, apprehended by the federal agency, pending their deportation from the United States. The additional funds would be used to add 564 personnel to the INS staff, including 236 Border Patrol agents.

Employer sanctions represented the second measure the Reagan administration recommended that Congress enact to address the problem of illegal immigration. Smith noted that jobs remain the primary magnet drawing illegal immigration to the United States: "The availability of employment in this country at relatively high wages, without regard to legal status, will continue to 'pull' illegal migration." Accordingly, Smith noted that the only means to eliminate incentives for aliens to reside in the United States illegally is to deprive them of employment. To this end, Smith announced that the Reagan administration was recommending employer-sanctions legislation, as outlined in the statement containing the White House's proposals on immigration reform.

Smith reiterated that "The administration is opposed to the creation of a national identity card. But, to make employer sanctions a workable deterrent, the administration recognizes the need for a means of compliance with the law that would provide an employer with a good-faith defense" should he or she ever be caught having hired an illegal alien. To enable employers to obtain such a defense, employers would be required to undertake the worker verification procedures which the Justice Department recommended in its statement.[39]

As we saw in the previous chapter, the pro-immigration lobby opposed employer sanctions. To avoid the possibility that they might be prosecuted for violating employer-sanctions legislation, many firms would refuse to hire immigrant workers, including those eligible to work in the United States. This would assure firms that they are in compliance with such legislation. Illegal alien workers may carry fraudulent documents which falsely verify their eligibility to work in the United States. As a result, employers cannot be sure of the authenticity of the documents presented to them. To assure that they are in compliance with employer-sanctions legislation, many employers would refuse to hire immigrants, including those eligible to work in the United States.

The President's Task Force on Immigration and Refugee Policy shared the pro-immigration lobby's concerns that employer sanctions might result in ethnic discrimination against legal immigrant workers. In its report presented to Reagan on July 1, 1981, the Task Force warned that "Employer sanctions could . . . result in discrimination against foreign-looking or-sounding Americans."[40] As we have seen, Latino immigrant workers are especially vulnerable to ethnic discrimination arising from employer sanctions. This results from the fact that an overwhelming majority of illegal aliens were born in Latin America, creating the false stereotype that most, if not all, Hispanic immigrants lack authentic documentation. Operating under this stereotype, many employers will automatically assume that any Latino immigrant who seeks work is an illegal alien, and refuse to hire him or her. In a preliminary draft of its report sent to members of the Cabinet on June 26, the Task Force expressed its fear that legal immigrant Latino workers would be especially vulnerable to ethnic discrimination arising from employer sanctions: "In order to minimize the risk of sanctions, employers may regard Hispanic [job] applicants without Social Security cards with suspicion increasing discrimination against Hispanics."[41]

However, the President's Task Force's concerns over the potential for ethnic discrimination against legal immigrant workers, especially those born in Latin

America, arising from employer sanctions were never made public. Rather, the official position of the Reagan administration was that employer sanctions carried no serious risk of resulting in ethnic discrimination against legal immigrant workers. The administration needed to take this position if it were to make a credible case for employer sanctions. The administration could only make a credible case for employer sanctions if it argued that there was no serious risk that they would result in ethnic discrimination against legal immigration workers; otherwise Congress would have been highly unlikely to pass immigration reform legislation imposing an employer-sanctions regime.

To be sure, employer sanctions promised, at least on paper, to deprive illegal aliens of jobs, resulting in a diminished flow of illegal immigration, in the face of declining employment opportunities for undocumented individuals. However, any benefits which employer sanctions would have provided, in terms of stemming the flow of illegal immigration, would have been offset by the costs resulting from ethnic discrimination against legal immigrant workers. Congress was likely to regard protecting the civil rights of legal immigrant workers to be a more important priority than stemming the flow of illegal immigration to the United States. As a result, Congress was highly unlikely to pass employer-sanctions legislation, if there was a serious risk that it might result in ethnic discrimination against legal immigrant workers. Accordingly, the Reagan administration needed to reassure Congress that, at least in its opinion, no such risk existed, if there was to be any hope of passing such legislation.

In his statement before a joint hearing of the immigration subcommittees of the Senate and House, Smith rejected the argument, which the pro-immigration lobby made, that employer sanctions would result in ethnic discrimination against legal immigrant workers. Employers who complied with their worker verification obligations need not fear federal prosecution under the employer-sanctions legislation which the Reagan administration was recommending. Such employers would have no reason to refuse to hire immigrant workers, including those eligibile to work in the United States, in order to assure they are in compliance with such legislation. As Smith put it, ''We believe that this new law can and will be enforced without discrimination. . . . Since employers may rely upon existing documents and will not be required to make judgments about the authenticity of the documents, they would have no occasion to make subjective, and possibly discriminatory, judgments about persons, who may appear to be foreign.''

The third measure the Reagan administration recommended that Congress enact to address the problem of illegal immigration was the establishment of a two-year experimental guest worker program, which would allow 50,000 Mexicans to enter the United States annually, for up to nine to twelve months, to obtain employment. By allowing Mexicans who wish to work in the United States the opportunity to do so legally, the Reagan administration hoped that the program would reduce incentives for them to illegally cross the American border. After the expiration of the two-year trial period, the administration would evaluate the effectiveness of the program in order to determine whether it should be extended.

Amnesty was the fourth measure the Reagan administration recommended to Congress. Congress not only had to consider measures to deter further illegal immigration, but it also had to address the problem of what to do about the millions of undocumented individuals who already resided in this nation. Smith argued that the only moral, humane, and practical means to address this problem was to grant amnesty to those undocumented individuals. The INS lacked the resources to deport the millions of illegal aliens who resided in the United States. By granting amnesty to those illegal aliens, Smith argued that Congress would allow the INS to devote its limited resources to deterring further illegal immigration to the United States.

We must find some practical way of dealing with the illegal aliens now residing in the United States. We have neither the resources, the capability, nor the motivation to uproot and deport millions of illegal aliens, many of whom have become, in effect, members of the community. By granting limited legal status to the productive and law-abiding members of this shadow population, we will recognize reality and devote our enforcement resources to deterring future illegal arrivals. Our purpose is to deter illegal immigration and prevent the recurrence of the circumstances we are now facing.

Smith announced that the Reagan administration was recommending that Congress grant illegal aliens, who had resided in the United States since prior to January 1, 1980, and were not subject to deportation under federal immigration law for reasons other than their legal status, the right to obtain temporary legal residence, which would be renewable every three years. Those illegal aliens would be granted the right to obtain permanent legal residence ten years after receiving amnesty, provided they demonstrated the necessary proficiency in English. In addition, Smith announced that the administration was recommending that Congress grant Cuban and Haitian refugees, who had resided in the United States since prior to January 1, 1981, the right to obtain temporary legal residence for three years, which would be subject to renewal. Those Cubans and Haitians would be allowed the right to obtain permanent legal residence after five years.

In addition to the four measures which Smith recommended to Congress, the Reagan administration believed that legislation was required to respond to the specific issue of illegal crossings along the Mexican border. To reduce incentives for Mexicans to immigrate to the United States illegally, Congress needed to take action to relieve the massive backlog of Mexicans waiting for permission to enter this nation. This was necessary in order to reduce the amount of time Mexicans had to wait before being granted such permission. To this end, Smith reiterated the Justice Department's recommendation for legislation which doubled the number of visas allotted to Mexico, as well as Canada, from 20,000 to 40,000, respectively.

Mexicans are not the only individuals who illegally cross the American border in massive numbers. As we have seen, many third-country nationals also use the Mexican border to illegally enter the United States. Accordingly, Smith announced that the State Department would pursue negotiations with the Mexican government. The purpose of the negotiations would be to achieve cooperation between the United States and Mexico in order to prevent third-country nationals from crossing the American border, and the smuggling of illegal aliens into this nation.[42]

Smith Concludes His Statement Elaborating on the Reagan Administration's Immigration Policy

Smith completed his statement before a joint hearing of the immigration subcommittees of the Senate and House by reiterating the need for measures to address the problem of illegal immigration: "The dilemmas of immigration and refugee policy require the prompt attention of the Congress and diligent efforts of the Executive branch in order to regain control of our borders. I am confident that, working together, we can present the nation an effective program of vigorous and fair enforcement of our immigration laws."

However, in pursuing measures to address the problem of illegal immigration, Smith argued that Congress should refrain from taking any action to restrict the open and liberal immigration policy pursued since 1965. Smith stated that such a policy was fully consistent with Reagan's philosophical commitment to maintaining the United States as a land of opportunity, which welcomes immigrants from every corner of the world.

We will continue to be a nation that is open to immigration and that does its share to assist and resettle the refugee. As President Ronald Reagan has said many times, quoting John Winthrop, "we shall be a city upon a hill. The eyes of all people are upon us." Like a beacon, our freedom still blazes forth in a world filled with too much darkness. That beacon beckons the immigrant and refugee to our shores—seemingly in ever greater numbers.

Smith concluded his statement by arguing that the Reagan administration had presented Congress with a fair and balanced immigration policy, which preserved America's tradition of maintaining an open and liberal immigration policy, while containing measures to enable the federal government to effectively enforce its immigration laws.

I believe that the proposals the President has offered are in keeping with our modern and historic appeal to the citizens of other lands. Yet they are also fair and realistic in their consideration for the citizens of this land. Only a realistic policy of the type outlined by the President can fully provide for the well-being of our people, while welcoming from throughout the world others, who truly desire to contribute to this nation's continuing experiment in liberty.[43]

CONGRESS PASSES THE IMMIGRATION REFORM AND CONTROL ACT

The Reagan administration's recommendations on immigration reform—as contained in the statements which the Justice Department, the president, and Smith all issued on July 30, 1981—completed the work of the White House in developing an immigration policy. That work had begun nearly five months earlier, with Reagan's establishment of the President's Task Force on Immigration and Refugee Policy. With the Reagan administration having introduced its long-awaited recommendations on immigration reform, the task of considering, and possibly implementing, those proposals through legislation fell upon the shoulders of members of Congress. With the administration's immigration policy having been defined, the political spotlight on immigration quickly shifted from the White House to Congess.

As we saw in the previous chapter, the two chairmen of the immigration subcommittees of the Senate and House, Alan K. Simpson of Wyoming and Romano L. Mazzoli of Kentucky, had expressed their commitment to work with the White House in passing immigration reform legislation. Accordingly, on March 17, 1982, Simpson and Mazzoli jointly introduced the Immigration Reform and Control Act (IRCA) in Congress, designed to implement the major recommendations on immigration reform which the Reagan administration had made on July 30, 1981.

However, the task of passing IRCA turned out to be a long, arduous, exceedingly difficult, and complicated task, which took four and one-half years. It was not until October 17, 1986 that Congress finally passed the conference report on IRCA. Why did Congress take so long to pass IRCA? The answer lies in the fact that IRCA contained a number of politically controversial, if not explosive, provisions. The three most controversial provisions pertained to the issues of employer sanctions, amnesty, and guest workers. Each of those provisions provoked fierce opposition from special interests and their allies in Congress. It took four and one-half years for the co-sponsors of IRCA to fashion the compromises concerning those three issues in order to build the bipartisan majorities in both houses of Congress necessary to pass the bill.

To be sure, broad support for IRCA existed in the Senate, which passed the bill three times—in 1982, 1983, and 1985. On each of those three occasions, IRCA commanded the support of over two-thirds of the Senate. However, powerful opposition to IRCA existed within the House, which delayed passage of IRCA until 1986. Why was the House so reluctant to pass IRCA? The answer is that the three most controversial provisions of IRCA provoked especially intense opposition within the House.

Liberal Democratic House members, representing the interests of the Latino community, rejected employer sanctions, charging that they would result in ethnic discrimination against legal Hispanic immigrant workers. This fear was based upon the fact that the overwhelming majority of illegal aliens were born in Latin America. Laboring under the false stereoptype that most, if not all, Latino immigrants reside in the United States illegally, many firms would respond to employer sanctions by refusing to hire foreign-born Hispanic workers.

Leading the Latino community's opposition to employer sanctions was MALDEF. It mounted an intense lobbying campaign to influence Congress to reject the employer-sanctions provisions of IRCA. Peter Skerry notes that MALDEF's opposition to employer sanctions was a major reason why passage of IRCA proved to be such a difficult, arduous, and time-consuming task.

MALDEF's . . . political clout was most evident in the decade-long battle that culminated in the Immigration Reform and Control Act of 1986. . . .

MALDEF focused Latino opposition to Simpson-Mazzoli onto the presumed racial dimension of the issue. Indeed, MALDEF argued that the legislation's proposed sanctions on employers hiring undocumented workers would lead to discrimination—not just against undocumented workers, but against "all brown-skinned people." This argument may have resonated among Mexican Americans who remembered family members (including U.S. citizens) being rounded up and deported in Depression-era repatriation efforts, or in Operation Wetback during the early 1950s. . . . Those charges allowed MALDEF to tie up congressional negotiations over Simpson-Mazzoli for months at a time at various critical junctures. Although the organization did not prevail, and employer sanctions were eventually enacted into law, MALDEF managed to dilute their effectiveness and secured creation of an office within the Justice Department to investigate complaints of discrimination. Perhaps most importantly, MALDEF succeeded in defining the terms of the debate [on immigration reform].[44]

House members of both parties, representing the interests of agribusiness, refused to accept employer sanctions unless they were coupled with the establishment of a large and generous guest worker program. Agribusiness interests, especially in the West, were heavily dependent upon illegal aliens as a vital source of cheap labor. Employer sanctions would require agribusiness interests to replace their illegal alien workers with American citizens and other permanent legal residents.

As a result, the replacement of illegal alien workers with American citizens and permanent legal residents would cost agribusiness substantial sums, in the form of higher wages and spending to improve working conditions in the field. Agribusiness interests were only willing to accept employer sanctions if they were coupled with a large and generous guest worker program which would allow growers to continue to have access to cheap Mexican labor. However, liberal Democratic House members, representing the interests of the Latino community and organized labor, rejected the establishment of such a program, charging that it would subject Mexican workers to exploitation by American employers and result in substantial job displacement of American workers.

In addition to employer sanctions and a guest worker program, amnesty was another emotional, hot-button issue, which served as a stumbling block to passage of IRCA in the House. House Republicans rejected amnesty, arguing that it would reward aliens for immigrating to the United States illegally by granting them the right to obtain permanent legal residence and eventual American citizenship. This was unfair to the millions of legal immigrants, who had to wait their turn before being admitted to the United States. House Republicans believed that aliens should be punished, not rewarded, for immigrating to the United States illegally. Granting amnesty to illegal aliens would only encourage further illegal immigration to the United States. Aliens would immigrate to the United States with the full expectation that they too would be granted amnesty the next time the issue was presented to Congress.

The amnesty provisions of IRCA divided the Latino community over the bill. While the Latino community remained united in its opposition to employer sanctions, its members were equally united in their support of amnesty. Many Latinos concluded that the benefits of amnesty outweighed the cost of employer sanctions, and threw their support behind IRCA. Support for IRCA was especially strong among illegal aliens eligible to receive amnesty if IRCA were passed. Those illegal aliens lobbied MALDEF to drop its opposition to IRCA because of the employer-sanctions provisions contained in the bill. As Skerry notes, "MALDEF . . . disregarded the pleas of many illegal immigrants who, according to a staff attorney in Los Angeles, called the organization daily and urged it to support Simpson-Mazzoli, employer sanctions and all, because of the bill's amnesty provisions."[45]

The amnesty provisions of IRCA undermined MALDEF's ability to lobby Congress to reject the bill. Many Latinos were willing to swallow their opposition to employer sanctions and support IRCA because of its amnesty provisions. Those Latinos recognized that the employer-sanctions provisions of IRCA would have to remain in the bill; otherwise Republican members of Congress would oppose the measure. Given the fact that they retained a majority in the Senate, Republicans probably had the votes to prevent passage of IRCA, absent its employer-sanctions provisions. In the unlikely event that Republican members of Congress lacked the votes to do so, Reagan was certain to veto IRCA, if it failed to contain employer-sanctions provisions. Two-thirds majorities in both houses of Congress did not exist to override such a veto.[46] Accepting employer sanctions was the political price many Latinos were willing to pay in order to assure the establishment of an amnesty program.

To be sure, Latinos incurred little political sacrifice in agreeing to accept employer sanctions, since illegal aliens have encountered almost no difficulty in continuing to find jobs. This is due to their ability to circumvent employer sanctions in finding jobs by engaging in document fraud. Accordingly, employer sanctions have failed to achieve their goal of depriving illegal aliens, the overwhelming majority of whom were born in Latin America, of jobs.

As a result, the decision of many Latinos to accept employer sanctions did not represent a substantive political concession to assure the passage of IRCA, since they have turned out to be ineffective and unworkable. On balance, IRCA represented a political victory for the Latino community, since it granted amnesty to 2.7 million illegal aliens, nearly 90 percent of whom were born in Latin America, while imposing a fraud-ridden employer-sanctions regime, which has utterly failed to achieve its goal. IRCA gave the Latino community the benefits of a large and generous amnesty program without requiring its members to pay the price of having to accept a credible and effective employer-sanctions regime capable of depriving illegal aliens of jobs.

With many Latinos supporting IRCA, MALDEF was unable to prevent passage of the bill. MALDEF could only succeed in this effort if its opposition had the united support of the Latino community. Absent such support, MALDEF could not legitimately claim to represent the Latino community in its opposition to IRCA, and without such a claim, MALDEF's lobbying campaign against the bill lacked credibility. MALDEF's failure to prevent passage of IRCA was due precisely to the divisions within the Latino community over the bill which the amnesty provisions of the bill created.[47]

Widespread disagreements over employer sanctions, a guest worker program, and amnesty thwarted the ability of the House to pass IRCA. Indeed, it was not until June 20, 1984 that the House finally passed IRCA for the first time. Even then, it was passed by an extremely narrow margin—216 to 211. The Senate and House passed differing versions of IRCA in the 98th Congress, which required the establishment of a conference committee to produce a report reconciling those differences. However, the committee was unable to reconcile the differences between the Senate and House versions of IRCA pertaining to the issue of reimbursing the states for the cost of providing social services to amnesty recipients. This prevented the committee from producing a conference report before the 98th Congress adjourned in October 1984.

New disagreements between the Senate and House developed over the issue of the guest worker program when the Senate passed IRCA for the third time in 1985. It took another year to resolve those disagreements before a conference report on IRCA could be produced, which Congress finally passed on October 17, 1986.[48] Passage of the conference report on IRCA ended the five-and-one-half-year effort to pass immigration reform legislation, which began on March 1, 1981 when SCIRP issued its final report containing its recommendations on immigration reform.

CONCLUSION

On March 1, 1981, SCIRP issued the final report containing its recommendations on immigration reform. However, Reagan was unwilling to accept SCIRP's recommendations as the basis for defining his administration's immigration policy. Rather, Reagan was determined that his administration define its own immigration policy, independent of the recommendations of SCIRP. Accordingly, on March 6, 1981, Reagan established the President's Task Force on Immigration and Refugee Policy in order to make recommendations to him on immigration reform, which would define his administration's immigration policy.

On July 1, 1981, SCIRP presented the report to Reagan. However, it contained few recommendations. Instead, the report presented Reagan with a confusing array of options for him to consider in defining his administration's immigration policy. Accordingly, during July, Reagan held a series of Cabinet meetings in order to enable his administration to make final recommendations on immigration reform which would comprise the basis of the president's immigration policy. On July 30 the administration finally presented its recommendations on immigration reform in three statements on immigration policy which the Justice Department, Reagan, and Smith issued.

With the Reagan administration having made its recommendations on immigration reform, the political spotlight on this issue quickly shifted to Congress. On March 17, 1982, Simpson and Mazzoli introduced IRCA, which contained provisions implementing the two major recommendations on immigration reform SCIRP and the Reagan administration had made pertaining to employer sanctions and amnesty. While the Senate had no difficulty passing IRCA, widespread disagreements existed within the House over the major issues, which the bill confronted, pertaining to employer sanctions, a guest worker program, and amnesty. It was not until October 1986 that those disagreements were finally resolved, paving the way for final passage of IRCA.

IRCA addressed the problem of illegal immigration through the carrot-and-stick approach, which SCIRP recommended in its final report. IRCA granted amnesty to illegal aliens who resided in the United States. Congress's decision to establish an amnesty program was in recognition of the fact that this was the only practical and humane solution to the problem of the millions of illegal aliens who resided in the United States. Congress was unwilling to order the mass deportation of those illegal aliens, given both their massive numbers and the fact that many of them had laid down roots in the United States and demonstrated their capacity to be productive, law-abiding American citizens.

However, Congress was determined to deter further illegal immigration to the United States. To this end, Congress imposed an employer-sanctions regime designed to deprive illegal aliens of jobs and eliminate incentives for foreign-born individuals to immigrate to this nation without authentic documentation. Insofar as illegal immigration is concerned, amnesty was the carrot which Congress used to respond to the problem of the millions of undocumented individuals who resided in the United States, while employer sanctions were the stick designed to deter further illegal immigration to this nation. The following two chapters will analyze how successful this carrot-and-stick combination of employer sanctions and amnesty has proven in addressing the problem of illegal immigration.

Chapter 4

The Immigration Reform and Control Act and the Challenge of Imposing Employer Sanctions

The 1986 Immigration Reform and Control Act represented the most sweeping change in U.S. immigration law in thirty-four years. Employer sanctions are one of [the] major policy innovations contained within IRCA that were intended to reduce the stock and flow of U.S. illegal immigration.[1]
—Michael Fix, The Urban Institute

The most important and lasting element of IRCA was the imposition of an employer-sanctions regime designed to deter further illegal immigration to the United States. Aliens immigrate to the United States illegally primarily in search of jobs. Employers find illegal aliens to be an attractive source of cheap labor. Illegal aliens are generally willing to work for lower wages than American citizens and permanent legal residents. Illegal aliens also often work in unsafe and unhealthful conditions, which American citizens and permanent legal residents would be unwilling to tolerate. As a result, firms save substantial sums through the employment of illegal aliens, both in terms of lower wages and avoiding having to make the expenditures necessary to comply with federal occupational safety and health regulations.

Through the imposition of federal civil and criminal sanctions upon employers who knowingly hire illegal aliens, IRCA was designed to deprive undocumented individuals of jobs. Firms would be expected to respond to employer sanctions by refusing to hire illegal aliens, resulting in a rapid loss of employment opportunities available to undocumented workers. In the absence of employment opportunities, aliens would have no incentive to reside in the United States illegally, resulting in a substantial reduction in the flow of illegal immigration to this nation. On paper, employer sanctions seemed to provide the Reagan administration and Congress with a solution to the problem of illegal immigration. As a result, the administration and Congress eagerly embraced employer sanctions, which became the central element of IRCA.

However, employer sanctions failed to fulfill their promise of stemming the flow of illegal immigration to the United States. The number of illegal aliens who currently reside in the United States is larger than it was in 1986, when IRCA was enacted into federal law. Moreover, the illegal alien population is rising at a more rapid rate than it was in the years prior to the enactment of IRCA into federal law.

The Urban Institute estimates that in 1986 between 3 million and 5 million illegal aliens resided in the United States. From 1980 to 1986, the illegal alien population was rising at an average annual rate of 200,000.[2] In 1997, the INS estimated that 5 million illegal aliens resided in the United States. The illegal alien population was rising at an average annual rate of 275,000.[3]

The growth in the illegal alien population since 1986 is actually substantially larger than the figures just cited would suggest. IRCA granted amnesty to illegal aliens, who had either resided in the United State since prior to January 1, 1982, or were eligible to obtain permanent legal residence under the Special Agricultural Worker (SAW) program. As we will see in the next chapter, 2.7 million illegal aliens ended up obtaining amnesty under IRCA.[4] With IRCA granting amnesty to such a large number of illegal aliens, the number of undocumented individuals who resided in the United States declined substantially in the years immediately following the enactment of IRCA into federal law in 1986.

On December 1, 1988, the last deadline for illegal aliens to file their amnesty claims expired.[5] The INS estimated that between 1.7 million to 2.9 million illegal aliens remained in the United States one month following this deadline.[6] Accordingly, the illegal alien population has actually doubled since the completion of the amnesty program on December 1, 1988, which is the very same day the employer-sanctions provisions of IRCA went into full effect. As a result, employer sanctions have had no discernible impact in stemming the flow of illegal immigration since they went into full effect in 1988.[7]

Why have employer sanctions failed to stem the flow of illegal immigration to the United States? The answer lies in the fact that there is no way for employers to meet their legal obligations under the employer-sanctions provisions of IRCA. Employers are required to solicit documents from individuals which verify their eligibility to work in the United States. To evade detection, illegal aliens use fraudulent documents, which falsely verify their eligibility to work in the United States. Lacking any means to determine the authenticity of those documents, employers have unwittingly accepted those documents as genuine, and proceeded to hire illegal aliens, in the false belief that they are eligible to work in the United States.[8]

Document fraud represents the single, central, overriding reason why the employer-sanctions provisions of IRCA have had no discernible effect in stemming the flow of illegal immigration to the United States. Congress recognized the potential for the employer-sanctions provisions of IRCA to be subject to massive document fraud. To this end, Congress required the attorney general to assess the effectiveness of the worker verification provisions of IRCA in establishing a secure means of determining the identity of individuals who seek employment. Congress authorized the president to recommend reforms in those provisions in order to improve their effectiveness. To accomplish this objective, IRCA authorized the president to establish worker verification pilot projects in order to determine their effectiveness in enabling employers to detect and crack down on document fraud.[9]

However, Reagan failed to exercise the authority granted him under IRCA to improve the effectiveness of its worker verification provisions. Reagan's failure to do so left the employer-sanctions provisions of IRCA subject to massive document fraud, as illegal aliens found it easy to illegally obtain jobs through the use of phony documents. In the absence of a fraud-resistant worker verification system, employer sanctions have proven to be an ineffective and unworkable means to deprive illegal aliens of jobs. And as long as illegal aliens continue to retain easy access to employment, they will have every incentive to reside in the United States in large numbers.

THE EMPLOYER-SANCTIONS PROVISIONS OF IRCA

IRCA prohibits employers from either knowingly hiring illegal aliens or refusing to meet the paperwork requirements under the bill. Those paperwork requirements compel all employers to solicit documents from each individual which verify his or her eligibility to work in the United States.[10] Employers are required to solicit a minimum of two documents: one to establish evidence of either American citizenship and authorization to work in the United States, and the other to determine the identity of individuals who seek employment.[11]

IRCA lists seventeen different documents, any one or more of which may be used by an individual to verify his or her eligibility to work in the United States.[12] Each individual who obtains employment must sign an I-9 form, in which he or she is required to attest to this eligibility. Employers are required to sign the I-9 form, affirming, under penalty of perjury, that they solicited specific documents from each individual whom they hired which verified this eligibility. Employers are required to accept any such document as authentic if it "appears reasonably on its face to be genuine."

Employers are required to maintain their I-9 forms on file, and make them available for inspection by either INS or Labor Department law enforcement officers, upon request. Those officers may request inspection of the I-9 forms of any employer without having to obtain a search warrant from a federal judge. IRCA makes it a civil offense, punishable by a fine, for any employer to reject a request by such officers to inspect his or her I-9 forms.

IRCA imposes federal civil fines upon employers who knowingly hire illegal aliens, which rise with each additional offense commited under the bill. The fines range from $250 to $2,000 per worker for the first offense; $2,000 to $5,000 per worker for the second offense; and $3,000 to $10,000 per worker for the third and each subsequent offense. Criminal penalties of up to six months in prison and a $3,000 fine may be imposed upon any employer who engages in a "pattern or practice" of knowingly hiring illegal aliens. The term "pattern or practice" is defined as "regular, repeated, or intentional activities but does not include sporadic or accidental acts." An employer need not have previously violated the employer-sanctions provisions of IRCA to be charged with a "pattern or practice" of hiring illegal aliens. A fine ranging from $100 to $1,000 is imposed upon employers who violate the paperwork requirements of IRCA.[13]

The INS is responsible for enforcement of the employer-sanctions provisions of IRCA.[14] The INS must refer all cases pertaining to civil violations of the employer-sanctions provisions of IRCA to the attorney general. He or she must determine whether a firm has violated those provisions before proceeding to inform all suspected offenders.

The attorney general must impose a penalty upon all suspected offenders, as prescribed by IRCA, thirty days following the issuance of a notice of violation of the employer-sanctions provisions of the bill. Employers charged with a violation of those provisions may request a hearing before a federal administrative law judge during the thirty-day period. If such a hearing is held, then the judge must determine by "a preponderance of the evidence" whether the alleged violation occurred. The judge's verdict is final, unless it was either modified or overturned by the attorney general within thirty days of its issuance. An employer could file an appeal against a negative verdict against him or her in federal appeals court within forty-five days following its issuance.[15]

EMPLOYER SANCTIONS AND THE PROBLEM OF DISCRIMINATION AGAINST LEGAL IMMIGRANT LATINO WORKERS

As we have seen, liberal Democratic members of Congress and interest groups representing the Latino community constituted a particularly powerful source of opposition to IRCA. That opposition was directed against the employer-sanctions provisions of IRCA. Liberal Democrats and Latinos feared that employer sanctions would result in widespread ethnic discrimination against legal immigrant Hispanic workers. Liberal Democratic members of Congress and interest groups representing the Latino community had good reason for this fear. Many employers undoubtedly operate under the false stereotype that most, if not all, immigrant Latino workers are residing in the United States illegally. This stereotype is an inevitable result of the fact that the overwhelming majority of illegal aliens were born in Latin America, as we saw in the previous chapter.

Accordingly, passage of employer-sanctions legislation could result in the refusal of many firms to hire Hispanic immigrants, including those eligible to work in the United States. Firms would not want to take the risk of hiring immigrant Latino workers, for fear that they might turn out to be illegal aliens, exposing those businesses to the severe civil and criminal penalties which employer-sanctions legislation would impose. Since the majority of Latino workers are foreign-born (51 percent in 1994),[16] millions of immigrant Latino workers could be subject to unlawful immigration-related employment discrimination arising from employer-sanctions legislation.

THE HOUSE PASSES THE FRANK AMENDMENT

The prospect that employer sanctions might result in widespread ethnic discrimination against legal immigrant workers, especially those born in Latin America, was a major source of concern to members of Congress in their consideration of IRCA. Congress responded to this concern by inserting new civil rights protections into IRCA designed to assure that employer sanctions did not result in such discrimination. The civil rights provisions of IRCA were introduced on June 12, 1984, as an amendment to the bill, by Barney Frank of Massachusetts, during the House debate on the measure. The House passed the amendment by a nearly unanimous margin of 404 to 9. The amendment made it an "unfair immigration-related employment practice" to discriminate on the basis of national orgin or alienage. A United States Immigration Board, headed by a Special Counsel, would be established in the Justice Department to investigate and prosecute immigration-related job discrimination complaints arising from the employer-sanctions provisions of IRCA.[17]

The Reagan administration strongly opposed the Frank amendment, arguing that it would represent an excessive and unwarranted expansion in federal civil rights regulations over employers. The administration believed that the amendment, if adopted by Congress, would expose employers to a flood of costly and frivolous litigation. The administration feared that many legal immigrant workers denied jobs would take advantage of the amendment in order to sue firms, claiming, however disingenuously, that they had been deprived of employment based upon their legal status as noncitizens. By opening a new avenue for costly and frivolous civil rights litigation against employers, the administration believed that the amendment would make it difficult for firms to conduct business. This was true, given the fact that employers faced the prospect of a lawsuit being filed against them every time they denied a legal noncitizen immigrant a job, and hired an American citizen instead, even if the American was better qualified for the job.

THE REAGAN ADMINISTRATION OPPOSES THE FRANK AMENDMENT

The Reagan administration feared that the Frank amendment might be retained in any final version of IRCA which Congress might pass. Accordingly, the administration decided to state its opposition to the amendment early on, before the 99th Congress had an opportunity to vote on IRCA. The administration hoped that by making its opposition to the Frank amendment clear from the very outset, Congress would delete it from IRCA. Congress might take such action in order to avoid a confrontation with the administration over the amendment, which might endanger prospects for passage of IRCA.

Accordingly, on September 12, 1985, Attorney General Edwin Meese III wrote Senate Judiciary Committee Chairman Strom Thurmond of South Carolina a letter which outlined the administration's position on IRCA. In his letter, Meese announced the Reagan administration's opposition to the Frank amendment.

[A] likely amendment which relates to employer sanctions would seek to establish a new cause of action for "unfair immigration-related employment practices" cognizable in a new office in the Department of Justice. The amendment would, for the first time, establish "alienage" as the basis for an action under our civil rights laws and would significantly expand the existing bar against employment discrimination based upon national origin. . . .

To establish a new agency-sized bureaucracy, complete with provisions providing for a private right of action, and attorneys' fees, in anticipation of a finding that coverage of our current civil rights laws will be inadequate, is inappropriate. The potential that such an approach promises for divergent and conflicting [civil rights] enforcement activities is in itself sufficient reason to counsel against its adoption.[18]

On September 12, 1985—the same day that Meese sent his letter to Thurmond—the Reagan administration issued a statement of policy on IRCA, in anticipation of the Senate vote on the bill held a week later. In its statement, the administration announced to the public what Meese had privately told Thurmond—that the White House strongly opposed the Frank amendment: "The administration would . . . strongly oppose any amendment . . . establishing a new bureaucracy in the Department of Justice to adjudicate 'unfair immigration-related employment practices' and establishing a new cause of action for 'alienage.' ''[19]

Consistent with the wishes of the Reagan administration, the Senate did not include the Frank amendment in its own version of IRCA, which passed on September 19, 1985. Nevertheless, the Senate version of IRCA did include important civil rights provisions of its own. The Senate version required the General Accounting Office (GAO) to monitor federal enforcement of the employer-sanctions provisions of IRCA to determine whether they had resulted in ethnic discrimination against legal immigrant workers.

The GAO would report its findings to the attorney general. He or she, in conjunction with the United States Civil Rights and Equal Employment Opportunity Commissions (EEOC), would make recommendations to Congress concerning reforms in the employer-sanctions provisions of IRCA, based upon the GAO's findings. Congress would be authorized to vote to terminate employer sanctions within three years of their establishment if the GAO found a widespread pattern of ethnic discrimination against legal immigrant workers which resulted from employer sanctions.[20]

In his letter to Thurmond, Meese announced the Reagan administration's support for the civil rights provisions of the Senate version of IRCA. Meese noted that the Senate version required the GAO to apprise Congress concerning whether employer sanctions were resulting in any ethnic discrimination against legal immigrant workers. Meese believed that the administration was fully capable, under existing civil rights laws, to effectively address any such discrimination which might arise from employer sanctions:

The concern that employer sanctions could result in discriminatory hiring practices persists and [IRCA] appropriately provides for careful monitoring of sanctions implementation by both the Executive Branch and the General Accounting Office. Any new pattern of employment discrimination which should arise would be noted in the regular reports required by the legislation and will be subject to vigorous enforcement actions under the comprehensive civil rights enforcement scheme currently in existence.[21]

THE HOUSE REJECTS THE SENSENBRENNER AMENDMENT

Opposition to the Frank amendment went beyond the Reagan administration to include the overwhelming majority of House Republicans. Those House Republicans shared the administration's concerns that the amendment would expose employers to a costly flood of new litigation. Accordingly, Republican Representative F. James Sensenbrenner, Jr., of Wisconsin, introduced a motion to delete the Frank amendment from IRCA hours before the final House vote on the bill on October 9, 1986.

The Democratic majority in the House opposed the Sensenbrenner amendment, believing that the civil rights provisions of IRCA were essential to preventing the potential for ethnic discrimination against legal immigrant workers arising from employer sanctions. Consistent with their strong support for civil rights, the Democratic majority in the House was unwilling to back IRCA without inclusion of the Frank amendment.

Accordingly, the House rejected the Sensenbrenner amendment by an overwhelming margin of 260 to 140. The House vote on the amendment fell largely along party lines, with most Republicans supporting it, and practically all Democrats opposing it. A total of 206 Democrats voted against the amendment, and 115 Republicans voted for it. Only twenty-five Democrats crossed party lines to join Republicans in voting for the amendment. Only fifty-four Republicans did the same in joining Democrats in voting against it.[22]

As the House vote on the Sensenbrenner amendment shows, IRCA could not have been passed without inclusion of its civil rights provisions. Indeed, the two major elements of IRCA—amnesty and employer sanctions—provoked bitter opposition within Congress from an unlikely coalition of liberal Democrats and conservative Republicans. Liberal Democrats opposed employer sanctions, believing that they would result in ethnic discrimination against legal immigrant Latino workers; conservative Republicans opposed granting amnesty to illegal aliens, believing that they should be punished, not rewarded, for living in this nation without authentic documentation. Liberals represent the dominant wing of the Democratic Party, and conservatives constitute the dominant wing of the Republican Party. Given their opposition to employer sanctions and amnesty, liberal Democrats and conservative Republicans could have joined together in creating bipartisan majorities in both houses of Congress to prevent passage of IRCA.

IRCA could only be passed if it commanded the support of a bipartisan coalition of moderates in Congress. However, moderates were sympathetic to the concern of liberal Democrats that employer sanctions would indeed result in ethnic discrimination against legal immigrant workers. To prevent such discrimination from occurring, moderates were unwilling to support IRCA unless it contained the Frank amendment.

The critical role which the Frank amendment played in guaranteeing passage of IRCA can be seen from the House votes on the Sensenbrenner amendment and the conference report on the bill. Of the 238 House members voting for the conference report, 172 opposed the amendment. A total of 142 of the 161 Democrats, and thirty of the seventy-seven Republicans, voted for the conference report, and against the amendment.[23]

House members voting against the Sensenbrenner amendment and for the conference report on IRCA were primarily moderates. They were willing to vote for IRCA, but only if it contained the Frank amendment. House members who both opposed the Sensenbrenner amendment and supported the conference report on IRCA represented nearly three-quarters of all House members who voted for final passage of the bill. It is highly unlikely that more than a handful of those moderates would have voted for the conference report on IRCA without the Frank amendment; and without the support of the overwhelming majority of those moderates, IRCA would have been rejected by the House.

THE REAGAN ADMINISTRATION CONTINUES TO OPPOSE THE FRANK AMENDMENT

As the House vote on the Sensenbrenner amendment shows, IRCA could not have been passed in the House without the civil rights provisions. Given the potential of employer sanctions to result in ethnic discrimination against legal immigrant workers, especially those born in Latin America, the House was unwilling to pass IRCA without those provisions. Given the Reagan administration's commitment to passage of IRCA, one would have expected the White House to abandon its opposition to those provisions. Instead, however, the administration persisted in its opposition to those provisions.

As we have seen, the Senate and House versions of IRCA contained different civil rights provisions. The Senate version required only that the GAO monitor federal enforcement of employer-sanctions provisions of IRCA to determine whether they had resulted in ethnic discrimination against legal immigrant workers. The House version went much further than this in establishing new civil rights protections for legal immigrant workers.

In his letter to Thurmond on September 12, 1985, Meese announced that, while the Reagan administration could accept the civil rights provisions contained in the Senate version of IRCA, it would continue to oppose the antidiscrimination amendments included in the House version. The administration's support for the civil rights provisions contained in the Senate version of IRCA is consistent with the fact that they would not affect existing federal civil rights laws, but only require the GAO to monitor enforcement of employer sanctions to determine whether they are resulting in ethnic discrimination against legal immigrant workers. As Congress prepared to take final action on IRCA in October 1986, the administration decided to maintain its position with respect to the civil rights provisions of IRCA. This decision was reflected in a memo Carol T. Crawford, Associate Director of Economics and Government in the OMB, sent to White House Chief of Staff Donald T. Regan. In her memo, Crawford reiterated that the administration could support the Senate version of IRCA, since it believed that "adequate protections currently exist" under federal civil rights laws to protect legal immigrant workers from immigration-related employment discrimination arising from the employer-sanctions provisions of IRCA.[24]

Attached to Crawford's memo was a document, which the OMB prepared, defining the Reagan administration's positions on the major provisions of the House and Senate versions of IRCA. The document made it clear that the administration "can support" the civil rights provisions contained in the Senate version of IRCA. However, the administration would continue to "strongly oppose" provisions in the House version of IRCA "establishing [a] new office in Justice to adjudicate unfair immigration-related employment practices and establishing a new right to sue based on 'alienage.' "[25]

On October 9, 1986—hours before the House rejected the Sensenbrenner amendment to delete the civil rights provisions from IRCA, subsequent to passing the bill—the Reagan administration issued a statement of policy on the measure reiterating its opposition to the antidiscrimination provisions: "The administration objects to . . . unnecessary provisions creating additional protections against discrimination by employers and establishing a new entity in the Department of Justice to enforce these protections. Existing law adequately addresses discrimination and there is no evidence indicating a significant problem in this area."[26]

Despite the Reagan administration's reiteration of its opposition to the civil rights provisions of IRCA in its October 9 statement, the House passed the measure containing the antidiscrimination amendments hours after the White

House released its announcement. Nevertheless, the administration still had hope that the civil rights provisions might be deleted from the conference report on IRCA, which was completed on October 14. Hours before the conference committee completed its report, the administration issued yet another statement of policy on IRCA reiterating its opposition to the civil rights provisions of the bill: "The administration believes that existing law adequately protects against discrimination by employers and that there is no evidence indicating a significant problem in this area; the administration therefore opposes the House provisions establishing a new entity within the Department of Justice to enforce those provisions."[27]

The Reagan administration's adamant opposition to the civil rights provisions of IRCA fell upon deaf ears on Capitol Hill. Hours after the administration issued that statement, the conference committee, which reconciled the differing Senate and House versions of the bill, issued its report. Much to the administration's dismay, the report, subsequently passed by Congress, combined the civil rights provisions contained in the earlier versions of the bill approved by the House and Senate, including the Frank amendment.

The civil rights provisions of IRCA made it an "unfair immigration-related employment practice" to "discriminate against" any individual in hiring, recruitment, job referral for a fee, or the act of discharging from employment, based upon national origin or alienage. The prohibition against discrimination in employment applies to all American citizens and legal noncitizen immigrants who demonstrate an intent to obtain American citizenship once they have met the legal requirements for doing so. Illegal aliens are specifically exempted from the prohibition against discrimination in employment. Employers would be allowed to grant a preference to hiring an American citizen over a legal noncitizen immigrant, provided both are equally qualified for the job in question.

To enforce the prohibition against discrimination in employment based on national origin or alienage, an Office of Special Counsel for Immigration-Related Unfair Employment Practices would be established in the Justice Department. The president would appoint the Special Counsel, subject to Senate confirmation, to serve a four-year term. The Special Counsel would be authorized to investigate and prosecute complaints arising from unlawful immigration-related employment practices pertaining to discrimination based upon national origin or alienage.[28] All individuals who believe they are the victims of unlawful immigration-related employment practices would have to file their discrimination complaints with either the Office of Special Counsel or the EEOC. Those individuals would be allowed to sue their employers directly in federal court, but only if either the Office of Special Counsel or EEOC refused to take their case.[29]

Both the federal agencies in charge of enforcing the civil rights provisions of IRCA and individuals filing lawsuits on their own would be authorized to bring their cases alleging unlawful immigration-related employment practices before a federal administrative law judge. He or she would conduct hearings to determine whether defendants charged with unlawful immigration-related employment practices were guilty of such an offense. The judge would be empowered to impose civil penalties upon employers found guilty of such practices, including requiring them to hire the immigrant worker who suffered discrimination, paying back pay awards, when appropriate, and paying a fine of $1,000 for each foreign-born worker experiencing discrimination.[30]

The GAO would monitor enforcement of the employer-sanctions provisions of IRCA to determine whether they were resulting in "widespread discrimination" against legal immigrant workers. The GAO would issue annual reports to Congress, concerning whether such discrimination was occurring, during the first three years employer sanctions were in effect. Congress could terminate employer sanctions should the GAO conclude, in its third and final annual report, that they had resulted in "widespread discrimination" against legal immigrant workers.

The termination of employer sanctions would be achieved through a joint resolution of Congress passed within thirty days of the GAO's third annual report stating such a conclusion.[31] Such action by Congress would automatically result in the elimination of the civil rights provisions of IRCA. Those provisions could also be eliminated should Congress pass a joint resolution which determined that employer sanctions either had not resulted in "widespread discrimination" against legal immigrant workers, or had "created an unreasonable burden on employers."[32]

Firms which employed three workers or fewer would be exempt from the civil rights provisions of IRCA. Nevertheless, firms employing four or more workers, which *are* required to comply with those provisions, still represent 48 percent of all employers in the United States. Title VII of the Civil Rights Act of 1964, which prohibits discrimination in employment, covers only firms employing fifteen or more workers, representing 13 percent of all employers in the United States.[33] As a result, the civil rights provisions of IRCA represented a major expansion in the number of firms subject to the prohibition against discrimination in employment existing under federal law.

REAGAN ACCEPTS THE CIVIL RIGHTS PROVISIONS OF IRCA

The conference committee's decision to include the civil rights provisions in its final report on IRCA, which Congress passed, confronted the Reagan administration with a particularly vexing dilemma. The administration had worked for over five years, since the Justice Department, Reagan, and Smith had issued their statements defining the White House's immigration policy (July 30, 1981), to win passage of immigration reform legislation. After several false starts and political setbacks, the administration's efforts finally bore fruit with the passage of IRCA in October 1986.

The House's rejection of the Sensenbrenner amendment by an overwhelming margin made it clear that its members would not pass IRCA unless it included the civil rights provisions contained in the final House version of the bill. As we have seen, the Reagan administration strongly opposed those provisions. However, had Reagan vetoed IRCA, because of his opposition to those provisions, there was little chance that Congress could have overridden the veto, since the House passed the bill by substantially less than the two-thirds majority required to overturn a presidential veto.

Even in the unlikely event that Congress had the capability to override a presidential veto of IRCA, Reagan still could have easily killed the bill. This is due to the fact that the 99th Congress adjourned after having passed IRCA in October 1986. As a result, Reagan would have vetoed IRCA after Congress adjourned, making his action a pocket veto. A pocket veto cannot be overridden by Congress, which goes out of business once it has adjourned. Since Reagan had the unilateral power to kill IRCA with a simple pocket veto, the bill could not have been enacted into law in 1986 unless it had the president's backing, regardless of the level of support which the measure enjoyed in Congress. Had Reagan chosen to kill IRCA, Congress would have had to resume its efforts to pass immigration reform legislation when its members reconvened in January 1987.

However, there was little prospect that immigration reform legislation could be passed during the remaining two years of the Reagan administration, if the president chose to veto IRCA. The Democratic majority in the House was completely unwilling to accept any immigration reform legislation which imposed an employer-sanctions regime without provisions protecting the civil rights of legal immigrant workers. With the Democratic Party assured of retaining its majority in the House following the 1986 congressional elections, House Democrats were in a position to kill any immigration reform legislation which failed to contain those provisions.

The intransigent position which the Democratic majority in the House adopted on the issue of civil rights protections for legal immigrant workers confronted Reagan with a difficult dilemma: either veto IRCA because of his objections to its civil rights provisions and destroy all prospects for passage of immigration reform legislation during the remaining two years of his presidency, or swallow his opposition to those provisions and sign the bill. Unwilling to destroy prospects for the passage of immigration reform legislation, which represented a key item on his domestic policy agenda from almost the very outset of his presidency, Reagan decided, however reluctantly, to accept those provisions and sign IRCA into federal law.

However, despite his decision to accept the civil rights provisions of IRCA, Reagan was determined to narrow their scope and application. He wanted to limit the power of the Special Counsel for Immigration-Related Unfair Employment Practices to investigate and prosecute cases of unlawful immigration-related employment discrimination. Reagan also intended to restrict the ability of legal immigrant workers to initiate lawsuits under the civil rights provisions of IRCA. This was designed to assure that those provisions would not open a new avenue for legal immigrant workers to initiate a flood of costly and frivolous litigation against employers who allegedly engaged in unlawful immigration-related employment discrimination.

Reagan's action to narrow the scope and application of the civil rights provisions of IRCA came in a statement which he issued following his signing of the bill on November 6, 1986. The statement contained Reagan's interpretation of the various provisions of IRCA and the regulations which would govern its enforcement. In his statement, Reagan announced that he was limiting the power of the Special Counsel for Immigration-Related Unfair Employment Practices to investigate and prosecute firms for employment discrimination only to those "cases involving discrimination apparently caused by an employer's fear of liability under the employer sanctions program."[34] The Special Counsel was prohibited from investigating and prosecuting employment discrimination cases which did not arise from employer sanctions.

Reagan also made it clear that legal immigrant workers who sued firms in federal court, alleging that they were the victims of unlawful immigration-related employment practices, would have to prove that the employers acted with "discriminatory intent." Firms could not be sued if their employment practices imposed a "disparate impact" upon immigrant workers, provided those firms operated without any "discriminatory intent."[35]

Reagan made it clear that legal immigrant workers would not be subject to the civil rights protections provided in the Supreme Court's decision on *Griggs v. Duke Power Company*, issued in 1971. In the Griggs decision, the Supreme Court ruled that employment practices which had a "disparate impact" upon minorities represented, in certain circumstances, a violation of the prohibition against job discrimination under Title VII of the Civil Rights Act of 1964. Such practices were only permissible if they could be justified on the basis of representing a "business necessity"—specifically, that such practices had a "manifest relationship" to the job in question.[36]

Reagan exempted legal immigrant workers from the civil rights protections contained in the Griggs decision by making it clear that employment practices which had a "disparate impact" upon legal immigrant workers would be permissible. This would be true, even if such practices were not justified by a "business necessity," and bore no "manifest relationship" to the job in question, provided that they are not designed to discriminate against legal immigrant workers.

A facially neutral employment selection practice that is employed without discriminatory intent will be permissible under the [civil rights] provisions of [IRCA]. For example, [IRCA] does not preclude a requirement of English language skill or a minimum score on an aptitude test even if the employer cannot show a "manifest relationship" to the job in question or that the requirement is a "bona fide occupational qualification reasonably necessary to the normal operation of that business or enterprise," so long as the practice is not a guise used to discriminate on account of national origin or citizenship status.[37]

As we have seen, the primary reason for Reagan's opposition to the civil rights provisions of IRCA was his fear that they would open a new avenue for legal immigrant workers to initiate a flood of costly and frivolous litigation against employers. Legal immigrant workers denied jobs for legitimate reasons might attempt to use those provisions to launch frivolous lawsuits against firms by falsely alleging that they were deprived of employment due to unlawful immigration-related job discrimination. By narrowing the scope and application of civil rights provisions of IRCA to only legitimate cases of unlawful immigration-related employment practices, Reagan took action to assure that the litigation arising from the bill would be kept to a minimum, and confined to cases where ethnic discrimination against legal immigrant workers may have actually occurred. Reagan's action allowed him to sign IRCA, containing its civil rights provisions, since he could be reasonably assured that the bill would not impose costly ligitigation burdens upon business, and would, therefore, have little, if any, disruptive impact upon the operation of private enterprise.

THE REAGAN ADMINISTRATION DENIES THAT EMPLOYER SANCTIONS RESULT IN DISCRIMINATION AGAINST LEGAL IMMIGRANT WORKERS

As we have seen, the purpose of the civil rights provisions of IRCA was to assure that its employer-sanctions provisions did not result in ethnic discrimination against legal immigrant workers. Had the Reagan administration accepted the premise that employer sanctions could serve as a source of ethnic discrimination against legal immigrant workers, especially those born in Latin American, then the White House would have undoubtedly supported the civil rights provisions of IRCA. In an interview with local television reporters in San Antonio on July 2, 1984, Reagan made it clear that he would not tolerate ethnic discrimination against legal immigrant Latino workers arising from employer sanctions: "I'm convinced that we can protect our Hispanic American citizens from discrimination . . . on the basis that an employer might be afraid to hire them [as a result of employer sanctions]. We're going to protect their rights."[38]

However, Reagan did not believe that new federal civil rights laws were required to protect legal immigrant Latino workers. Rather, he believed that existing federal civil rights laws were adequate to achieve this objective. This was consistent with the fact that the Reagan administration challenged the very premise that employer sanctions might serve as a source of widespread ethnic discrimination against legal immigrant workers. Indeed, in his letter to Thurmond on September 12, 1985, Meese rejected this premise. As a result, Meese argued that the civil rights provisions of IRCA were unnecessary, since there was little, if any, possibility that employer sanctions might serve as a source of widespread ethnic discrimination against legal immigrant workers: "The premise for these additions to existing [civil rights] law—a premise we reject—is that employer sanctions will result in dramatically increased employment discrimination."[39]

However, the Reagan administration's public position on employer sanctions stands in sharp contrast to the White House's private views on this issue. As we saw in the previous chapter, the President's Task Force on Immigration and Refugee Policy believed that employer sanctions *would* result in ethnic discrimination against legal immigrant workers, especially those born in Latin America. However, the Reagan administration could not make this view public for fear that Congress might respond by rejecting the employer-sanctions provisions of IRCA.

Congress was highly unlikely to accept employer sanctions if the Reagan administration believed there was a serious risk that they might result in ethnic discrimination against legal immigrant workers. To assure inclusion of employer-sanctions provisions in IRCA, the administration took the public position that they would not result in such discrimination, fully recognizing in private that this was not the case. This disingenuous position was conveyed to members of Congress by the two attorneys general who served in office during the four-and-a-half-year effort on Capitol Hill to pass IRCA—William French Smith and Edwin Meese III. Indeed, as we saw in the previous chapter, in 1981 Smith assured members of Congress that employer sanctions would not result in ethnic discrimination against legal immigrant workers, without revealing that the members of the President's Task Force, which he chaired, held the opposite view. The Reagan administration's success in securing the inclusion of employer-sanctions provisions in IRCA was largely due to the deceit which Smith and Meese had engaged in on the issue.

THE GAO CONFIRMS THAT EMPLOYER SANCTIONS RESULT IN DISCRIMINATION AGAINST LEGAL IMMIGRANT WORKERS

As we have seen, IRCA required the GAO to issue annual reports to Congress, during the first three years the bill was in effect, determining whether employer sanctions had resulted in "widespread discrimination" against legal immigrant workers. In March 1990 the GAO issued its third and final report to Congess, which concluded that employer sanctions had indeed resulted in such discrimination. The GAO argued that such discrimination was "serious but not pervasive," and attributed a "substantial amount" of it to employer sanctions.[40] The GAO based its conclusion on a survey, which it had conducted, of 9,000 employers, who were asked what actions they had taken "as a result of the 1986 immigration law." Five percent of all employers surveyed admitted that they had responded to IRCA by initiating a practice of refusing to hire workers who had either a foreign appearance or accent.

IRCA requires employers to solicit documents from all individuals, including native-born Americans, that verify their eligibility to work in the United States. Employers are prohibited from complying with the worker verification provisions of IRCA on a selective basis, soliciting such documents only from immigrants whom they wish to hire. However, 8 percent of all employers surveyed admitted that they complied with their worker verification obligations under IRCA on a selective basis, soliciting such documents only from individuals who have either a foreign appearance or accent. Fourteen percent of all employers surveyed admitted that they had responded to IRCA by initiating a practice of either only hiring native-born Americans, or refusing to hire immigrants eligible to work in the United States on a temporary basis.[41]

The GAO report confirmed what liberal Democratic members of Congress and interest groups representing the Latino community had feared from the very beginning: that many employers would respond to employer sanctions by refusing to hire immigrant workers, including those eligible to work in the United States.

As we have seen, IRCA authorized Congress to terminate employer sanctions if the GAO concluded, in its third and final annual report, that they had resulted in ''widespread discrimination'' against legal immigrant workers. With the GAO having reached such a conclusion in its third and final annual report, Congress was free to terminate employer sanctions. Senators Edward M. Kennedy of Massachusetts and Orrin Hatch of Utah introduced legislation to terminate employer sanctions following issuance of the 1990 GAO report. However, Congress failed to take any action on the Kennedy-Hatch bill, leaving the employer-sanctions provisions of IRCA intact.[42]

THE REASONS WHY EMPLOYER SANCTIONS RESULT IN DISCRIMINATION AGAINST LEGAL IMMIGRANT WORKERS

Why do employer sanctions serve as a source of ''widespread discrimination'' against immigrant workers, as the 1990 GAO report found? The answer lies in the fact that the employer-sanctions provisions of IRCA require employers to assume primary responsibility for enforcement of the prohibition against the hiring of illegal aliens. Firms can be prosecuted for hiring illegal aliens who present fraudulent documents in cases where it can be proven that the employer knew the documents to be false, or should have known this to be so, where actual knowlege cannot be established.[43]

Accordingly, it is possible for firms to be prosecuted for hiring illegal aliens who presented them with fraudulent documents, even when they believed such documents to be authentic. This would be true should an administrative law judge, hearing an employer-sanctions case, determine that the firm should have known that such documents were fraudulent, and had failed to prove that it believed the documents to be authentic. As a result, all employers face legal jeopardy when they hire immigrant workers, since no employer has any real way of knowing whether the documents presented are actually authentic. This places firms at risk of being prosecuted for violating the employer-sanctions provisions of IRCA, should such documents turn out to be fraudulent.

Given the legal jeopardy employers face under IRCA, many firms have decided that the best way to avoid violating the employer-sanctions provisions of the bill is to refuse to hire immigrant workers, including those eligible to work in the United States, and employ only native-born Americans instead. This is the only way firms can guarantee that all the workers they hire are American citizens, and therefore eligible to work in the United States. By making firms liable for hiring an illegal alien, even in certain cases where the business actually believed the worker to be residing in the United States with authentic documentation but could not prove it, employer sanctions have served as a source of ethnic discrimination against legal immigrant workers, much as the GAO concluded in its 1990 report on this issue.

Some members of Congress believe that the most appropriate response to rectifying the potential for employer sanctions to serve as a source of ethnic discrimination against legal immigrant workers is to eliminate employer sanctions altogether. This was precisely the response of some members of Congress to the release of the GAO report in 1990. Despite the introduction of legislation to eliminate employer sanctions, Congress has refused to take such action.

EMPLOYER SANCTIONS AND THE CHALLENGE OF ESTABLISHING A WORKER VERIFICATION SYSTEM

Congress's refusal to act on the Kennedy-Hatch bill to terminate employer sanctions is consistent with the fact that its members fully recognize that employer sanctions remain the most credible and effective deterrent existing against illegal immigration to the United States. It would be wrongheaded to eliminate employer sanctions only because of the ethnic discrimination they have created. To be sure, such discrimination remains a problem which must be addressed. However, the best means to address this problem is not through elimination of employer sanctions, which would leave the United States without any effective deterrent against illegal immigration. Rather, this problem can best be addressed by establishing a fraud-resistant worker verification system, which would enable firms to enforce employer sanctions in a nondiscriminatory manner. Congress has the means to establish such a system, which would enable employers to determine the authenticity of the documents provided to them by individuals verifying their eligibility to work in the United States.

Perhaps the most promising worker verification proposal involves the establishment of a telephone verification system. In 1994 the Commission on Immigration Reform (CIR), which Congress established to make recommendations on immigration reform, issued an interim report proposing the creation of such a system. It would be based upon a computerized national registry consisting of all the valid Social Security numbers held by individuals eligible to work in the United States.

Each individual who seeks employment would have to present his or her Social Security number to the employer. He or she would in turn call the federal agency in charge of maintaining the national computerized registry in order to confirm whether the Social Security number was indeed valid. Each individual who seeks employment would also have to present documents, such as a birth certificate or driver's license, establishing identity in order to verify that he or she is indeed the person named on the Social Security card. The CIR recommended that all documents which individuals may use to establish their identity be made tamper-proof.[44]

A telephone verification system would enable firms to determine the authenticity of the documents presented to them. This would prevent illegal aliens from illegally obtaining jobs by presenting their employers with fraudulent documents. Since employers could rest assured, under a telephone verification system, that all immigrants whom they wish to hire are in fact eligible to work in the United States, they need not worry about the possibility that some of their foreign-born workers might be illegal aliens. Accordingly, employers would no longer feel any need to refuse to hire immigrant workers.

To be sure, some employers will intentionally violate the employer-sanctions provisions of IRCA either by knowingly hiring illegal aliens, who serve as a vital source of cheap labor for many firms, or by refusing to meet their paperwork requirements. Some firms will also continue to discriminate against legal immigrant workers for reasons other than the need to comply with the employer-sanctions provisions of IRCA. Nevertheless, any firm which knowingly hires illegal aliens, refuses to meet its paperwork requirements, or practices ethnic discrimination against legal immigrant workers who either are American citizens or demonstrate an intent to obtain citizenship, based upon national origin or alienage, stands in violation of those provisions. A telephone verification system would enhance the capability of the federal government to enforce those provisions.

It is virtually impossible for the federal government to enforce the two major elements of the employer-sanctions provisions of IRCA. Employers who hire illegal aliens can argue that they were duped into believing that their undocumented workers are actually eligible to work in the United States, whether or not this is actually true. The use of such a defense makes it almost impossible for the Justice Department to prosecute firms that knowingly hire illegal aliens under the employer-sanctions provisions of IRCA. Indeed, the Justice Department did not issue its first felony indictment against an employer until 1994, six years after employer sanctions went into full effect.

Most firms that hire illegal aliens do so unwittingly, having been duped by document fraud. However, many other firms have hired their undocumented workers intentionally, recognizing there is little chance they will ever be caught and prosecuted for violating the employer-sanctions provisions of IRCA. Illegal aliens represent a vital source of cheap labor in many industries. As a result, firms will have every incentive to hire them, especially if there is little chance they will ever be caught and prosecuted. As a representative of the Amalgamated Clothing and Textile Workers Union in New York put it, ''If a guy running a sewing loft or a laundry or a restaurant needs to cut labor costs, he knows he can hire a few illegal workers, pay them less than the minimum wage, and get away with it.''[45]

In addition to being unenforceable, the employer-sanctions provisions of IRCA continue to represent a source of ethnic discrimination against legal immigrant workers. Firms that refuse to hire immigrant workers due to their national origin or alienage can continue to argue that such discriminatory employment practices are necessary to assure their compliance with the employer-sanctions provisions of IRCA. One could argue that because the employer-sanctions provisions of IRCA are unenforceable, firms need not fear ever being caught and prosecuted for violating employer sanctions, whether knowingly or unintentionally. This eliminates the need for firms to refuse to hire immigrant workers in order to assure that they are in compliance with the employer-sanctions provisions of IRCA.

However, firms, like individuals, wish to obey the law, whether or not it is enforceable. Few firms wish to violate the employer-sanctions provisions of IRCA, even if there is little, if any, chance they will ever be caught and prosecuted. Practically all firms regard it as their civic duty to obey the law, including the employer-sanctions provisions of IRCA. Those firms will take every precaution to assure that they are in compliance with those provisions, which could result in their refusal to hire immigrants.

To be sure, the employer-sanctions provisions of IRCA prohibit discrimination against legal immigrant workers based upon national origin or alienage. Firms that engage in such discrimination are in violation of those provisions even if the discrimination is designed to enable the business to comply with employer sanctions. However, firms will tend to see the prohibition against knowingly hiring illegal aliens, and not the ban on ethnic discrimination against legal immigrant workers, as their primary legal obligation under the employer-sanctions provisions of IRCA. Those firms can easily rationalize such discrimination as necessary to assure they are in compliance with their legal obligations under those provisions. As a result, employer sanctions have driven firms to engage in ethnic discrimination against legal immigrant workers, which they would otherwise not do, absent employer sanctions.

It is true that some employers engage in ethnic discrimination for reasons of prejudice, and not in response to employer sanctions. But in general, employers are disinclined to engage in ethnic discrimination in employment, and will only tend to do so in order to assure that they are in compliance with their legal obligations under the employer-sanctions provisions of IRCA.

By providing employers the means to detect and crack down on document fraud, a telephone verification system would eliminate any legal defenses they might use to escape prosecution for having violated the employer-sanctions provisions of IRCA, either by knowingly hiring illegal aliens or refusing to hire legal immigrant workers based upon their national origin or alienage. Employers of illegal aliens can currently defend themselves against federal prosecution based upon the argument that they had been duped through document fraud. The employer can legitimately argue that he or she mistakenly believed those documents to be authentic, since firms currently lack the means to detect document fraud. A telephone verification system would enable employers to verify the authenticity of those documents, depriving them of any legal defense for hiring illegal aliens.

As a result, with a telephone verification system in place, firms could only hire illegal aliens by intentionally failing to comply with their legal obligations under the employer-sanctions provisions of IRCA—either by failing to solicit documents from individuals which verify their eligibility to work in the United States or by accepting as valid such documents that they know to be fraudulent. Deprived of all legal defenses for hiring illegal aliens, firms which did so would face the virtual certainty that they would be successfully prosecuted under the employer-sanctions provisions of IRCA.

By the same token, firms that discriminate against legal immigrant workers could no longer justify this employment practice as essential to assure that they are in compliance with their legal obligations under the employer-sanctions provisions of IRCA. If firms continued to engage in employment discrimination once a telephone verification system was established, it would be for reasons other than the need to comply with their legal obligations under the employer-sanctions provisions of IRCA.

A telephone verification system would eliminate the two major problems with employer sanctions: the widespread and pervasive use of fraudulent documents and the equally widespread and pervasive ethnic discrimination against legal immigrant workers resulting from employer sanctions. By eliminating those two problems, a telephone verification system would enable employer sanctions to be enforced in a fair and effective manner in meeting Congress's primary objective under IRCA: to deter further illegal immigration by depriving undocumented individuals of jobs.

The Reagan administration fully recognized that a fraud-resistant worker verification system was essential to avert the potential of employer sanctions to result in ethnic discrimination against legal immigrant workers. In a a preliminary draft of its report, which was circulated to the entire Cabinet on June 26, 1981, the President's Task Force on Immigration and Refugee Policy argued that "employer sanctions without some agreed identifier would likely be . . . discriminatory because employers might fear hiring those who look or sound like foreigners."[46] As we will see, in its final report presented to Reagan on July 1, the Task Force recommended that the president consider proposing the creation of a tamper-proof Social Security card. Employers would use the card to verify the eligibility of individuals, whom they wish to hire, to work in the United States.

In the preliminary draft of its report, the Task Force rejected the notion that its recommendation that employers use a tamper-proof Social Security card for worker verification purposes would impose substantial regulatory burdens upon business. The Task Force noted that employers already use the Social Security cards of their workers for tax and identification purposes. The Task Force argued that use of a tamper-proof Social Security card would assure firms that they are in compliance with their legal obligations under the employer-sanctions provisions of IRCA, without the need to refuse to hire immigrant workers, including those eligible to work in the United States, for fear that they might lack authentic documentation.

The President's Task Force expressed its belief that Congress should not refrain from passing employer-sanctions legislation because of the potential that firms might respond to such action by refusing to hire immigrant workers. Rather, employers need not respond in this manner if they had a means to verify document authenticity. The President's Task Force emphasized that employer sanctions remained the most credible deterrent to further illegal immigration to the United States.

While no one expects employer sanctions to be a panacea, they are the only mechanism viewed as having some chance of being effective [against illegal immigration]. Requiring a showing of an improved Social Security card is only slightly more intrusive and burdensome to business than the current requirements [for workers] to provide a Social Security number. Such a requirement is necessary if employers are to have a defense against [employer] sanctions when acting in good faith and if we are to prevent discrimination against those who look and sound foreign. The polls show most Americans are willing to go this route. . . . Using the Social Security card as an ID would limit discrimination against foreign-looking Americans.[47]

WHY DID REAGAN FAIL TO TAKE THE FIRST STEP TOWARD THE ESTABLISHMENT OF A WORKER VERIFICATION SYSTEM?

Given the need for a worker verification system, and in light of the fact that such a system, especially one operated through a computerized national registry consisting of all valid Social Security numbers existing in the United States (as the CIR recommended), is feasible, one would have expected Reagan to establish a worker verification pilot project, as he was authorized to do under IRCA. This would enable the federal government to take the necessary first step toward the establishment of a nationwide worker verification system. However, Reagan failed to establish a worker verification pilot project, thereby thwarting the ability of the federal government to move toward creation of a nationwide worker verification system during his presidency. Reagan's failure to do so makes no sense, given the problems involved in enforcing employer sanctions. Given the ability of illegal aliens to illegally obtain jobs through document fraud and the widespread discrimination against legal immigrant workers resulting from employer sanctions, a worker verification system is vitally needed to rectify those two problems, as we have argued.

The Reagan Administration Opposes the Creation of a National Identity Card

Why, given the need for a worker verification system, did Reagan fail to take the first step toward the establishment of one? One major reason for this failure is that any such system would require individuals who seek employment to use a single document, most likely the Social Security card, in order to establish their identity. The Reagan administration feared that this would result in the creation of a national identity card, representing an invasion of individual privacy. The administration believed that such an invasion of individual privacy would simply be too high a price to pay in order to establish a secure means to deprive illegal aliens of jobs through the effective enforcement of the employer-sanctions provisions of IRCA.

Indeed, the Reagan administration was willing to accept the failure of employer sanctions as a means to deprive illegal aliens of jobs, if this were necessary, in order to avoid creation of a national identity card. Insofar as the administration was concerned, preserving individual privacy represented a far more important goal in the development of immigration policy than depriving undocumented workers of employment in order to deter further illegal immigration to the United States. Indeed, as Reagan emphasized in his statement of July 30, 1981, which defined his administration's immigration policy, any steps taken to deter further illegal immigration must ''be consistent with our values of individual privacy and freedom.''[48]

No worker verification proposal which any credible policymaker has ever recommended would have provided for the outright creation of a national identity card. Rather, proponents of a worker verification system have recommended that a single existing document be used as a means to verify the eligibility of individuals to work in the United States. The document most preferred for such purposes is the Social Security card.

However, the Reagan administration rejected the use of the Social Security card, or any other single document, as a means to verify the eligibility of individuals to work in the United States. If, for example, the Social Security card was used for worker verification purposes, then this would, for all intents and purposes, transform the Social Security card into a national identity card. The Reagan administration was strongly opposed to even this indirect means of creating a national identity card.

In his memo to Reagan on July 24, 1981, Baker noted that ''no standard form of identification in the U.S.'' currently exists. Baker warned that the creation of a secure and reliable means to verify the eligibility of individuals to work in the United States could result in the use of a specific document to establish personal identity. Baker expressed his fear that if Congress granted a preference for a certain document to establish individual identity, then the document could rapidly evolve into a national identity card. This is especially true if the document were to be the Social Security card: "The fear is that if any particular form of identification is preferred over others, one of the preferred forms (especially the Social Security card) could evolve into a national identity card."[49]

In the report containing its recommendations on immigration reform, which it presented to Reagan on July 1, 1981, the President's Task Force on Immigration and Refugee Policy did not directly advise the president to propose passage of employer-sanctions legislation. Rather, the Task Force recommended that Reagan only consider proposing such legislation among the many options on immigration reform which it presented to him. A major reason why the Task Force failed to recommend such legislation was concern among its members that the worker verification requirements, which firms would have to meet in complying with their legal obligations under employer-sanctions legislation, might result in the creation of a national identity card. Members of the Task Force were especially concerned that use of the Social Security card to establish individual identity under an employer-sanctions regime might result in the transformation of the Social Security card into a de facto national identity card.

The concerns which members of the President's Task Force had about the creation of a national identity card were fully expressed in a preliminary draft of its final report, which was circulated among the entire Cabinet on June 26, 1981. In the draft, the Task Force recommended that the Reagan administration consider the arguments against employer-sanctions legislation. The Task Force noted that employer-sanctions legislation would necessarily require firms to solicit documents from individuals which verify their eligiblity to work in the United States. One of those documents would have to be a Social Security card.

The Task Force noted that critics of employer sanctions are adamantly opposed to use of the Social Security card as a means to verify the eligibility of individuals to work in the United States. The Task Force cited a number of reasons why this was so.

Opponents of this option argue use of a Social Security card for identification purposes is a de facto national identification card, which many feel is inconsistent with fundamental American principles of freedom, individual privacy, and limited central government. While the polls are favorable regarding use of a Social Security card [to establish individual identification], they are negative on a national identity card.

Opponents of this option argue requiring new hires to show a Social Security card (in addition to stating the number) is in direct opposition to the President's stated views on personal privacy.

Use of the Social Security card for identification is contrary to the original intent of the card. . . .

While providing a means of defense for employers, the principle of requiring new hires to show their Social Security card (in addition to providing the number) could lead to use of the card for other purposes, such as registration of guns and registration for the draft.[50]

The White House shared the concerns of the members of the President's Task Force regarding the potential of a worker verification system for transforming the Social Security card into a de facto national identity card. Accordingly, the White House recommended that a variety of different documents be used to verify the eligibility of individuals to work in the United States. The Social Security card would represent one, but by no means the only, such document which could be used for worker verification purposes. Indeed, no single document would be preferred in verifying an individual's eligibility to work in the United States. This would assure that neither the Social Security card, nor any other document, would serve as the preferred means to establish individual identity under an employer-sanctions regime. This would prevent the Social Security card, or any other document, from being transformed into a de facto national identity card under employer-sanctions legislation.

To assure the successful enforcement of employer sanctions, firms need a means to establish that the documents presented to them by individuals are indeed authentic. This necessarily requires that employers be allowed to solicit a single document, most likely the Social Security card, from each individual to establish his or her identity. However, the Reagan administration flatly rejected allowing employers to solicit such a document. Rather, the only worker verification system the Reagan administration was willing to accept would be one which involved the use of any combination of a variety of different documents to establish an individual's eligibility to work in the United States. No system of any kind would be established to enable employers to determine the authenticity of documents presented to them.

The Reagan Administration Raises Concerns over the Cost of Establishing a Credible Worker Verification System

Hostility to a national identity card was only one major reason why the Reagan administration opposed establishment of a fraud-resistant worker verification system. Another major reason was the cost of such a system. That cost was illustrated in a memo two officials of the administration, Robert Goldfarb and Thomas Lenard, sent to Anderson on June 28, 1981.

In its final report issued on July 1, 1981, the President's Task Force recommended that Reagan consider proposing employer-sanctions legislation. Employers would solicit documents from individuals to verify their eligibility to work in the United States. One of those documents would be the Social Security card. To reduce the potential for document fraud, the President's Task Force recommended that Reagan consider proposing making the Social Security card tamper-proof.[51]

Goldfarb and Lenard sent Anderson a memo estimating the cost of the employer-sanctions legislation which the President's Task Force recommended that Reagan consider. In that memo they attempted to estimate the cost of the employer-sanctions proposal, and argued that the federal government would have to incur substantial costs in hiring additional INS investigators to enforce employer-sanctions legislation.

The costs to the government involve the process of finding and prosecuting violators. The explicit government costs involved depend on the enforcement mechanism chosen. . . . It is important to recognize that minimizing government costs may not be desirable, since the effectiveness of employer sanctions in reducing use of illegal aliens depends crucially on the level of enforcement. This suggests that, if effective enforcement is desired, a sizable program of inspections, based upon a random sample of firms, is required.

In addition to the federal government, firms and workers would also have to incur costs in complying with employer sanctions.

Private sector costs fall on employers and employees. Employer costs involve the extra costs associated with monitoring the new hire process to make sure that the law is being complied with. . . . Each employer must ask for a set of documents. A sensible employer would set up a recordkeeping system, which contained the required evidence. . . . There are also inventory costs associated with keeping the collected records. Note that much of this burden would appear to be imposed on employers who voluntarily comply (do not hire illegal aliens) in any case.

An additional regulatory burden is imposed on employers because of employer time that must be devoted to cooperating with INS investigators. We do not know the magnititude of this cost per investigation, and the number of investigations depends on the chosen level of enforcement.

Employee costs involve the extra requirements involved in the job search process because of the new requirements. These costs are of two types: (1) a one-time cost associated with obtaining a new Social Security card for someone who already has one. . . . (2) A second cost for employees involves the extra time required each time they apply for a job to fill out the required forms. . . .

In summary, costs associated with employer sanctions include: an annual paperwork burden on employers . . . some inventory costs, and time costs of undergoing inspections; one-time costs to workers associated with obtaining Social Security cards . . . and costs to government which depend crucially on level of enforcement.

In addition to the costs of enforcement and compliance with employer sanctions, Goldfarb and Lenard noted that the creation of a tamper-proof Social Security card, which represented one means to establish a secure and reliable worker verification system, would generate new costs of its own. The creation of a tamper-proof Social Security card would require the replacement of all

existing cards with the new tamper-proof card. Goldfarb and Lenard noted that
"A Dec. 1980 GAO report . . . indicated that [Social Security Administration]
SSA estimated the cost of replacing all cards in 5–10 years at $850 million.
GAO argues that this is an underestimate, and true costs might be as much as
$2 billion."[52]

The GAO's 1980 estimate that it would cost up to $2 billion to reissue every
existing Social Security card underestimates the actual cost of such an operation.
In 1995 the SSA issued a new estimate, claiming that it would cost between $3
billion and $6 billion to reissue the 250 million Social Security cards which
existed that year. The SSA estimated that it would take over ten years to complete such an operation. Testifying before the Subcommittee on Immigration
and Claims of the House Judiciary Committee on March 3, 1995, Shirley S.
Chater, Commissioner of Social Security, claimed that such an operation would
pose "a tremendous challenge for the agency and its employees . . . and could
not be handled in the SSA's 1,300 local offices, because it would interfere with
the ability of the offices to properly serve the people needing help with Social
Security."[53]

In addition to incurring substantial costs for the federal government, Goldfarb
and Lenard doubted that the SSA could actually create a tamper-proof Social
Security card.

There is considerable skepticism about the effectiveness of a tamper-proof card. First,
the GAO report stresses that such a card does not prevent misuse, since such misuse
stems from inappropriate uses (for example, by other individuals) of legitimate cards.
The dollar estimates cited above are for cards without photos. Cards with photos are
more expensive (partially because new cards would be required periodically) and raise
new civil rights-type issues. . . . If cards do not contain pictures, illegal aliens can continue to borrow legitimate cards of their friends. Second, the documents used in obtaining
a "more secure" card are themselves subject to fraud.

In addition to all the costs listed in their memo, a final cost of employer
sanctions, which Goldfarb and Lenard cited, pertained to the increased litigation
which employer-sanctions legislation would trigger. A major such cost would
involve discrimination lawsuits brought by legal immigrant workers, who
charged that they were unlawfully denied jobs because their prospective employers suspected them of lacking authentic documentation. Goldfarb and Lenard noted that employer-sanctions legislation "would increase the volume of
immigration law litigation significantly."[54]

The Goldfarb-Lenard memo made it clear that an employer-sanctions regime
would be costly for the federal government, employers, and workers. The most
substantial cost which an employer-sanctions regime would impose pertains to
worker verification. Employers would need some means to determine whether
the documents presented to them by individuals are indeed authentic. One such
means would involve the use of a tamper-proof Social Security card. However,

1980 GAO estimates, which Goldfarb and Lenard cited, and subsequent estimates the SSA provided in 1995, make it clear that the creation of a tamper-proof Social Security card would cost the federal government billions of dollars, and years of effort, which would tax the limited resources of the SSA. Moreover, there would be no way to make the Social Security card completely tamper-proof, since cards could always fall into the wrong hands, as Goldfarb and Lenard noted. The enormous costs and uncertainty of establishing a fraud-resistant worker verification system, based upon the use of a tamper-proof Social Security card, in addition to the threat it posed to individual privacy, led the Reagan administration to strongly oppose such a system.

CONGRESS FAILS TO IMPOSE A CREDIBLE EMPLOYER-SANCTIONS REGIME UNDER IRCA

By rejecting the establishment of a fraud-resistant worker verification system, the Reagan administration supported the imposition of an employer-sanctions regime, under IRCA, which has become riddled with fraud. Illegal aliens use fraudulent documents to illegally obtain employment. Employers have no means to verify the authenticity of the documents presented to them. As a result, many employers end up unwittingly hiring illegal aliens in the mistaken belief that those documents are valid.

The Justice Department cannot prosecute firms which hire illegal aliens unless it can prove that their employment of undocumented individuals was intentional. However, there is no way of proving this, as long as employers lack the means to determine the authenticity of the documents presented to them. If caught, employers of illegal aliens can argue, whether truthfully or not, that their un-documented workers had provided them with fraudulent documents which the employers mistakenly believed to be authentic. In the absence of a fraud-resistant worker verification system, there is no way to successfully prosecute employers of illegal aliens. As a result, there is no way that the federal government can enforce the employer-sanctions provisions of IRCA.

The Reagan administration supported the imposition of a fraud-ridden employer-sanctions regime which has failed to achieve its goal of depriving illegal aliens of jobs. Retaining easy access to employment, aliens have had every incentive to immigrate to the United States illegally since employer sanctions have been in effect in 1987. As a result, employer sanctions have had no discernible effect in stemming the flow of illegal immigration to the United States. Accordingly, it is little wonder that the illegal alien population has doubled during the first decade in which employer sanctions were in effect.

In fairness to the Reagan administration, it must be pointed out that the failure of employer sanctions did not become apparent until after the president left office on January 20, 1989. Indeed, employer sanctions did not go into effect until very late in the administration. Employer sanctions went into partial effect on June 1, 1987. Firms guilty of their first offense under the employer-sanctions provisions of IRCA were to receive only a citation. Those firms were to be fined for each offense committed thereafter. On June 1, 1988, employer sanctions went into full effect for all industries except the agricultural sector. All non-agricultural industrial firms, including first-time offenders, were to be fined for violating the employer-sanctions provisions of IRCA. On December 1, 1988, employer sanctions were extended to all firms in the agricultural sector, including first-time offenders.[55]

Accordingly, employer sanctions did not even begin to go into effect until the final year and a half of the Reagan administration. Reagan had no idea whether employer sanctions would be effective in deterring further illegal immigration during his presidency. As a result, he was unable to determine whether it was necessary to invoke the authority granted him under IRCA to recommend establishment of a credible and effective worker verification system which would enable firms to meet their legal obligations under the employer-sanctions provisions of the bill.

However, while Reagan had no idea whether the employer-sanctions provisions of IRCA would prove effective during his presidency, he still had every reason to believe that they would fail to deter further illegal immigration to the United States. Indeed, the Reagan administration fully understood that employer sanctions had little chance of proving effective in depriving illegal aliens of jobs without being coupled with a fraud-resistant worker verification system. In the preliminary draft of its report circulated to the entire Cabinet on June 26, 1981, the President's Task Force expressed its belief that illegal aliens would attempt to circumvent employer sanctions by obtaining fraudulent documents, which they would use to illegally secure jobs: "Employer sanctions may increase the demand for forged documents. . . . Social Security, or other identification cards, based on birth certificates, can be easily . . . forged. This problem is not correctable."

As the preliminary draft of the report of the President's Task Force clearly shows, the Reagan administration fully understood that illegal aliens would respond to the imposition of an employer-sanctions regime by obtaining fraudulent documents. Accordingly, the administration fully recognized that employers must have a secure and reliable means to determine the authenticity of the documents presented to them. As the President's Task Force noted in the preliminary draft of its report, "Employer sanctions without some agreed identifier would likely be burdensome to employers because they would have no clear-cut way under the law to avoid penalties for hiring an illegal immigrant."[56]

The Reagan administration's position that employer sanctions would fail unless they were coupled with a fraud-resistant worker verification system was never made public. Rather, the administration's official position was that employers could meet their legal obligations under employer-sanctions legislation by soliciting documents from individuals which verify their eligibility to work in the United States. Employers need not be required to take the extra step of having to verify the authenticity of those documents. In the statement issued before the immigration subcommittees of the Senate and House, Smith expressed the Reagan administration's belief that employer-sanctions legislation, which would require employers to solicit and inspect, but not determine the authenticity of such documents, would be sufficient to assure that illegal aliens are deprived of jobs: "We believe . . . that a system that relies on existing forms of documentation will effectively screen out illegal aliens, who will not ordinarily have the necessary documents."[57]

However, Smith deceived members of Congress when he assured them that the Reagan administration believed that employer sanctions could be effectively enforced without any means to determine the authenticity of documents. The draft of the preliminary report of the President's Task Force, which Smith chaired, clearly shows that the administration did not believe this to be true. Rather, the administration believed that employer sanctions would fail to achieve their objective of depriving illegal aliens of jobs unless they were coupled with the establishment of a fraud-resistant worker verification system. This was based upon the administration's recognition that illegal aliens would successfully attempt to circumvent employer sanctions in illegally obtaining jobs through document fraud. A fraud-resistant worker verification system was necessary to enable firms to detect and crack down on document fraud in assuring that they are in compliance with employer-sanctions legislation.

THE REASONS FOR THE REAGAN ADMINISTRATION'S OPPOSITION TO A CREDIBLE WORKER VERIFICATION SYSTEM

However, the Reagan administration could not make public its belief that employer sanctions would fail unless they were coupled with a fraud-resistant worker verification system; to do so would mean that Congress would have to couple the imposition of an employer-sanctions regime with such a system. This would be necessary to assure that employer sanctions are effectively enforced. However, the Reagan administration remained adamantly opposed to the establishment of a fraud-resistant worker verification system for philosophical and fiscal reasons.

Indeed, Reagan's failure to take the first step toward the establishment of a fraud-resistant worker verification system was not due to his desire to wait to see whether the employer-sanctions provisions of IRCA would prove effective before deciding whether such a project was needed—a decision which would, in any case, have to be made by his successor, George Bush. Reagan was unwilling to take the first step toward establishment of such a system because it would necessarily entail the use of a single document. In addition, the Reagan administration was concerned over the costs and uncertainties of such a system, as outlined in the Goldfarb-Lenard memo to Anderson.

Accordingly, Reagan was unwilling to go beyond acceptance of the weak and ineffective worker verification provisions of IRCA, which have become riddled with fraud. Despite its deficiencies, this system met the two tests which Reagan believed were essential to the operation of any such system: first, that it not compromise individual privacy; and second, that it not impose substantial additional costs upon the federal government. The worker verification provisions of IRCA met those two tests. They allowed individuals to choose from a wide variety of documents to verify their eligibility to work in the United States. This assures that no single document would be used for worker verification purposes. The worker verification provisions of IRCA also impose little additional costs upon the federal government. They do not involve the establishment of a costly new system to enable employers to determine the identity of individuals.

Unwilling to accept any alternative to the fraud-ridden worker verification system established under IRCA, Reagan supported the imposition of a weak and ineffective employer-sanctions regime, which has proven almost completely ineffective in depriving illegal aliens of jobs. As a result, while the Reagan administration promised to recommend effective measures to deter further illegal immigration, the president effectively sabotaged this effort. Indeed, the employer-sanctions provisions of IRCA represented a symbolic, rather than substantive, effort to deter further illegal immigration to the United States.

Employer sanctions confronted Reagan with having to make a difficult choice between deterring further illegal immigration and preserving individual privacy and restraining the growth of federal spending. Deterring further illegal immigration required the imposition of a workable and effective employer-sanctions regime. Reagan had to decide whether the compromises in individual privacy, and the additional costs to the federal government, were worth the reduction in the flow of illegal immigration which such a regime would achieve. Reagan ultimately decided that the costs of such a regime outweighed its benefits. As a result, Reagan accepted the imposition of a regime which he fully knew would fail to achieve its objective of stemming the flow of illegal immigration to the United States.

The Reagan administration waged a largely rhetorical fight against illegal immigration, since the president failed to support the imposition of a credible and effective employer-sanctions regime. Insofar as Reagan was concerned, measures which compromised individual privacy or imposed substantially additional costs upon the federal government in any way were unacceptable, regardless of what their value may be in deterring further illegal immigration to the United States. This decision assured that future presidents and Congresses would have to revisit this issue in the future. Rather than representing the final solution to the problem of illegal immigration, IRCA constituted only the initial phase of a two-decades-long effort to address this issue, which began in 1981, and continues to this very day.

THE REAGAN ADMINISTRATION'S OPPOSITION TO THE ESTABLISHMENT OF AN EFFECTIVE WORKER VERIFICATION SYSTEM LACKS CREDIBILITY

A worker verification system, such as the one established under IRCA, which is based upon the use of a wide variety of documents to establish the identity of individuals, is sure to be ripe with fraud, and cannot be effectively enforced. This is true, since there is no single document which employers can use to verify the eligibility of individuals to work in the United States. A fraud-resistant worker verification system requires individuals to establish their personal identity through the use of a single document, which can be made tamper-proof, or whose authenticity can be determined by the employer. The worker verification system established under IRCA does not provide for any such secure means of individual identification, but instead allows individuals seeking employment to choose from among seventeen different documents for this purpose, as we have seen. Any one of those seventeen documents can be fraudulently produced and disseminated among the illegal alien population. This has allowed illegal aliens to easily circumvent employer sanctions in order to illegally obtain jobs through document fraud.

Perhaps the most credible worker verification proposal made thus far has been the CIR's recommendation for the establishment of a telephone verification system, which would make the Social Security card the means to establish the identity of individuals seeking employment, and enable employers to verify the authenticity of each card presented by individuals through a computerized national registry consisting of all valid Social Security numbers existing in the United States.

The Lack of Credibility of the Reagan Administration's Concerns over Threats to Individual Privacy

However, the Reagan administration rejected the use of any single document for worker verification purposes, claiming it would result in the creation of a de facto national identity card, which would lead to an invasion of individual privacy. This argument is groundless, a fact fully recognized by none other than the administration itself. As we have seen, on July 1, 1981, the President's Task Force issued its report, which contained a list of options for Reagan to consider in making his final recommendations on immigration reform to Congress. One of those options involved the imposition of an employer-sanctions regime. The President's Task Force recommended that Reagan consider proposing the establishment of a tamper-proof Social Security card, which would be used by individuals to verify their eligibility to work in the United States.

In the analysis of its employer-sanctions proposal, the President's Task Force questioned the Reagan administration's assumption that use of a single document, most likely the Social Security card, to establish personal identity would result in an invasion of individual privacy. The Task Force argued that workers must already present their Social Security cards to their employers for identification and tax purposes. No credible individual has ever argued that this requirement represents an invasion of individual privacy.

Accordingly, the President's Task Force concluded that the requirement that persons who seek employment be compelled to present their Social Security cards in order to verify their eligibility to work in the United States would not result in any invasion of individual privacy. This is true precisely because those individuals are already required to present their Social Security cards to their employers for the reasons just mentioned: "An improved Social Security card system is a national identity card by another name, an intrusion of government. But the current Social Security number and [Internal Revenue Service] IRS tax systems already provide for intrusion; new hires must already provide their Social Security number." Given the fact that individuals who seek employment are already required to present their Social Security cards to their employers, the President's Task Force concluded that "a new system" requiring use of the Social Security card for the purposes of worker verification "would only add marginally" to any compromises in individual privacy which exist through current use of the card.[58]

However, Baker rejected the Task Force's argument that use of the Social Security card to establish personal identity for worker verification purposes would not result in any invasion of individual privacy. To be sure, in his memo to Reagan on July 24, 1981, Baker conceded that "Employees are already required to give their Social Security numbers when hired; employers are already required to document employees for tax, Social Security, and employment insurance." However, Baker insisted "that, since there is no standardized form of identification in the U.S., any commonly accepted proof of identity should stand on equal footing with every other. The fear is that if any particular form of identification [for worker verification purposes] is preferred over others, one of the preferred forms (especially the Social Security card) could evolve into a national identity card," resulting in an invasion of individual privacy.

Accordingly, Baker recommended that the Social Security card be only one among the five specific documents which the Reagan administration proposed be used to verify the eligibility of individuals to work in the United States. No preference for any single document would exist under the worker verification system which the administration recommended, since any one or more of those five documents could be used to establish the identity of individuals who seek employment. This would assure that the worker verification requirements, which firms would have to meet under employer-sanctions legislation, would not result in the creation of a de facto national identity card. Given the fact that the Reagan administration's worker verification proposal would prevent the creation of a de facto national identity card, Baker assured the president in his memo that the White House's recommendation "does not add much in terms of government intrusiveness or burden."[59]

In the end, Reagan rejected the Task Force's recommendation that he consider proposing the establishment of a worker verification system based upon use of a tamper-proof Social Security card as a secure and reliable means to determine identity of individuals who seek employment. Rather, Reagan accepted the White House's alternative proposal, which Baker presented to him, allowing a variety of different documents to be used in verifying the eligibility of individuals to work in the United States. As we have seen, the worker verification provisions of IRCA, which are consistent with the White House's proposal, have proven to be riddled with fraud, and have served as an ineffective means to enforce the employer-sanctions amendments to the bill.

As the President's Task Force readily conceded, the White House's argument that use of a single document, like a tamper-proof Social Security card, for worker verification purposes would represent an invasion of individual privacy is groundless. The fact that the White House would accept such a groundless argument in determining the design of a worker verification system under IRCA represents a severe indictment of the president's conduct of immigration policy. This is especially true given the fact that the worker verification system the administration recommended, which was ostensibily designed to preserve individual privacy, has proven to be a dismal failure as a means to enable firms to comply with their legal obligations under the employer-sanctions provisions of IRCA.

To be sure, the White House's concern over the adverse impact a worker verification system based upon the use of a single document would have on individual privacy was based upon legitimate fears that the government might misuse the information which such a system would contain. As we have seen, in the preliminary draft of its report, the President's Task Force warned that personal information contained in such a system might be misused ''for other purposes such as registration of guns and registration for the draft.'' Two leading critics of employer sanctions, John J. Miller and Stephen Moore, have expanded the list of purposes for which personal information contained in a worker verification system might be misused, including determining an individual's eligibility for entitlement programs, running background checks on persons wishing to purchase firearms, and tracking down children who have missed their immunizations and absent fathers who have skipped their child support payments. Miller and Moore warn that ''Once a system of information on all Americans is in place, it will become ubiquitous in American life, presenting an enormous threat to the privacy and liberty of Americans.''[60]

However, Miller's and Moore's warnings concerning the potential misuse of personal information contained in a worker verification system based upon the use of a single document, which the Reagan administration shared, are groundless. The federal government already possesses personal information on all working Americans through their Social Security and tax records. No evidence exists that this information has been substantially misused to invade the individual privacy of Americans. Accordingly, there is no reason to believe that the personal information contained in a worker verification system would ever be substantially misused in a manner seriously compromising individual privacy.

The Lack of Credibility of the Reagan Administration's Concerns over the Cost of a Worker Verification System

In addition to its concerns over individual privacy, the Reagan administration's belief that the establishment of a fraud-resistant worker verification system would be too costly lacks credibility. As we saw from the Goldfarb-Lenard memo, the administration's concerns over those costs pertain to the expense of making the Social Security card tamper-proof. All Social Security cards currently in existence are not tamper-proof. As a result, many such cards are fraudulent, and used by undocumented individuals to illegally obtain employment. The creation of a tamper-proof Social Security card would require the replacement of all cards currently in existence with new cards. The Goldfarb-Lenard memo cited a 1980 GAO report, which estimated the cost of replacing all existing Social Security cards with a new tamper-proof card as high as $2 billion. However, a 1995 SSA assessment raised this estimate to as high as $6 billion.

The CIR recommended that the Social Security card be used as the means to verify the eligibility of individuals to work in the United States; however, the CIR did not recommend that the Social Security card be made tamper-proof. Rather, it recommended the establishment of a national computerized registry, containing all valid Social Security numbers existing in the United States, which employers would use to verify the authenticity of the Social Security cards presented to them. Such a registry would avert the need to create a tamper-proof Social Security card, but not the necessity of replacing all existing Social Security cards with new ones. The reason for this is that a GAO report issued in 1989 found that 60 percent of all existing Social Security cards were issued to individuals who failed to prove their identity and legal status to the SSA.[61] Many of those individuals provided the SSA with a false identity in obtaining fraudulent cards.

Many undocumented individuals falsely claimed that they were residing in the United States legally in order to obtain fraudulent cards. As a result, many fraudulent Social Security cards are currently in existence, some of which are used by undocumented individuals to illegally obtain employment.

Given the large number of fraudulent Social Security cards which currently exist, use of the card as a secure and reliable means to establish individual identity will necessarily require the replacement of all cards presently held by the public with new cards. As the SSA estimated in 1995, this would cost up to $6 billion. The question confronting Congress is clear: Are the benefits of establishing a worker verification system, based upon use of the Social Security card as a secure and reliable means of individual identification, worth the enormous cost of instituting such a system? The answer to this question is unequivocally yes.

A fraud-resistant worker verification system would enable employers to detect and crack down upon document fraud, thereby depriving illegal aliens of jobs. Absent employment opportunities, aliens would have no incentive to immigrate to the United States illegally, resulting in a substantial decline in the flow of illegal immigration to the United States. This would save the states billions of dollars, which they must currently spend, in providing social services to illegal aliens.

Consider the case of California, home to 40 percent of all illegal aliens who resided in the United States in 1995.[62] The state of California estimates that it spent \$2.6 billion to provide social services to illegal aliens in fiscal 1996, including \$1.7 billion for K–12 public education and \$414 million for health care. In addition, the state spent \$503 million to incarcerate illegal aliens either accused or convicted of committing crimes. The state also spent \$954 million to provide social services to the American-born children of illegal aliens, who are automatically entitled to citizenship, including \$599 million for K–12 public education, \$278 million for welfare, and \$77 million for health care. The state received \$732 million in federal reimbursements for the cost of providing social services to illegal aliens, including \$422 million for incarcerating undocumented individuals either accused or convicted of crimes, and \$310 million for health care.[63] Altogether, the state spent \$1.9 billion in unreimbursed costs to provide social services for illegal aliens in fiscal 1996. This figure climbs to \$2.8 billion when the cost of providing social services to the American-born children of illegal aliens is factored into the equation.

As we have seen, the federal government would have to spend between \$3 billion and \$6 billion to establish a credible and effective worker verification system, which would enable firms to comply with their legal obligations under the employer-sanctions provisions of IRCA. This represents the total unreimbursed cost which the state of California *alone* must spend to provide social services to illegal aliens and their American-born children during the course of between one and two years.

In 1996, 80 percent of all illegal aliens resided in only six states—California, Texas, New York, Florida, Illinois, and New Jersey.[64] As a result, the financial burden of providing social services to illegal aliens falls disproportionately on those six states. The cost of establishing and operating a fraud-resistant worker verification system would be extremely low when one considers the enormous amounts those six states must spend to provide social services to illegal aliens. This is especially true of California, which far and away has the largest illegal alien population of any state. Indeed, the financial burdens which illegal immigration have imposed upon California have grown so large that voters of the state approved, by an overwhelming margin of 59 percent to 41 percent, Proposition 187 in November 1994.[65] Proposition 187, among other things, denies illegal aliens state social services, with the exception of those public health care services which the Director of the Department of Health Services deems "necessary to protect the general public from threats to the public health."[66]

When measured against the enormous cost of providing social services to illegal aliens and their American-born children in California alone, a fraud-resistant worker verification system which would enable firms to meet their legal obligations under the employer-sanctions provisions of IRCA would pay for itself. This would be true once such a system succeeded in depriving illegal aliens of jobs, deterring further illegal immigration and inducing a substantial part of the undocumented population who currently reside in the United States to return to their native nations in the face of diminishing employment opportunities. Such a development would reduce the enormous fiscal strain which the six states with the largest illegal alien populations must bear in having to spend substantial sums providing social services to undocumented individuals; as the numbers of illegal aliens who reside in those six states decline, so would their social welfare burdens. Accordingly, the Reagan administration's concerns over the cost of establishing and operating a fraud-resistant worker verification system were groundless.

To be sure, opponents of employer sanctions have shared the Reagan administration's concerns over the cost of establishing and operating a fraud-resistant worker verification system. Miller and Moore point out that the cost of the worker verification proposal which the CIR recommended "would carry a price tag in the billions of dollars."[67] However, Miller and Moore ignore the enormous cost which the six states with the largest illegal alien populations must spend to provide social services to undocumented individuals and their American-born children. When measured against this cost, the establishment of a fraud-resistant worker verification system represents a wise investment for the federal government.

To be sure, the taxes which illegal aliens pay may very well offset the cost of the social services they use. However, most of the taxes illegal aliens as well as legal immigrants pay go to the federal government. However, the Personal Responsibility and Work Opportunity Reconciliation Act (PRWORA) of 1996 makes illegal aliens ineligible for all but a very few entitlement programs.[68] As a result, practically all the social services which illegal aliens use are financed by the states.[69]

In addition to having to bear a disproportionate share of the cost of providing social services to illegal aliens, the states have no power to deny undocumented individuals public services. As the data which the state of California has provided clearly shows, K–12 public education represents the most costly of the very few social services which illegal aliens are entitled to. Illegal aliens gained entitlement to K–12 public education as a result of the Supreme Court's decision in the case of *Plyer v. Doe* in 1982. In *Plyer v. Doe*, the Supreme Court ruled, by a vote of five to four, that illegal aliens have a constitutional right to K–12 public education.[70] Consistent with *Plyer v. Doe*, Judge Marianna Pfaelzer of the Federal District Court of Los Angeles imposed an indefinite injunction which prevented the state of California from enforcing those provisions of Proposition

187, denying social services to illegal aliens, following its approval by California voters in November 1994.[71]

In the meantime, Congress has rejected legislation, which Representative Elton Gallegly of California introduced in 1996, authorizing the states to deny K–12 public education to illegal aliens.[72] Congress has also rejected requests by Governor Pete Wilson of California that the state be fully reimbursed for the cost of providing social services to illegal aliens. This forced Wilson to launch a series of unsuccessful lawsuits in federal court in 1994 in an effort to obtain such reimbursement.[73]

Given the fact that various congressional and judicial actions have made the federal government liable for the enormous sums which the six states with the largest illegal alien populations must spend to provide social services to undocumented individuals, the Reagan administration should have insisted upon the establishment of a credible and effective employer-sanctions regime, which would deny illegal aliens jobs and curtail the flow of illegal immigration to the United States. However, the administration failed to do so, in large part due to its concerns over the cost of establishing a fraud-resistant worker verification system. In deciding to oppose the establishment of a fraud-resistant worker verification system, the administration failed to consider the enormous cost which the six states with the largest illegal alien populations are incurring in providing social services to undocumented individuals.

Such a system would substantially reduce the number of illegal aliens who resided in the United States over the long term by depriving them of employment. This reduction in the illegal alien population would save the states untold billions of dollars. Accordingly, the Reagan administration was short-sighted in its decision not to recommend establishment of such a system, in part because of its cost. In failing to do so, the administration showed a gross disregard for the negative fiscal consequences which illegal immigration is having on the six states with the largest illegal alien populations.

CONCLUSION

By promising to deprive illegal aliens of jobs, employer sanctions seemed to offer the solution which Congress needed to deter further illegal immigration to the United States. Accordingly, employer sanctions represent the central element of Congress's strategy to stem the flow of illegal immigration under IRCA. It prohibits employers from knowingly hiring illegal aliens and requires that they solicit documents from individuals which verify their eligibility to work in the United States. However, illegal aliens have been able to circumvent employer sanctions by engaging in document fraud. As a result, employer sanctions cannot serve as a workable and effective means to deprive illegal aliens of jobs unless they are coupled with a fraud-resistant worker verification system. Employers must have a means to determine the authenticity of the documents presented to them by individuals. This would enable employers to detect and crack down on document fraud, thereby depriving illegal aliens of the ability to use phony documents to illegally obtain jobs.

Recognizing the need for a fraud-resistant worker verification system, IRCA authorized Reagan to seek congressional approval for the establishment of worker verification pilot projects designed to determine their effectiveness in enabling firms to meet their legal obligations under the employer-sanctions provisions of the bill. However, Reagan failed to exercise this authority granted him under IRCA because his administration opposed the establishment of a fraud-resistant worker verification system.

The Reagan administration's arguments against the establishment of a fraud-resistant worker verification system were groundless. As we argued earlier, such a system would not result in an invasion of individual privacy, a fact fully recognized by the president's own Task Force. Moreover, the billions of dollars which the federal government would have to spend to establish and operate such a system is not too costly when one considers the substantially greater sums the states with large illegal alien populations, especially California, must spend to provide social services to undocumented individuals. By depriving illegal aliens of jobs, deterring further illegal immigration, and inducing a substantial share of the illegal alien population to return to their native nations in the face of diminishing employment opportunities, a fraud-resistant worker verification system would save the states untold billions of dollars in reduced spending on social services. As a result, such a system would pay for itself over the long run, and would represent a very wise investment for the federal government to make.

The Reagan administration simply failed to clearly think through the need for a fraud-resistant worker verification system, and did not subject its flimsy arguments to any critical scrutiny. As a result, the administration supported the imposition of a fraud-ridden employer-sanctions regime which has failed to achieve its goal of depriving illegal aliens of jobs. Retaining easy access to jobs, aliens have had every incentive to immigrate to the United States illegally, resulting in a doubling of the illegal alien population since employer sanctions went into full effect in 1988. The employer-sanctions provisions of IRCA have proven to be a complete and unmitigated failure, so much so that the 104th Congress was forced to confront the issue of how to make the employer-sanctions provisions of IRCA workable and effective when its members considered immigration reform legislation in 1996.

As we saw, the CIR recommended the establishment of a telephone verification system, based upon the use of the Social Security card as a secure and reliable means of individual identification, which would enable employers to meet their legal obligations under the employer-sanctions provisions of IRCA by providing them the ability to detect and crack down upon document fraud. However, opponents of employer sanctions made many of the same arguments against such a system that the Reagan administration advanced a decade earlier: that it would represent a costly, ineffective, and error-prone means to deter further illegal immigration and result in an invasion of individual privacy.[74] Many members of Congress accepted those arguments. Accordingly, the 104th Congress failed to take any meaningful and genuine action to make the employer-sanctions provisions of IRCA effective and workable when its members took up the issue of illegal immigration, which resulted in passage of the Illegal Immigrant Reform and Immigrant Responsibility Act (IIRIRA) of 1996.[75]

Chapter 5

The Immigration Reform and Control Act and the Challenge of Granting Amnesty

The main legalization provisions of IRCA were the product of considerable congressional conflict and last minute compromise.[1]
—Susan Gonzalez Baker, The Urban Institute

As we have seen, IRCA adopted a carrot-and-stick approach to immigration reform. The stick was employer sanctions designed to deter further illegal immigration by imposing federal civil and criminal penalties upon employers who knowingly hire undocumented workers. The carrot was the granting of amnesty to illegal aliens residing in the United States who had demonstrated their potential to be productive, law-abiding citizens.

IRCA granted the right to obtain temporary legal residence to all illegal aliens who had lived continuously in the United States since prior to January 1, 1982, and could not be excluded from securing legal residence under federal immigration law for reasons other than their legal status. Illegal aliens would be allowed to obtain permanent legal residence eighteen months after being granted amnesty, provided they possessed both a minimal fluency in English and a basic knowlege of the government and history of the United States, or were enrolled in a course of instruction designed to enable them to attain such lingustic skills and civics education. The attorney general would be authorized to exempt any illegal alien age sixty-five or older from having to meet the linguistic skills and civics education requirements as a condition for being granted amnesty. IRCA also granted Cubans and Haitians who had entered the United States illegally prior to January 1, 1982 the right to obtain immediate permanent legal residence in the United States.

Illegal aliens granted amnesty, with the exception of Cuban and Haitian refugees, would be denied eligibility to all but a very few entitlement programs for five years. Exceptions would be made only for SSI, Medicaid coverage for emergency and prenatal health care, and welfare benefits for individuals under the age of eighteen. The federal government would provide the states $1 billion annually during fiscal years 1988 through 1991 to finance the cost of providing social services to illegal aliens granted amnesty.[2]

REAGAN DEFIES HOUSE REPUBLICANS OVER THE ISSUE OF AMNESTY

The amnesty provisions of IRCA provoked strong opposition from House Republicans, who believed that aliens should be punished, not rewarded, for immigrating to the United States illegally. As a result, the amnesty provisions of IRCA could not have been been passed without presidential support. Indeed, the House was sharply divided over the issue of amnesty, as we will see.

Had Reagan chosen to oppose amnesty and veto IRCA, should it provide for a legalization program, he could have easily killed the bill, since a veto-proof majority in support of the measure, containing its amnesty provisions, did not exist in the House. However, far from opposing amnesty, the Reagan administration announced its support for granting amnesty to illegal aliens who resided in the United States in statements which the Justice Department, the president, and Smith issued defining the White House's immigration policy on July 30, 1981, as we saw in Chapter 3. Moreover, Reagan remained steadfast in his support of amnesty during the five years Congress took to pass immigration reform legislation, after the administration's announcement of its immigration policy.

In supporting amnesty, Reagan defied the wishes of the overwhelming majority of House Republicans, who vociferously opposed legalization. House Republicans remained adamant in their belief that aliens should be punished, not rewarded, for residing in the United States illegally. On October 9, 1986, hours before the House passed IRCA, Republican Representative Bill McCollum of Florida introduced an amendment to delete the amnesty provisions from the bill. The House rejected the amendment by a narrow margin of 199 to 192. The House vote on the amendment fell largely along party lines, with most Republicans supporting it, and most Democrats opposing it. A total of 124 Republicans and sixty-eight Democrats voted for the amendment; 159 Democrats and forty Republicans voted against it.[3] Fully three-quarters of all House Republicans who voted on the McCollum amendment supported it—clear evidence that amnesty had little support among House Republicans.

In addition to House Republicans, opposition to the amnesty provisions of IRCA existed within the White House, despite its long-standing commitment to the establishment of a legalization program. In a memo sent on October 8, 1986 to Charles D. Hobbs, Assistant to the President for Policy Development, Charles P. Smith, a White House aide, argued that "[The] amnesty provision [of IRCA] is too liberal and rewards people for breaking the law by illegal entry.''[4] Smith was especially opposed to amnesty because it rewarded aliens who entered the United States illegally, while millions of foreign-born individuals, who wish to obey federal immigration law, must wait their turn, often spanning a period of years before being granted admission to this nation. In another memo to Hobbs on October 20, Smith argued that ''Providing amnesty . . . rewards law breakers for entry into the U.S., and . . . reduces [the] chance for entry into the U.S. for many persons waiting a long time for legal entry.''[5]

Why did Reagan defy the wishes of the overwhelming majority of House Republicans, and even some members of his own White House staff, and remain steadfast in his support for amnesty? The answer to this question is simple: IRCA could not have been passed without its amnesty provisions. Liberal Democratic members of Congress opposed the employer-sanctions provisions of IRCA; they were only willing to accept employer sanctions if they were linked to the granting of amnesty to illegal aliens.

As we saw in Chapter 3, employer sanctions provoked intense opposition from liberal Democratic members of Congress and interest groups representing the Latino community. They feared that employer sanctions would result in ethnic discrimination against legal immigrant workers, especially those born in Latin America. As we saw in the previous chapter, those fears were well-founded; the GAO confirmed, in its third and final report on employer sanctions in 1990, that they had indeed resulted in ''widespread discrimination'' against legal immigrant workers.

While opposing employer sanctions, liberal Democratic members of Congress and interest groups representing the Latino community strongly supported the granting of amnesty to illegal aliens who resided in the United States. The Latino community's support for amnesty was based upon the fact that the overwhelming majority of illegal aliens who stood to be legalized were born in Latin America. Fully 74.3 percent of all illegal aliens who received amnesty under IRCA were born in Mexico, 5.7 percent in El Salvador, 4.6 percent in Cuba, 2.4 percent in Guatemala, and 0.9 percent in the Domincan Republic.[6] Amnesty would represent a major benefit to the Latino community by allowing many of its members, who were illegal aliens, the opportunity to obtain permanent legal residence and eventual American citizenship, thereby securing all the rights to voting and access to entitlement benefits attached to citizenship. Accordingly, interest groups representing the Latino community and their liberal Democratic allies in Congress strongly supported amnesty.

Liberals represent the dominant ideological constituency within the Democratic Party. The Democrats controlled the House throughout the Reagan administration. The Democratic majority in the House, which was dominanted by liberals, was not about to support passage of IRCA without including amnesty provisions. As a result, Reagan had strong political reasons to support amnesty. Without amnesty, IRCA would not command the support of the Democratic majority in the House. And without this support, IRCA stood no chance of passage.

The employer-sanctions provisions of IRCA were essential to deterring further illegal immigration, which represented a top domestic policy priority of the Reagan administration. Accordingly, Reagan needed Congress to pass IRCA containing its employer-sanctions provisions, which required that the bill also grant amnesty to illegal aliens who resided in the United States. Support for amnesty was the major political concession which Reagan had to make in order to assure that IRCA would be able to garner the backing of a sufficient number of liberal Democratic members of Congress, who would otherwise oppose the bill because of its employer-sanctions provisions, to assure its passage.

The vote on the McCollum amendment makes it clear that the House would not have passed IRCA without its amnesty provisions. Of the 238 House members voting for the conference report on IRCA, 159 opposed the amendment. A total of 126 of the 161 Democrats, and thirty-three of the seventy-seven Republicans, voted for the conference report and against the amendment.[7]

Many, if not most, House members who voted for the conference report on IRCA did so because of its amnesty provisions. This was especially true of House Democrats, who saw their support for amnesty as a means of winning favor with the rapidly growing Latino community. House members who both supported the conference report on IRCA and opposed the McCollum amendment represented two-thirds of all House members who voted for final passage of the bill.

Many, if not most, House members who supported amnesty were not about to vote for IRCA unless its amnesty provisions were retained in the conference report on the bill. Those House members would have almost certainly voted against IRCA had the McCollum amendment, which deleted the amnesty provisions of the bill, been passed. Without the support of those House members, IRCA could not have been passed.

Throughout the four-and-a-half-year debate in Congress on IRCA, which culminated with its passage in October 1986, the Reagan administration emphasized the need for amnesty on both practical and humanitarian grounds. The overwhelming majority of illegal aliens who resided in the United States at the time IRCA was passed had demonstrated their ability to become productive, law-abiding American citizens. As a result, the granting of amnesty to those illegal aliens made practical sense.

It would have also been morally unconscionable to undertake the mass deportation of the millions of illegal aliens who resided in the United States in 1986, when IRCA was enacted into federal law. The same would have been true if those illegal aliens were allowed to remain in the United States permanently without authentic documentation. Federal law essentially consigns illegal aliens to the status of second-class citizens, insofar as they are prohibited from voting and denied eligibility for all but a very few entitlement programs. The Reagan administration, along with a bipartisan majority in Congress, believed that it would be morally unconscionable to allow those illegal aliens, who had demonstrated their capacity to become productive, law-abiding Americans, to remain in the United States permanently without the basic legal and political rights which all citizens enjoy. From Reagan's viewpoint, amnesty made practical and moral sense.

However, Reagan also knew that amnesty made political sense. He may very well have personally shared the view of most House Republicans that illegal aliens should not be granted amnesty, since it represented a reward to foreign-born individuals who had violated federal immigration law in order to reside in the United States. However, Reagan also knew that IRCA could not have been passed without its amnesty provisions, as the House vote on the McCollum amendment clearly showed. As a result, Reagan had no alternative but to support amnesty if there was to be any hope of passing IRCA.

By imposing federal civil and criminal sanctions upon employers who knowingly hire illegal aliens, IRCA promised, at least on paper, to deter further illegal immigration, which remained a fundamental objective of the Reagan administration's immigration policy. Accordingly, Reagan had no choice but to swallow whatever reservations over amnesty he may have shared with House Republicans and support legalization, in order to assure passage of the employer-sanctions provisions of IRCA, which represented the cornerstone of the administration's policy to deter further illegal immigration to the United States. Amnesty was the political price Reagan had to pay in order to secure the single, central, overriding element of immigration reform which he wanted most—employer sanctions. Reagan was quite willing to defy the wishes of the overwhelming majority of House Republicans and support amnesty, if he had to do so in order to obtain employer sanctions.

Reagan found that he could support the amnesty provisions of IRCA despite whatever reservations he may have had about legalization, since the bill imposed stringent conditions which limited an illegal alien's ability to obtain permanent legal residence in the United States. The purpose of IRCA was to grant amnesty only to those illegal aliens who had demonstrated their capacity to become productive, law-abiding American citizens. Accordingly, IRCA made illegal aliens who had been either convicted of one felony or three or more misdemeanors in the United States, or were likely to become dependent upon the welfare system, ineligible for amnesty.

As we saw in the previous chapter, Reagan issued a statement following his signing of IRCA on November 6, 1986, outlining the regulations which would govern his administration's enforcement of the bill. In his statement, Reagan made it clear that no illegal alien would be eligible for amnesty who possessed a criminal record which would disqualify him or her from obtaining permanent legal residence under IRCA. The same would be true of illegal aliens "likely to become a public charge." Reagan made it clear that illegal aliens would be eligible for amnesty only if they demonstrated the capacity to be financially self-sufficient and remained independent of the welfare system: "A likelihood that an [amnesty] applicant would become a public charge would exist, for example, if the applicant had failed to demonstrate either a history of employment in the United States of a kind that would provide sufficient means without public cash assistance for the support of the alien and his likely dependents who are not United States citizens or the possession of independent means sufficient by itself for such support for an indefinite period.''

In addition to criminals and welfare recipients, IRCA made illegal aliens who applied for amnesty ineligible for permanent legal residence unless they had been "continuously physically present in the United States since the date of enactment" of the bill into federal law. However, illegal aliens who resided continuously in the United States since that date would not become ineligible for amnesty if they had only undertaken "brief, casual, or innocent absences from the United States."[8] Reagan made it clear that no illegal alien who leaves the United States following the enactment of IRCA into federal law would be eligible for amnesty unless he or she had first obtained IRS authorization for a departure from and reentry to the United States, consistent with procedures which the federal agency established to enforce this provision of IRCA.[9]

IRCA AND THE CHALLENGE OF MEETING THE LABOR NEEDS OF AMERICAN AGRICULTURE

One of the most contentious and controversial issues confronting Congress in its deliberations over IRCA pertained to the special labor needs of American agriculture. The agricultural sector is especially dependent upon illegal aliens as a vital source of cheap labor. Through the imposition of federal civil and criminal sanctions upon employers who knowingly hire illegal aliens, IRCA threatened to deprive the agricultural sector of its access to cheap foreign farm labor. As a result, Congress needed to create a legal mechanism in which the agricultural sector would be able to retain its access to cheap foreign farm labor once employer sanctions went into effect. To this end, the versions of IRCA which the 97th and 98th Congresses passed would have expanded and liberalized the H-2 program.[10]

As we saw in Chapter 2, the H-2 program permits foreign workers to enter the United States on a temporary basis to fill shortages existing within the domestic labor market. However, the H-2 program imposes stringent regulatory barriers, making it a difficult and time-consuming task for employers to gain access to temporary foreign workers. IRCA would have eased and streamlined regulations which governed the H-2 program in order to assure employers access to temporary foreign workers more easily and quickly.[11]

The Reagan administration was acutely aware of the fact that certain industries, especially the agricultural sector, are heavily dependent upon illegal aliens as a vital source of cheap labor. By prohibiting firms from hiring illegal aliens, employer sanctions would impose financial burdens upon those industries. To comply with employer sanctions, those industries would have to replace their illegal alien workers with American citizens and permanent legal residents.

Illegal aliens are willing to work for substantially lower wages, and under less safe and healthful conditions than American citizens and permanent legal residents. Accordingly, employers of illegal aliens would have to spend substantial sums in higher wages and to undertake improvements in working conditions if they are required to replace their undocumented workers with American citizens and permanent legal residents. As a result, employer sanctions promised to impose substantial financial harship upon industries which are heavily dependent upon illegal alien labor. This financial hardship would have been especially severe in the agricultural sector.

The Reagan administration fully recognized the potential for employer sanctions to disrupt the ability of industries heavily dependent upon illegal alien labor to meet their labor needs. To avert such a disruption, on June 14, 1985, Meese appeared before the Subcommittee on Immigration and Refugee Policy of the Senate Judiciary Committee to announce the administration's support for an expansion and liberalization of the H-2 program in order to assure employers an adequate supply of temporary foreign workers. To assure that the agricultural sector retained its access to cheap foreign farm labor, Meese also announced the Reagan administration's support for the establishment of a Special Agricultural Worker (SAW) program. It would provide a legal means for growers to retain their access to foreign farm workers, who would enter the United States on a temporary basis in order to meet the labor needs of American agriculture.

The labor needs of certain sectors of our economy have been filled over the past few years by a sizable number of illegal aliens. . . . As we prohibit the employment of illegal aliens, it is important that we also provide a legal mechanism for employers to hire temporary foreign workers when they are unable to find American workers.

The administration supports statutory authorization of a distinct H-2 temporary agricultural worker program. This program may be particularly important for agriculture during the transition period from dependence on illegal alien labor to reliance on domestic labor. Over the past several years the Departments of Justice, Labor, and Agriculture have been reviewing both the existing H-2 program and proposed statutory modifications. We seek a balanced program that would ensure an adequate source of foreign labor, but would not exploit employees or provide an added incentive to hire foreign, rather than resident, workers. The program should also provide safeguards to ensure that American workers are not adversely affected by foreign labor. And it should protect the rights and welfare of all workers.

As we have seen, the versions of IRCA passed in the 97th and 98th Congresses would have allowed the agricultural sector to retain its access to cheap foreign farm labor through an expansion and liberalization of the H-2 program. It permits alien workers to enter the United States on a temporary basis to fill shortages existing within the domestic labor market. Meese expressed his belief that such reform in the H-2 program "represents a suitable approach" in assuring that the labor needs of the agricultural sector would continue to be met.

However, Meese argued that an expansion and liberalization of the H-2 program would not alone be sufficient to meet those labor needs. Rather, Meese insisted that those labor needs could only fully be met through the establishment of a SAW program, which would operate independently of the H-2 program. The versions of IRCA passed in the 97th and 98th Congresses would have permitted foreign farm workers to enter the United States on a temporary basis through an expanded and liberalized H-2 program; however, they would not have established a separate SAW program.

To reconcile the differences between the Reagan administration and Congress on the issue of a temporary farm worker program, Meese urged both sides to pursue

continued discussion of the specifics in this sensitive area. We also urge that an extra effort be made by representatives of growers and labor, in conjunction with the administration and Congress, to develop an acceptable and workable agricultural temporary worker program. This can be accomplished if all parties proceed in good faith and recognize the broader national need for [immigration] reform.[12]

As we saw in the previous chapter, on September 12, 1985, Meese wrote Thurmond outlining the Reagan administration's position on the major provisions of IRCA. Attached to the letter was a "statement of principles," which defined the administration's position on the issue of guest farm workers. Meese revealed that the statement "had been agreed to by the affected agencies in the administration," with an interest in the issue of guest farm workers. He expressed the administration's belief that the statement "should provide the framework for the temporary admission of foreign workers for agricultural employment, while at the same time insuring that American workers are not adversely affected" by the entry of large numbers of foreign farm workers to the United States.[13]

In its statement of principles, the Reagan administration announced its support for "the creation of a seasonal worker program to address the particular labor needs of growers of perishable commodities. Any workers admitted under such a program would be admitted only for the purpose of doing field harvest labor for truly perishable commodities. MSAPA [The Migrant and Seasonal Agricultural Protection Act] shall apply to any such field harvest laborers admitted under such a program, with regard to job disclosure, working conditions, housing, transportation, and wage determination."

The Reagan administration recommended the establishment of an Agricultural Worker Commission two years following the creation of a SAW program. The commission "will set a cap on the total number of workers to be admitted" to the United States annually, beginning the first year following its establishment. IRCA "will provide that the commission lower the cap by not less than 5%, nor more than 20%; the commission will have the discretion to determine the precise percentage decline within that range and could, for one year only, suspend the decline altogether if exceptional circumstances warranted such a suspension. In setting the cap, and subsequent rates of decline, the commission will consider labor market conditions and the abundance of crops." Finally, "State Department concerns with respect to the operation of such a program will be appropriately addressed."

In addition to a SAW program, the Reagan administration issued a statement of principles, which would govern the expansion and liberalization of the H-2 program: "DOL [Department of Labor], acting independently and in response to recommendations from the Agricultural Workers' Commission, will take meaningful steps to improve the H-2 program as a workable and acceptable means of meeting shortages in the domestic agricultural market."[14] The version of IRCA which the Senate passed in 1985 provided that the attorney general, in consultation with the secretaries of Labor and Agriculture, issue regulations governing the H-2 program. The attorney general would be responsible for certifying the need for guest workers, in response to applications made by employers unable to find Americans qualified to perform certain jobs.[15]

The Reagan administration recommended that the Secretary of Labor, rather than the attorney general, be responsible for issuing regulations governing the H-2 program. However, the Secretary of Labor would be required by federal law to consult with the attorney general and Secretary of Agriculture before issuing such regulations: "The administration supports [IRCA's] temporary worker reforms, except that the Secretary of Labor will issue the regulations governing labor certification under this program after meaningful consulation with the Departments of Justice and Agriculture. Both the regulatory provision and the consultation requirement will be statutory."[16]

WILSON INTRODUCES AN AMENDMENT TO IRCA ESTABLISHING A GUEST FARM WORKER PROGRAM

Consistent with the Reagan administration's wishes, on September 12, 1985, the same day Meese sent his letter to Thurmond, Pete Wilson of California introduced an amendment to IRCA, which would have established a SAW program, during the Senate floor debate on the bill. The amendment would have permitted an unlimited number of foreign farm workers to enter the United States for up to nine months in order to obtain employment within specified agricultural regions to be defined by the attorney general. To assure that foreign farm workers left the United States after the expiration of their nine-month visas, 20 percent of their paychecks would be held in escrow, and could not be collected until after they had departed this nation. The Wilson amendment confronted powerful opposition from two key groups with an interest in immigration policy—organizations representing labor and the Latino community.

Organized labor strongly opposed the Wilson amendment because it would have established a large new guest worker program modeled after the bracero program. The Mexican farm workers admitted to the United States under the bracero program were willing to work for substantially lower wages and under less safe and healthful conditions than their American counterparts. This allowed employers of Mexican farm workers to save substantial sums in lower wages and by avoiding the spending necessary to improve the working conditions of their laborers. As a result, agribusiness found it profitable to replace its American farm workers with Mexicans, resulting in substantial job displacement of natives in the agricultural sector.

Accordingly, organized labor successfully lobbied the Johnson administration to terminate the bracero program. The Wilson amendment essentially represented an effort to restore the defunct bracero program. As a result, the amendment confronted intense opposition from organized labor.

Organized labor was joined in its opposition to the Wilson amendment by interest groups representing the Latino community. The bracero program subjected Mexican farm workers to harsh treatment; they had to work for meager wages, and under unsafe and unhealthful conditions. Interest groups representing the Latino community charged that the establishment of a large new guest worker program would result in a repetition of the experience of the bracero program.

The Christian and civil rights communities were concerned over the adverse impact a large new guest worker program would have on Mexican and American workers alike, and joined organized labor and the Latino community in mounting an intense lobbying campaign to defeat the Wilson amendment. As a result, a powerful coalition of interest groups representing liberals and organized labor emerged to lobby against the amendment. The liberal community and organized labor retain powerful, if not dominant, influence over the Democratic Party; they succeeded in steering most Democratic senators to oppose the amendment.

The Wilson amendment promised to benefit growers financially by allowing them to retain their access to cheap foreign farm labor. As a result, growers strongly supported the amendment, and lobbied the Senate to pass it. In introducing his amendment in the Senate, Wilson warned that growers faced financial bankruptcy as a result of employer sanctions if they were deprived of access to foreign farm workers.

Employer sanctions would prohibit growers from continuing to hire illegal aliens. Without guest workers to replace those illegal aliens, growers would have to employ American citizens and permanent legal residents. Growers lacked the means to pay the higher wages and make improvements in their working conditions which American citizens and permanent legal residents would demand. Accordingly, growers faced financial collapse unless Congress gave them a legal means to retain their access to cheap foreign farm labor.

Wilson appealed to the Senate to pass his amendment, arguing that it was necessary ''to save an industry.'' The Republican Party maintains a strong relationship with the business community, including growers. Accordingly, growers were able to steer most Republican senators to support the Wilson amendment.

However, a minority of Republican senators broke ranks with their other Republican colleagues and joined the Democrats in opposing the Wilson amendment. Republican senators opposing the Wilson amendment were generally immigration restrictionists who feared that the provision would exacerbate the problem of illegal immigration. Leading this group of Senate Republican immigration restrictionists was Alan K. Simpson. He argued that many foreign farm workers admitted to the United States under the Wilson amendment would remain in this nation after the expiration of their nine-month visas, in violation of federal immigration law.

Accordingly, Simpson strongly opposed the Wilson amendment, arguing that it would only add more illegal aliens to the millions of foreign-born individuals who reside in the United States without authentic documentation. Simpson branded the amendment "an open-ended guest worker program," which would "repeat the most serious errors we have ever made in immigration policy. It would legalize the status quo of illegal alien labor in agriculture, and in my mind, that is not immigration reform."[17]

With the Wilson amendment confronting powerful opposition from a Left-Right coalition of liberals, organized labor, and immigration restrictionists, the Senate rejected the provision, but only by the barest of margins—fifty to forty-nine. The Senate vote on the amendment fell largely along party lines: Most Democrats opposed it, while most Republicans supported it. Thirty-one Democrats opposed the amendment; thirty-nine Republicans supported it. Nineteen Republicans crossed party lines to oppose the amendment; fifteen Democrats did the same to support it.[18]

Wilson remained undaunted by the Senate's rejection of his amendment. Indeed, the Wilson amendment would have been passed with a switch of only two Senate votes. Following the defeat of his amendment, Wilson opened negotiations with his colleagues to develop a revised version of his amendment, which could gain majority support in the Senate.

On September 17, 1985, Wilson introduced a revised version of the amendment. The new version was the same as the original version, with one important exception. The original version would have allowed an unlimited number of foreign farm workers to enter the United States on a temporary basis. The new version would have limited that number: No more than 350,000 foreign farm workers would be allowed to enter the United States at any given time.

Many foreign farm workers who enter the United States to work in American agriculture remain in this nation beyond the expiration of their visas. Accordingly, by allowing an unlimited number of foreign farm workers to enter the United States, the original version of the Wilson amendment threatened to make a substantial contribution to the growth of the illegal alien population. By imposing a strict limit on the number of foreign farm workers who would be allowed to enter the United States at any given time, the new version of the

Wilson amendment assured that the number of foreign farm workers overstaying their visas would be kept to an absolute minimum. This would assure that the amendment would not add substantially to the number of illegal aliens who resided in the United States. Wilson hoped that by addressing concerns in the Senate over the potential that his amendment had to open a new flood of illegal immigration, the revised version of his provision would enable enough senators who opposed the original version to switch their votes in supporting the new version.[19]

The Senate passed the revised version of the Wilson amendment by a vote of fifty-one to forty-four. As with the original version, the Senate vote on the revised version broke down largely along party lines: Most Republicans supported it, while most Democrats opposed it. Thirty-six Republicans supported the amendment; twenty-nine Democrats opposed it. Fifteen Republicans and Democrats, respectively, crossed party lines to vote with the majority of the opposing party on the amendment.[20]

Four Republican senators and one Democratic senator, who opposed the original version of the Wilson amendment, switched their votes to support the revised version. Only two Democratic senators, who supported the original version of the amendment, did the same, to oppose the revised version. This provided the revised version its margin of victory in the Senate. Opposition to the Wilson amendment was further undermined by the fact that three senators who voted against the original version of the measure failed to appear on the Senate floor to oppose the revised version.[21] By imposing a strict limit on the number of foreign farm workers who could enter the United States at any given time, Wilson succeeded in enabling enough Senators who opposed the original version of his amendment to switch their votes in supporting the revised version, assuring its passage.

However, the Wilson amendment confronted powerful opposition in the House. Liberal Democratic House members made it clear that they would oppose any immigration reform legislation which established a guest farm worker program, such as that contained in the amendment. The enormous political obstacles preventing passage of the amendment were perhaps best summed up by Kitty Calavita: "When Senator Alan K. Simpson was shepherding immigration reform through the 1985 Congress, then-Senator Pete Wilson, responding to pressure from the Western Growers' Association, introduced an amendment to import 350,000 workers annually. Likening it to the old bracero program, Simpson ridiculed the idea as 'exploitation deluxe'; House Democrats called it a 'de facto slave labor program.' "[22]

Republican members of Congress generally supported a guest farm worker program, while their Democratic counterparts tended to oppose it. As a result, it was relatively easy to pass legislation which established a guest farm worker program, like the Wilson amendment, in the Senate, which remained under the firm control of the Republican Party from 1980 to 1986. However, this was not the case in the House, which remained under the equally firm control of the Democratic Party during this period.

Accordingly, House members needed to come up with some other alternative to a guest worker program which would allow the agricultural sector to retain its access to cheap foreign farm labor once employer sanctions went into effect. In the absence of such an alternative, no immigration reform legislation could be passed. The Democratic majority in the House was determined to kill any immigration reform legislation which established a guest farm worker program, especially one as large as the Wilson amendment. Immigration reform legislation, which imposed an employer-sanctions regime without providing the agricultural sector a legal means to retain its access to cheap foreign farm labor, would confront powerful opposition from growers. Responding to the interests of growers, Republican members of Congress would strongly oppose such legislation, assuring that it would be killed in the Republican-controlled Senate.

As a result, the issue of guest workers represented the major stumbling block to passage of IRCA in the 99th Congress. Members of Congress needed to find a way that they could impose an employer-sanctions regime while enabling the agricultural sector to meet its labor needs in the process. Moreover, this had to be done without establishing a guest worker program, which the Democratic majority in the House adamantly opposed. The trick to passing IRCA remained how to impose an employer-sanctions regime without establishing a new guest worker program in the process. That was the task that members of Congress undertook, once the Senate passed IRCA on September 19, 1985, and sent the bill on to the House for its consideration.[23]

SCHUMER INTRODUCES AN AMENDMENT TO IRCA GRANTING AMNESTY TO ILLEGAL ALIEN FARM WORKERS

Following Senate passage of IRCA, Representative Charles Schumer of New York, who served on the Judiciary Committee (which retained jurisdiction over immigration reform legislation in the House), launched an initiative to break the political impasse over the establishment of a SAW program, which threatened to derail passage of IRCA in the 99th Congress. Schumer attempted to do so by brokering a compromise between interest groups representing labor and agribusiness. To achieve such a compromise, Schumer worked closely with Howard Berman of California, another member of the House Judiciary Committee, who represented the interests of organized labor, and one of his colleagues from the state, Leon Panetta, a member of the Agriculture Committee, who represented the interests of agribusiness. Schumer, Berman, and Panetta joined together in crafting an amendment to IRCA which would establish a SAW program acceptable to organized labor and agribusiness.

After seven months of delicate negotiations, in June 1986, Schumer introduced an amendment to IRCA which established a SAW program. The amendment would grant the right to obtain permanent legal residence to illegal alien farm workers who had been employed in American agriculture for at least sixty days during the year-long period ending on May 1, 1986. If large numbers of illegal alien farm workers left the agricultural sector to seek employment in the industrial economy, then the amendment provided for the admission to the United States of replacement agriculture workers (RAW) in order to assure that the labor needs of American agriculture would continue to be met.

Foreign farm workers who enter the United States under the RAW program would do so on a temporary basis. However, those workers would be allowed to obtain permanent legal residence, once they were employed in the agricultural sector for at least ninety days annually during their first two years in the United States. They would have to work at least sixty days annually for an additional three years to obtain American citizenship.[24]

Schumer had good reason to propose that illegal alien farm workers be granted amnesty. Illegal aliens are easily subject to exploitation, since they have no power to assert their rights. Illegal aliens have no way to file complaints against employers who abuse and mistreat them in a manner which violates federal labor law. Illegal aliens who do so stand a good chance of being caught and turned over to the INS for deportation. Unlike illegal aliens, American citizens and permanent legal residents can report violations of federal labor law to the appropriate government agencies without fear of exposing their identity and legal status. This makes it less likely that growers would abuse and mistreat their American workers in a manner which violates federal labor law.

Recognizing that illegal aliens must maintain anonymity, employers pay their undocumented workers substantially lower wages and subject them to much harsher working conditions than would be the case with American citizens and permanent legal residents. Illegal alien farm workers might seek higher wages and improved working conditions through the collective bargaining process. However, illegal alien farm workers who do so risk being fired and replaced by other undocumented agricultural laborers.

By granting amnesty to illegal alien farm workers, the Schumer amendment was designed to provide them with the same bargaining power to press for higher wages and improved working conditions as that which American citizens and permanent legal residents enjoy. Indeed, Schumer defended his amendment as "the only way to assure [illegal alien farm] workers that they will have the freedom of movement and bargaining power that is enjoyed by every other worker in every other industry in this nation." By enabling illegal alien farm workers to bargain effectively with their employers to improve their economic well-being, Schumer added that his amendment represented "an attempt to get the free market principle into agriculture."

The Schumer amendment served the interests of American farm workers. Illegal immigration represented a threat to the economic well-being of American farm workers. As we have seen, illegal aliens are willing to work for substantially lower wages and under much poorer conditions than American citizens and permanent legal residents. As a result, growers have strong incentives to replace their American farm workers with illegal aliens.

By granting amnesty to illegal alien farm workers, the Schumer amendment would deprive growers of the ability to exploit their undocumented laborers, who would now be entitled to obtain permanent legal residence in the United States. Moreover, the employer-sanctions provisions of IRCA would, at least on paper, deprive growers of access to any additional illegal alien farm workers which they might use as an alternative to higher-cost American workers. By protecting American farm workers from the competitive threat posed by illegal immigration, the Schumer amendment promised to safeguard the economic well-being of American citizens and permanent legal residents employed in the agricultural sector. Accordingly, organized labor strongly supported the amendment.

Joining organized labor in its support for the Schumer amendment were interest groups representing the Latino community. Practically all illegal alien farm workers are Mexicans. To secure employment, Mexican illegal alien farm workers have been required to work for lower wages and under less safe and healthful working conditions than those which Americans citizens and permanent legal residents would be willing to accept. Because they profit from the employment of illegal alien labor, growers prefer to hire Mexicans over Americans. If illegal aliens were to demand the same wages and working conditions as those enjoyed by Americans, growers would replace their undocumented Mexican workers with Americans. To secure employment, Mexican illegal alien farm workers must be willing to work for lower wages, and under harsher conditions, than those which would be acceptable to American citizens and permanent legal residents.

By obtaining amnesty, Mexican illegal alien farm workers would be able to assume the same collective bargaining leverage which their American counterparts enjoy. This would allow Mexican illegal alien farm workers to secure higher wages and improved working conditions, comparable to those enjoyed by their American counterparts. Because the Schumer amendment promised to improve the economic well-being of illegal alien farm workers, who are practically all Mexican, interest groups representing the Latino community strongly supported the provision.

Joining the coalition of liberal interest groups which supported the Schumer amendment was agribusiness. Its members demanded that any immigration reform legislation imposing an employer-sanctions regime must allow growers to retain their access to foreign farm workers. By granting amnesty to many, if not most, illegal alien farm workers, the Schumer amendment would assure growers an abundant supply of cheap foreign farm labor. As a result, agribusiness added its own conservative voice to the coalition of liberal interest groups supporting the amendment.[25]

Republicans supported the McCollum amendment, which would have deleted provisions of IRCA granting amnesty to illegal aliens who had resided continuously in the United States since prior to January 1, 1982. House Republicans generally opposed this general amnesty program. They were not about to accept a second amnesty program, established under the Schumer amendment, which would grant illegal alien farm workers the right to obtain permanent legal residence in the United States.

House Republicans were joined in their opposition to the Schumer amendment by a powerful Democrat—Representative Mazzoli, who chaired the House immigration subcommittee. Mazzoli objected to the RAW program, which would allow foreign farm workers to enter the United States to replace the agricultural laborers granted amnesty under the SAW program. Mazzoli charged that the SAW and RAW programs amounted to a "rolling legalization program," which would grant amnesty to illegal alien farm workers while providing a legal avenue for new waves of foreign agricultural laborers to replace those who left the agricultural sector to seek employment in the industrial economy.[26]

Mazzoli's concerns over the potential of the Schumer amendment to trigger a wave of "rolling legalization" was echoed by Smith in his memo to Hobbs on October 8, 1986: "[The] guest worker compromise may still have [a] flaw because it still may permit 'group' legalization for aliens and their supposed families unless better identification is made of aliens (and family members) classified as guest workers. It also may permit workers to leave agricultural work to take other work and still permit growers to hire others as replenishment, thus creating a form of 'rolling' legalization."[27]

Defying Republican opposition, on June 25, 1986, the House Judiciary Committee approved the Schumer amendment by a vote of nineteen to sixteen during its markup of IRCA. On July 16 the committee approved IRCA, containing the amendment, by a vote of twenty-five to ten, and sent the bill on to the House floor for a final vote. However, before IRCA could reach the House floor it had to go to the Rules Committee for the adoption of rules, which would govern House debate on the bill.

The Rules Committee voted to prohibit House members from holding a separate vote to either amend or delete the Schumer measure. The committee's decision to prohibit such a vote reflected the desire of the Democrats, who controlled the committee, to force Republicans to accept the Schumer amendment. To kill the Schumer measure, House Republicans would have to vote against IRCA; they could not hold a separate vote to amend or delete the provision before voting on the entire bill itself.

However, House Republicans found the Schumer amendment unacceptable. House Republicans wanted an opportunity to delete the amendment from IRCA without having to vote against the entire bill. To achieve this objective, Republicans needed to kill the rule governing House debate on IRCA, which prohibited its members from holding a separate vote to either amend or delete the Schumer measure.

Growers insisted that any immigration reform legislation which imposed employer sanctions must allow them to retain their access to foreign farm workers.

As a result, House Republicans needed to develop an alternative to the Schumer amendment, which would allow the agricultural sector to retain its access to foreign farm workers. The alternative House Republicans agreed to was the establishment of a guest worker program.

However, the Democratic majority in the House was completely unwilling to permit passage of IRCA without inclusion of the Schumer amendment in the bill. Democrats would also reject any amendment to IRCA which established a guest worker program as an alternative to the Schumer measure.[28] The refusal of House Democrats to permit the deletion of the Schumer amendment from IRCA left the Republicans with a difficult choice: Either they accept the amendment, or allow the 99th Congress to adjourn without passage of any immigration reform legislation.

Congress had worked long and hard to pass IRCA, spanning a period of four and one-half years, by the time its members were given an opportunity to vote on the bill in October 1986. With Congress on the threshold of finally passing IRCA, House Republicans were not about to kill the bill merely because they objected to one of its provisions—the Schumer amendment. As a result, House Republicans agreed to accept the amendment as the price they would have to pay in order to assure passage of IRCA.

Democrats adopted an all-or-nothing strategy on IRCA: Either the Republicans accept IRCA, including the Schumer amendment, or the entire bill would be rejected by the Democratic majority in the House. House Democrats gambled that Republicans would be unwilling to kill IRCA simply because they objected to the Schumer amendment, and would be willing to accept the provision as the price they would pay to assure passage of the bill. Democrats recognized that Republicans needed to pass IRCA in the 99th Congress, because the bill contained critical provisions designed to deter further illegal immigration through the imposition of an employer-sanctions regime. House Republicans were committed to stemming the flow of illegal immigration to the United States. Employer sanctions represented a critical component in the Republican strategy to fight illegal immigration.

To be sure, the employer-sanctions provisions of IRCA were sure to fail to achieve their objective of stemming the flow of illegal immigration to the United States. This is true, since Congress failed to couple employer sanctions with the establishment of a fraud-resistant worker verification system. Nevertheless, despite the fact that they had no practical value as a deterrent against illegal immigration, the employer-sanctions provisions of IRCA were still symbolically important to Congress. At the very least, employer sanctions created the illusion that Congress was doing something to address increased public concern over the flood of illegal immigration existing since 1965. That illusion was especially important to House Republicans.

Immigration restrictionists represent an important constituency in the Republican Party. House Republicans needed to demonstrate to their party's immigration restrictionist constituency that Congress was doing something to address the problem of illegal immigration. House Republicans could point to the employer-sanctions provisions of IRCA as a demonstration of their resolve to address this problem.

Given the symbolic importance of employer sanctions to them, House Republicans were willing to accept the Schumer amendment as the price they would have to pay to assure passage of IRCA, with its employer-sanctions provisions. By maneuvering Republicans into reluctantly accepting the Schumer amendment, the Democrats' all-or-nothing strategy to assure passage of IRCA, containing the provision, was an unqualified success.

IRCA represented a bargain between Democratic and Republican members of Congress. Democrats wanted amnesty because it served the interests of their labor and Latino constituencies. Republicans wanted employer sanctions because it served the interests of their immigration restrictionist constituency. Accordingly, IRCA gave both the Democrats and Republicans what they wanted: amnesty and employer sanctions. The only disagreement remaining was how expansive the amnesty program should be.

Republicans were originally unwilling to go beyond the general amnesty program, which granted illegal aliens who resided in the United States continuously since prior to January 1, 1982 the right to obtain permanent legal residence in the United States. While Republicans attempted to kill the general amnesty program through their support of the McCollum amendment, they were still willing to accept it. Democrats wanted illegal alien farm workers to be included in the amnesty program. With Republican acceptance of the Democratic position on amnesty, the way was now clear for House passage of IRCA.

DEMOCRATS AND REPUBLICANS IN THE HOUSE REACH AGREEMENT ON A REVISED VERSION OF THE SCHUMER AMENDMENT

The original Schumer amendment represented a Democratic measure drafted by Schumer, Berman, and Panetta. To secure bipartisan support for his amendment in the House, Schumer joined four other Democrats—Rodino, Mazzoli, Panetta, and Berman—and two Republicans—Representatives Dan Lungren of California and Hamilton Fish of New York—to draft a revised version of the measure. On October 7, 1986, Schumer and the six other representatives in Congress announced agreement on a new revised version of the Schumer amendment, which would be included in IRCA. Rules which the House adopted two days later prohibited the Schumer measure from being either amended or deleted.[29]

The final version of the Schumer amendment granted the right to obtain temporary legal residence to up to 350,000 illegal aliens, who could prove they had lived in the United States during the three-year period ending on May 1, 1986, and had been employed in the agricultural sector for at least ninety days in each of those years. Those illegal aliens could obtain permanent legal residence one year thereafter. The Schumer amendment also granted the right to obtain temporary legal residence to illegal aliens who were employed in the agricultural sector for at least ninety days during the one-year period ending on May 1, 1986. Those illegal aliens could obtain permanent legal residence two years thereafter.

Illegal aliens who obtained temporary legal residence under the SAW program would have to remain in agricultural employment before they could receive permanent legal residence in the United States. However, once they received permanent legal residence, those illegal aliens would be free to leave the agricultural sector in order to pursue employment in the industrial economy. If large numbers of illegal aliens who obtained amnesty under the SAW program left the agricultural sector, then new shortages of farm labor would develop. To prevent this from occurring, the Schumer amendment required the Secretaries of Labor and Agriculture, beginning in fiscal 1990, to jointly determine whether additional foreign replenishment farm workers were needed to replace those who had left the agricultural sector. If the Secretaries of Labor and Agriculture determined that replenishment workers were needed, then the attorney general would allow foreign farm laborers to enter the United States on a temporary basis.

Foreign farm workers who entered the United States under the RAW program could obtain permanent legal residence if they were employed in the agricultural sector for at least ninety days annually during their first three years in the United States. Those workers would be allowed to obtain American citizenship once they were employed in the agricultural sector for at least ninety days annually for an additional two years. The RAW program would be terminated at the end of fiscal 1993. Illegal aliens who obtained permanent legal residence under the SAW and RAW programs would be ineligible for most entitlement programs until five years after receiving amnesty, with the exception of SSI, Food Stamps, and Medicaid coverage for emergency and prenatal health care.[30]

The revised version of the Schumer amendment differed little from the original version: It slightly lengthened, from sixty to ninety days, the amount of time illegal alien farm workers would have to be employed in the agricultural sector during the year-long period ending on May 1, 1986, before obtaining permanent legal residence in the United States. In one important respect the revised version of the Schumer amendment actually expanded and liberalized the provisions of the original version—by establishing a new amnesty program for up to 350,000 illegal alien farm workers who had been employed in the agricultural sectors for at least ninety days annually during any given three-year period.

The revised version of the Schumer amendment was ostensibly designed to meet House Republican concerns over the excessively liberal and generous amnesty provisions contained in the original version. However, by essentially adding a second amnesty program to the program contained in the original version, the revised version of the Schumer amendment was actually more liberal and generous in its legalization provisions than the original version. The revised version of the Schumer amendment was fully consistent with House Democratic support for the provision of a liberal and generous amnesty program for illegal alien farm workers, and represented a complete triumph and victory for the Democrats in their dispute with Republicans over the issue of amnesty for undocumented agricultural laborers.

The Reagan administration and the Senate originally conceived the SAW program as a legal means to assure that foreign farm workers would be allowed to enter the United States to meet the labor needs of American agriculture—but only on a temporary basis. This would be necessary, since the agricultural sector would no longer have access to its illegal alien farm workers, once the employer-sanctions provisions of IRCA went into effect. The temporary foreign farm workers entering the United States under the SAW program would be used to replace the illegal aliens, who have traditionally served as the major source of labor for the agricultural sector. Neither the Reagan administration nor the Senate envisioned that foreign farm workers who resided in the United States illegally would be allowed to obtain permanent legal residence in this nation. By transforming the SAW program into a new amnesty program for illegal alien farm workers, the Schumer amendment went far beyond the SAW program which the Reagan administration and the Senate originally envisaged.

THE REAGAN ADMINISTRATION OPPOSES THE SCHUMER AMENDMENT

The Reagan administration had swallowed hard in accepting provisions within IRCA which granted amnesty to illegal aliens who had resided continuously in the United States since prior to January 1, 1982. Indeed, the administration supported such amnesty in defiance of the wishes of the overwhelming majority of House Republicans, as we have seen. By including the Schumer amendment in IRCA, the House was now proposing to establish a new amnesty program for illegal alien farm workers in addition to the general amnesty program for undocumented individuals.

As we have seen, the Reagan administration accepted the general amnesty program originally contained in IRCA primarily because the bill could not be passed without it. However, the administration was not about to accept another amnesty program established for illegal alien farm workers under the Schumer amendment. The administration viewed the amendment as a reckless and irresponsible effort to liberalize and expand the amnesty provisions of IRCA beyond the bounds dictated by the practical, moral, and political considerations which had led Reagan to support the original amnesty program. The result of the amendment would be to enable large numbers of illegal alien farm workers to obtain permanent legal residence, thereby rewarding them for residing in this nation without authentic documentation. Accordingly, the administration mounted an intense lobbying campaign to defeat the amendment.

The Reagan administration's lobbying campaign to defeat the Schumer amendment came literally at the last moment, following the negotiation of a bipartisan agreement on a final version of the measure, which came on October 7, 1986. As we saw in the previous chapter, the administration issued a statement of policy on IRCA hours before the House voted on the bill on October 9, 1986. Included in the statement was a declaration of the administration's opposition to the Schumer amendment: "The administration objects to . . . the 'Schumer amendment,' which provides permanent residency status after one or two years to certain alien agricultural workers. The provision, while well-intentioned, is an inequitable, ineffective, and costly scheme for meeting the needs of domestic agricultural employers. The administration is seriously concerned about both the cost and policy implications of this provision."

As an alternative to the Schumer amendment, the Reagan administration repeated its support for "a limited seasonal worker program," which would allow foreign farm workers to enter the United States on a temporary basis in order to "provide field harvest labor for perishable commodities."[31] However, the administration's opposition to the amendment was symbolic rather than substantive. As we have seen, House rules prohibited the Schumer measure from either being amended or deleted from IRCA. Accordingly, the only way the House could have killed the Schumer amendment was to reject IRCA. The Reagan administration was committed to the passage of IRCA, and was not about to support its rejection simply because the White House opposed one provision of the bill—the Schumer amendment. As a result, the administration's opposition to the Schumer amendment represented an empty gesture designed to satisfy House Republicans who opposed the provision, since the only way that the House could have killed the measure was through its rejection of IRCA, which Reagan was committed to signing.

Hours following the administration's issuance of its statement of policy on IRCA, announcing its opposition to the Schumer amendment, the House passed the bill which contained the provision.[32] Despite the House's action, the Reagan administration remained adamant in its opposition to the amendment. In a memo to White House Chief of Staff Donald T. Regan, Carol T. Crawford, Associate Director of the OMB for Government and Economics, made clear that "the administration supports a program to admit a limited number of seasonal workers to harvest perishable crops. They would have no rights to permanent residency."[33]

Attached to Crawford's memo was a document, prepared by the OMB, which noted that the Reagan administration's opposition to the Schumer amendment was based upon the fact that it would establish a second amnesty program, targeted toward illegal alien farm workers, in addition to the general amnesty program available to other undocumented individuals under IRCA: "INS estimates that Schumer will legalize an additional 1 million aliens at an estimated cost of $2.1 billion over five years (1987–1991). We believe that this may be an underestimate. Also, aliens may be able to fraudulently claim eligibility for participation under Schumer."[34]

Crawford reiterated that "the administration supports a program to admit a limited number of seasonal workers to harvest perishable crops. They would have no rights to permanent residency." Crawford noted that the Wilson amendment, contained in the Senate version of IRCA, "would allow up to 350,000 foreign workers into the U.S. to harvest perishable crops."[35] Those workers would be ineligible for permanent legal residence in the United States. Accordingly, the OMB document attached to Crawford's memo announced that the Reagan administration would "support [a] Wilson amendment-type program limited to harvesting perishable crops," since foreign farm workers who entered the United States under this program would do so on a temporary basis and be ineligible for permanent legal residence in this nation.[36]

Attached to Crawford's memo was another document, prepared by the OMB, which defined the Reagan administration's position on the major provisions of the House and Senate versions of IRCA. In the document, the OMB reiterated that the administration would "strongly oppose [the] Schumer amendment," since it "provides citizenship to people whose only commitment to this country is that they performed illegal farm work for ninety days last year." The OMB noted that the "INS estimates 500,000 people would meet this criteria," thereby becoming eligible for permanent legal residence and eventual American citizenship. The OMB also argued that since the documents which illegal aliens would be required to provide the INS in order to qualify for amnesty under the Schumer amendment "are minimal, many more can be expected to fraudulently claim [permanent residency] status" under the provision. As an alternative to the Schumer amendment, the OMB reiterated that the "administration supports a . . . limited program to harvest persihable crops, such as is provided by the Wilson amendment," which would allow foreign farm workers to enter the United States in order to fill labor shortages existing within American agriculture—but only on a temporary basis.[37]

Despite the House's passage of IRCA, which contained the Schumer amendment, the Reagan administration continued its opposition to the provision. The Senate and House passed differing versions of IRCA, which had to be reconciled by a conference committee, composed of representatives of both houses of Congress. This gave the Reagan administration an opportunity to defeat the Schumer amendment by pressing the committee to delete the provision from the final version of IRCA contained in the conference report on the bill.

As we saw in the previous chapter, the Reagan administration issued another statement of policy on IRCA on October 14, 1986, hours before the final conference report on the bill was released. Included in the statement was the administration's reiteration of its opposition to the Schumer amendment: "The special agricultural worker program contained in the House-passed version [of IRCA] is particularly objectionable because it . . . offers preferential treatment to aliens who otherwise would not be eligible for federal benefits or resident status under the legalization provisions of the bill and . . . does not adequately limit the number of persons who may participate in the program.''

The Reagan administration repeated its support for the establishment of a SAW program, which would allow foreign farm workers to enter the United States to meet the labor needs of American agriculture—but only on a temporary basis: ''The administration supports the creation of a special agricultural worker program to address the particular labor needs of growers of perishable commodities. However, these workers should be admitted only on a temporary basis for the express purpose of harvesting perishable commodities.''[38]

However, the Reagan administration's opposition to the Schumer amendment fell upon deaf ears on Capitol Hill. The conference committee failed to delete the amendment from its final report on IRCA, which Congress subsequently passed.[39] The committee had good reason to ignore the Reagan administration's opposition to the amendment.

Congress's decision to pass IRCA, containing the Schumer amendment, confronted Reagan with a politically difficult decision. As we saw in the previous chapter, Reagan could have killed IRCA with a simple pocket veto thereby also preventing passage of the amendment. Any congressional action on immigration reform would have had to await the convening of the 100th Congress in January 1987.

However, Reagan had worked long and hard with Congress, spanning a period of four and one-half years, to pass IRCA. This was in addition to the intense work, spanning nearly four months in 1981, the President's Task Force on Immigration and Refugee Policy undertook to enable the Reagan administration to develop an immigration policy, which was largely implemented by Congress through its passage of IRCA. With IRCA having been passed at last in October 1986, Reagan was extremely reluctant to kill the bill with a pocket veto simply because he objected to one provision of the measure—in this case, the Schumer amendment.

In addition to his desire not to squander the substantial time and energy his administration had devoted to the issue of immigration reform, Reagan had good political reasons to sign IRCA into federal law. Given the Reagan administration's fervent and long-standing commitment to immigration reform, any presidential veto of IRCA would have undermined the political credibility of the White House. To be sure, IRCA contained provisions which the administration opposed—most notably the Frank and Schumer amendments. However, IRCA also contained the two essential elements which the administration had insisted since 1981 be part of any immigration reform legislation passed—employer sanctions and amnesty. IRCA, on balance, implemented the basic elements of the administration's immigration policy, as defined in the statements on immigration reform which the Justice Department, Reagan, and Smith issued on July 30, 1981. Accordingly, any presidential veto of IRCA would have undermined Reagan's political credibility on the all-important issue of immigration reform by calling into question his commitment to immigration reform. As Smith noted in his memo to Hobbs on October 20, 1986, "The President has publicly stated his support for immigration reform in general since 1981 and for employer sanctions and amnesty."[40]

REAGAN DECIDES TO SIGN IRCA INTO FEDERAL LAW

Reagan fully understood that, with only two years remaining in his presidency, it was highly unlikely that Congress would have passed new immigration reform legislation before he left the White House, had he killed IRCA with a pocket veto. IRCA was likely to be the only immigration reform legislation Reagan would ever have the opportunity to sign; and the president was neither willing to squander the time and energy which he had devoted to passage of such a bill, nor risk damaging his political credibility on the issue of immigration reform by killing IRCA with a pocket veto. Accordingly, Reagan decided to sign IRCA.

Despite his decision, however reluctant, to accept the Schumer amendment, Reagan remained concerned about the potential this provision had to trigger a new flood of illegal immigration to the United States. IRCA granted illegal aliens an eighteen-month period ending on November 30, 1988, in which to apply for amnesty under the SAW program.[41] IRCA prohibited the Justice Department from denying amnesty to, or deporting from the United States, any illegal alien eligible for amnesty under the SAW program whom the INS apprehended during this application period.

However, Reagan feared that the provisions of IRCA, which granted illegal alien farm workers immunity from either deportation or being denied amnesty, might encourage agricultural laborers who resided in their native nations to enter the United States without authentic documentation in order to apply for legalization under the SAW program. This could result in a flood of new illegal immigration to the United States. To prevent this from occurring Reagan made it clear, in his statement issued following his signing of IRCA on November 6, 1986, that no illegal alien eligible for amnesty under the SAW program would be allowed to enter the United States without authentic documentation in order to apply for temporary, and eventual permanent, legal residence under the provision. Rather, those illegal aliens would have to apply for amnesty at an appropriate consular office outside the United States, pursuant to procedures established by the attorney general for enforcing the amendment.[42]

Like House Republicans, Reagan was leery about the amnesty provisions of IRCA, believing that aliens should be punished, not rewarded, for residing in the United States illegally. Nevertheless, Reagan was willing to accept, however reluctantly, the general amnesty program for illegal aliens for practical, humanitarian, and political reasons. By signing IRCA, Reagan was forced to establish a second amnesty program for illegal alien farm workers, pursuant to the Schumer amendment. This resulted in a substantial increase in the number of illegal aliens eligible for amnesty, far beyond the level which Reagan would have been willing to accept, had political considerations not dictated otherwise.

As of December 1, 1991, 1,526,814 illegal aliens were granted permanent legal residence as a result of the general amnesty program which IRCA established for undocumented individuals who had lived continuously in the United States since prior to January 1, 1982. In addition, 997,429 illegal aliens were granted permanent legal residence through the SAW program. Another 129,000 illegal aliens were granted amnesty under provisions of IRCA which extended permanent legal residence to Cubans and Haitians who entered the United States illegally prior to January 1, 1982.

As we have seen, the Schumer amendment established the RAW program. It extended permanent legal residence to foreign replenishment farm workers needed to replace illegal aliens granted amnesty under the SAW program, who had left the agricultural sector to pursue employment in the industrial economy. The RAW program went into effect in fiscal 1990, and was terminated at the end of fiscal 1993. However, no foreign replenishment farm workers were ever needed during the four years the RAW program was in effect. This was due to the fact that many, if not most, of the one million illegal alien farm workers granted amnesty under the SAW program remained employed in American agriculture, assuring that the labor needs of growers would continue to be met.[43] Given the fact that no foreign farm workers were able to enter and gain permanent legal residence through the RAW program, the Schumer amendment resulted in the legal admission to this nation of substantially fewer foreign farm workers than the Reagan administration had feared.

Nevertheless, despite the failure of the RAW program to go into effect, the Schumer amendment still resulted in a 38 percent increase in the number of illegal aliens eligible for amnesty under IRCA as a result of the SAW program. This increase fully justifies the Reagan administration's claim that the amendment would result in a massive expansion in the amnesty program, extending well beyond the illegal alien population who had resided continuously in the United States since prior to January 1, 1982, to include nearly one million undocumented farm workers.

DEVELOPING A SOCIOECONOMIC PROFILE OF THE AMNESTY POPULATION

While Reagan found it politically necessary to support amnesty, were the legalization provisions of IRCA in the national economic interest? To answer this question, we need to obtain a socioeconomic profile of the amnesty population. As we have seen, the socioeconomic characteristics of the immigrant population are largely linked to the national origin of each alien community: A large disparity exists in the economic performance of the various immigrant ethnic groups who reside in the United States. As a result, we are able to easily attain a socioeconomic profile of the amnesty population, since it is ethnically homogenous. Over 80 percent of the amnesty population was born in one of only three nations—Mexico, El Salvador, and Guatemala. Nearly three-quarters of the amnesty population was born in only one of those nations—Mexico. The amnesty population represents a substantial share of the Mexican immigrant community which resides in the United States. In 1996, 30 percent of all Mexican immigrants were granted amnesty under IRCA.[44]

The overwhelming majority of the amnesty population was born in either Mexico or Central America; and amnesty recipients represent a substantial share of the Mexican and Central American immigrant communities. Accordingly, the socioeconomic makeup of the amnesty population almost certainly reflects that of the Mexican and Central American immigrant communities. To derive a socioeconomic profile of the amnesty population, we need only analyze the socioeconomic characteristics of the Mexican and Central American immigrant communities.

California represents perhaps the best place to obtain a socioeconomic profile of both the amnesty population and the Mexican and Central American communities. California serves as home to 57 percent of the entire amnesty population which resided in the United States in 1995.[45] Moreover, a disproportionate share of immigrants born in Mexico and Central America reside in California. The state serves as home to 51 percent of Mexican immigrants who reside in the United States.[46] Moreover, California serves as a good place to conduct a comparative analysis between Mexicans and Central Americans, and the other immigrant communities, since the state serves as home to one-third of all foreign-born individuals who reside in the United States, as we saw in Chapter 1.

In their analysis of the data profiling the socioeconomic characteristics of the immigrant population which resides in California, as well as the rest of the United States, Robert F. Schoeni, Kevin F. McCarthy, and Georges Vernez find that Mexicans and Central Americans stand at the bottom of the socioeconomic ladder among all the foreign-born ethnic groups living in the state. Mexicans and Central Americans are less educated, less fluent in English, and earn a lower average income than virtually every other major immigrant ethnic group, as well as native-born Americans. Moreover, since 1970 the average income of Mexicans and Central Americans has declined substantially, relative to that of native-born Americans, while the average income of all the other major immigrant ethnic groups has risen in this regard during the same period.[47]

Summarizing their findings on the incomes of the major immigrant ethnic groups since 1970, McCarthy and Vernez conclude that

The picture one draws of immigrants' economic performance over the past 20 years depends entirely upon which group of immigrants one is describing. European-heritage immigrants have traditionally done very well relative to native-born workers and continue to do so. Asian immigrants, who have historically lagged behind natives, are now doing much better in the labor market and are generally at parity with natives. The one exception to this improvement is the Indochinese refugee population, whose wages continue to lag behind those of natives. Mexican and Central American immigrants, who together constitute over half of California's immigrants, present a very different picture. Their wages, traditionally well below those of natives, have fallen even further behind over the past 30 years.[48]

The analysis of the data on immigrant incomes, which Schoeni, McCarthy, and Vernez conducted, provides a strong empirical foundation to refute the conclusions of Chiswick, who, in his influential 1978 study of immigrant incomes, concluded that "Immigrants start with earnings about 17 percent below that of natives, but, after 10–15 years working in the U.S., they tend to 'overtake' the average wage level and thereafter rise above the average wage."[49] Chiswick mistakenly treats immigrants as an economically homogeneous group, with all ethnic groups within the alien community possessing the same socioeconomic characteristics and rates of economic assimilation.

However, McCarthy and Vernez make clear that, far from being homogeneous, the immigrant community represents a socioeconomically heterogeneous group: the socioeconomic characteristics and rates of economic assimilation of the immigrant community are highly differentiated according to the national origin of each alien ethnic group. The socioeconomic status of Europeans generally exceeds that of native-born Americans. Asians enter the United States with substantially lower incomes than those of native-born Americans, and enjoy rapid socioeconomic mobility, which enables them to achieve economic parity with natives after twenty years, consistent with the findings of Chiswick. On the other hand, Mexicans and Central Americans represent the most socioeconomically disadvantaged ethnic group within the immigrant community, whose incomes have continued to deteriorate in relation to other immigrant groups, as well as native-born Americans.

THE EMPIRICAL EVIDENCE SHOWING THE LOW SOCIOECONOMIC STATUS OF THE AMNESTY POPULATION

As we have seen, the overwhelming majority of amnesty recipients were born in Mexico and Central America. As a result, it is safe to assume that the amnesty population reflects the same low socioeconomic status as the Mexican and Central American immigrant communities. The data suggests this to be the case.

Consider the amnesty population in California, which serves as home to the overwhelming majority of amnesty recipients. In their analysis of the data measuring the socioeconomic characteristics of the amnesty population in California, McCarthy and Vernez find that amnesty recipients are less educated, less fluent in English, and earn a lower average income than other nonrefugee immigrants. The same is generally true of the amnesty population in relation to refugees, though the incomes of the two groups are roughly the same.[50] Without question, the amnesty population represents the most socioeconomically deprived segment of the entire immigrant community, even in relation to refugees, whose socioeconomic status is substantially lower than that of nonrefugee immigrants.

Congress's decision to grant amnesty to 2.7 million illegal aliens, mostly born in Mexico and Central America, was clearly not in the national economic interest. The data clearly shows that those illegal aliens are generally poorly educated, unskilled, and earn lower incomes than virtually every other immigrant group. It is difficult to see what economic benefit the United States has derived from the granting of amnesty to those illegal aliens.

As the data from California clearly illustrates, Mexicans and Central Americans represent the most impoverished, least educated and fluent in English, and most socioeconomically deprived immigrant ethnic group who reside in the United States. Given their relatively low incomes, it is safe to assume that Mexican and Central American immigrants have made substantial use of the welfare system. As we have seen in Chapter 1, a substantially higher share of immigrants use various welfare benefits than is the case for native-born Americans. Given their low socioeconomic status, Mexicans and Central Americans represent a major source of the relatively high welfare participation rates among immigrants. The same is true of two other major ethnic groups who obtained amnesty under IRCA—Cubans and Dominicans.[51]

As we have seen, nearly 90 percent of the illegal aliens granted amnesty under IRCA were born in either Mexico, Central America, Cuba, or the Dominican Republic. As a result, it is safe to assume that the socioeconomic characteristics of the amnesty population mirrors that of the Mexican, Central American, Cuban, and Dominican immigrant communities which reside in the United States. Like the Mexican, Central American, Cuban, and Dominican immigrant communities as a whole, we can assume that the amnesty population is plagued by poor education, a lack of fluency in English, and low earnings. The analysis of the data profiling the socioeconomic characteristics of the amnesty population, which McCarthy and Vernez conducted, clearly shows this to be the case.

It is reasonable to assume that a substantial share of the amnesty population has become dependent upon the welfare system, both because of the low socioeconomic status of amnesty recipients and the high welfare participation rates among the immigrant ethnic groups which serve as the source of the overwhelming majority of the amnesty population. To be sure, IRCA made illegal aliens ineligible for all but a very few entitlement programs until five years after they had obtained amnesty, as we have seen. However, that five-year period has long since expired, and the amnesty population is now eligible for all the entitlement programs available to American citizens and permanent legal residents. Given their low socioeconomic status, we can expect the amnesty population to take full advantage of their right to welfare benefits, as reflected in the high welfare participation rates among the major immigrant ethnic groups granted amnesty—Mexicans, Central Americans, Dominicans, and Cubans.

The empirical evidence clearly shows that the amnesty provisions of IRCA were not in the national economic interest. The United States is making the transition from an economy based upon the production of manufactured goods to one based upon the dissemination of information. The newly emergent information-based economy demands a substantially better-educated and more highly skilled labor force than was the case with the old industrial economy. To serve the national economic interest, immigration policy should be geared toward serving the labor needs of the newly emergent information-based economy. This would entail granting the right to immigrate to the United States only to well-educated aliens, who have critically vital skills to provide to the newly emergent information-based economy, have the capacity to earn relatively high incomes, and are not likely to use any welfare benefits.

Few, if any, of the 2.7 million illegal aliens granted amnesty under IRCA have the education and skills required to make any contribution to the newly emergent information-based economy. Rather, those illegal aliens for the most part are poorly educated, possess few, if any, skills, and are qualified only for menial jobs which pay low wages. Having now been granted amnesty under IRCA, and gained eligibility for all the entitlement benefits available to American citizens five years after obtaining temporary legal residence in the United States, many of those illegal aliens have become dependent upon the welfare system.

Congress granted amnesty to 2.7 million illegal aliens under IRCA, not because lawmakers believed that such action was in the national economic interest, but rather due to politics. Interest groups representing the Latino community strongly supported amnesty, since nearly 90 percent of those who would obtain permanent legal residence under IRCA were born in Latin America. Eager to please the Latino community, and perhaps be rewarded in the future with Hispanic votes, Democratic members of Congress insisted that amnesty provisions be included in IRCA.

To be sure, Republican members of Congress, especially in the House, opposed amnesty, as the vote on the McCollum amendment illustrates. This was fully consistent with the fact that immigration restrictionists represent an important constituency within the Republican Party. Republican opposition to amnesty within the House was designed to satisfy the desires of the party's immigration restrictionist constituency.

However, the Republican Party has fully recongized that the rapidly growing Latino community represents a rich source of potential votes. Republicans have been increasingly eager to compete with Democrats for the Latino vote. To assure that they remain competitive with the Democrats within the Latino community, Republican members of Congress decided to accept the inclusion of amnesty provisions in IRCA. Republican members of Congress hoped that they would be rewarded for their willingness to accept amnesty with Latino votes.

With both parties eager to cultivate the support of the Latino community through their willingness to accept, if not demand, amnesty, the Reagan administration had no alternative to backing amnesty, even though the White House remained adamantly opposed to the legalization provisions of IRCA which derived from the SAW program. Given the fact that few, if any, of the 2.7 million illegal aliens granted amnesty under IRCA have the education and skills to make any contribution to the newly emergent information-based economy, and that many of them have become dependent upon the welfare system, the long-term effect of the amnesty program has been to damage the national economic interest. The amnesty program is a clear example of how immigration policy has been determined by politics, especially ethnic politics, and not the national economic interest.

THE NEED FOR THE REAGAN ADMINISTRATION TO HAVE CONSIDERED THE ESTABLISHMENT OF A DEFERRED AMNESTY PROGRAM

Given the potential for the amnesty provisions of IRCA to impose substantial long-term financial burdens upon the welfare system, Reagan should have opposed the unconditional granting of amnesty to the 2.7 million illegal aliens who obtained permanent legal residence under the bill. Rather, Reagan should have insisted that the amnesty be granted on a deferred basis—only after employer-sanctions provisions of IRCA had proven effective in substantially reducing the flow of illegal immigration to the United States. It simply made no sense to grant amnesty to illegal aliens who resided in the United States until effective measures had been imposed to deter further illegal immigration to this nation. Otherwise, amnesty could only serve to encourage further illegal immigration, as aliens entered the United States without authentic documentation to wait their turn to be legalized the next time Congress established an amnesty program. Indeed, the argument in favor of amnesty was that the federal government could not, from either a practical or humanitarian standpoint, engage in the mass deportation of the millions of illegal aliens who resided in the United States; nor could Washington permit such a large undocumented population to continue to reside in the United States without the legal and political rights available to American citizens.

Amnesty was necessary to allow the illegal alien population to assimilate legally, politically, and economically into American society. However, for such amnesty to be justified, the federal government would have had to establish effective measures to deter further illegal immigration to the United States. Otherwise, a rapidly growing post-amnesty illegal alien population would develop, forcing Congress to confront the same political and moral considerations, concerning whether to grant amnesty to this new illegal alien population, which lawmakers had to face in 1986 when they established the amnesty program under IRCA.

Unless the problem of illegal immigration was solved, Congress would be forced to confront each decade the dilemma of whether to grant amnesty to each new population of aliens. The result would be the willful and wanton abuse of federal immigration law, as aliens, ineligible to immigrate to the United States legally, entered this nation illegally, with the hope and expectation that they would obtain permanent legal residence once Congress established its next amnesty program. As a result, the amnesty provisions of IRCA needed to be the first and *last* legalization program which Congress established; and its members needed to institute effective measures to deter further illegal immigration in order to prevent the growth of a new illegal alien population in the wake of amnesty.

IRCA was designed to solve the problem of illegal immigration by granting amnesty to undocumented individuals who resided in the United States while imposing an employer-sanctions regime designed to deter further illegal immigration to this nation. However, as we saw in the previous chapter, employer sanctions have proven to be an unmitigated failure, having had no discernible effect in stemming the flow of illegal immigration to the United States. This is due to the absence of a secure and reliable worker verification system, which would allow employers to detect and crack down on the massive document fraud illegal aliens have engaged in. As a result, IRCA has failed to solve the problem of illegal immigration. Indeed, the number of illegal aliens currently residing in the United States is double the number who lived in this nation in 1988, when employer sanctions went into full effect, as we saw in the previous chapter.

A deferred amnesty program would have forced Congress to establish a credible and effective employer-sanctions regime to deter further illegal immigration by depriving undocumented individuals of jobs. Liberal Democratic members of Congress supported amnesty, but opposed employer sanctions. A deferred amnesty program would have forced liberal Democrats to make a difficult choice: Either support establishment of a credible and effective employer-sanctions regime, or accept the termination of the amnesty program. No amnesty would be granted unless an employer-sanctions regime, capable of substantially reducing the flow of illegal immigration, was established.

Reagan and conservative Republican members of Congress supported IRCA primarily because of its employer-sanctions provisions. Few of those conservative Republicans supported amnesty; and Reagan's own support for amnesty was in large measure a political calculation designed to enlist liberal Democratic support for the bill in Congress. Such support was necessary given the fact that the Democratic majority in the House, which was dominated by liberals, remained completely unwilling to permit passage of IRCA without its amnesty provisions.

Reagan needed to use a deferred amnesty program to force liberal Democrats to join more moderate members of Congress of both parties in supporting the establishment of a credible and effective employer-sanctions regime. Its establishment would have been the political price which liberal Democrats would have had to pay to obtain implementation of the amnesty provisions of IRCA, which they strongly supported. Reagan could have used deferred amnesty as his trump card to coerce liberals into accepting a credible and effective employer-

sanctions regime, thereby assuring that IRCA would achieve its goal of providing a viable and lasting solution to the problem of illegal immigration.

To be sure, the major roadblock to the establishment of a credible and effective employer-sanctions regime came not from liberal Democratic members of
Congress, but from the Reagan administration. As we saw in the previous chapter, employer sanctions cannot be effectively enforced unless they are coupled
with a fraud-resistant worker verification system. The most promising worker
verification proposal involves the use of a single document, most likely the
Social Security card, as a secure and reliable means to establish the identity of
individuals who seek employment. A worker verification system promised to
assure firms the capability to detect and crack down on document fraud, in
guaranteeing that they comply with their legal obligations under employer-
sanctions provisions of IRCA. However, the Reagan administration opposed the
establishment of such a system, charging that it would result in an invasion of
individual privacy and would be too costly.

Nevertheless, despite the Reagan administration's opposition to the establishment of a credible and effective worker verification system, the president still
needed to make the granting of amnesty to illegal aliens conditional upon the
success of employer sanctions in stemming the flow of illegal immigration to
the United States. This would force Congress to consider ways to make employer sanctions workable and effective if its members wanted the amnesty
provisions of IRCA to go into effect. Employer sanctions did not go into full
effect until the closing weeks of the Reagan administration. As a result, the
administration would not have to confront the possibility of having to impose a
fraud-resistant worker verification system, which the White House adamantly
opposed. Rather, this possibility would have to be confronted by a future president who succeeded Reagan, since the failure of the worker verification provisions of IRCA did not become apparent until they had been in effect for
several years, well after Reagan had left the White House.

Because employer sanctions did not go into full effect until the closing weeks
of the Reagan administration, the president knew that he would not have to be
the one to take responsibility for establishing a fraud-resistant worker verification system; rather, that burden would have to be assumed by one of his successors. As a result, Reagan need not have worried about whether he might
disapprove of the final worker verification system which Congress established
to make employer sanctions effective and workable, since he would be out of
office when that occurred. Rather, Reagan needed to create conditions which
would force Congress to consider ways to make employer sanctions effective
and workable, once the failure of the worker verification provisions of IRCA
became fully apparant after he left office. A deferred amnesty program would
do just that, by forcing Congress to make employer sanctions a workable and
effective means to stem the flow of illegal immigration as a condition for allowing the amnesty provisions to go into effect.

Reagan needed to use a deferred amnesty program to coerce liberal Democratic members of Congress to support a fraud-resistant worker verification system, which would enable the employer-sanctions provisions of IRCA to be enforced. Liberal Democrats would have to support such a system in order to guarantee the success of employer sanctions; otherwise, the amnesty provisions of IRCA would not go into effect. Given their strong commitment to amnesty, liberal Democrats would have, in all likelihood, reluctantly accepted the establishment of a fraud-resistant worker verification system in order to guarantee implementation of the amnesty program. Accordingly, Reagan could have influenced Congress to establish a credible and effective employer-sanctions regime, had he only used the leverage which a deferred amnesty program would have given him, in order to buy liberal Democratic support for a fraud-resistant worker verification system. By agreeing to an unconditional, rather than deferred, amnesty program, Reagan squandered the political leverage, which he could have used to wrench political concessions from liberal Democratic members of Congress.

DISAGREEMENTS EMERGE WITHIN SCIRP OVER THE ISSUE OF AMNESTY

The amnesty program, which SCIRP recommended in its final report containing its proposals on immigration reform issued in 1981, was to have been linked in an unspecified way to progress made in reducing the flow of illegal immigration to the United States. In their report, the sixteen members of SCIRP unanimously recommended that "legalization begin when appropriate enforcement mechanisms [to deter further illegal immigration] have been instituted." To assure unanimous support within SCIRP, the language of this recommendation was deliberately worded in a vague manner: It was not clear from the commission's proposal how much progress had to actually be made in reducing the flow of illegal immigration before the amnesty provisions of IRCA would go into effect.

As a result, both supporters and opponents of mass immigration, who served as members of SCIRP, had differing interpretations of the commission's recommendation on amnesty. The leading immigration restrictionist member of SCIRP, Senator Simpson, interpreted this recommendation as meaning that the implementation of amnesty must be made conditional on the success of employer sanctions in substantially reducing the flow of illegal immigration to the United States: "No amnesty program should be adopted until effective additional enforcement measures are in place—not merely 'implemented,' but shown actually effective in substantially eliminating illegal immigration. It was in this context that I supported the concept [of amnesty]."

However, the leading pro-immigration member of SCIRP, Senator Kennedy, took strong exception to Simpson's interpretation of the commission's recommendation on amnesty. Kennedy challenged Simpson's contention that the implementation of amnesty be made conditional upon the success of employer sanctions in stemming the flow of illegal immigration to the United States. Rather, Kennedy insisted that amnesty and employer sanctions be implemented simultaneously: "This does not mean that the legalization program should be delayed until the implementation of all the other . . . enforcement procedures recommended by the commission. Rather, the legalization program should be undertaken at the same time new enforcement efforts are initiated and funds are authorized."[52]

Had Congress adopted Simpson's recommendation—that the amnesty program which SCIRP proposed not go into effect until employer sanctions had proven successful in substantially curtailing the flow of illegal immigration to the United States—then the amnesty provisions of IRCA would never have been implemented. This is true since the employer-sanctions provisions of IRCA have had no discernible effect in curbing the tide of illegal immigration to the United States, due to the ability of illegal aliens to illegally obtain jobs through document fraud. Pro-immigration members of SCIRP, led by Kennedy, were committed to implementing amnesty on an unconditional basis, regardless of how ineffective employer sanctions would ultimately prove in curtailing the flow of illegal immigration to the United States. They certainly recognized that employer-sanctions legislation, which SCIRP recommended, had a good chance of failing, given the fact that the commission did not recommend the establishment of a secure and reliable worker verification system.

With illegal aliens maintaining easy access to jobs by engaging in document fraud, Kennedy and other pro-immigration members of SCIRP could have easily predicted that employer sanctions would have no discernible effect in stemming the flow of illegal immigration to the United States. As a result, pro-immigration members of SCIRP were unwilling to recommend that the implementation of amnesty be linked to the success or failure of employer sanctions. Rather, they insisted that amnesty be implemented on an unconditional basis. This would assure that undocumented individuals would be granted amnesty even if employer sanctions failed miserably to reduce the flood of illegal immigration to the United States, as was certain to be the case.

From 1980 to 1986, the Democrats remained a minority in the Senate, and lacked a veto-proof majority in the House. As a result, no immigration reform legislation could pass both houses of Congress unless it had the support of Reagan and substantial numbers of Republican members of Congress. This required that the Democrats accept employer sanctions as the price they would have to pay to establish an amnesty program.

However, Democratic members of Congress were reluctant to accept anything more than the weak and ineffective employer-sanctions regime established under IRCA. The only way Democrats would have been willing to accept a credible and effective employer-sanctions regime was if Congress tied the implementation of amnesty to the success of employer sanctions in curbing the flow of illegal immigration to the United States. Democratic members of Congress wanted amnesty so badly that there is a good chance that they would have cooperated with their Republican colleagues, led by Simpson, in designing a workable and effective employer-sanctions regime. To assure such cooperation, Simpson insisted that the implementation of amnesty must not be allowed to go forward until employer sanctions had proven successful.

The versions of IRCA passed by the Senate in the 97th Congress, and the Senate and the House in the 98th Congress, which Simpson co-sponsored, would have established an unconditional amnesty program.[53] Though he supported deferred amnesty, as we have seen, Simpson recognized that the Democratic members of Congress were unwilling to accept anything less than unconditional amnesty. As a result, Simpson reluctantly dropped his earlier demands for deferred amnesty, deciding to include provisions within the Senate version of IRCA requiring the implementation of amnesty on an unconditional basis.

However, by the time the 99th Congress convened in January 1985, Simpson had a change of heart on the issue of amnesty. Simpson's latest version of IRCA, introduced on May 23, would have established a deferred amnesty program. Congress would have established a bipartisan Legalization Commission to determine whether employer sanctions had proven effective in substantially reducing the flow of illegal immigration to the United States. The amnesty provisions of IRCA would not have gone into effect until the commission certified that employer sanctions were in fact working in significantly stemming the tide of illegal immigration to the United States.[54]

The Reagan administration responded in a confused and inconsistent manner to the deferred amnesty provisions of Simpson's latest version of IRCA. In his statement issued before the Subcommittee on Immigration and Refugee Policy of the Senate Judiciary Committee on June 14, 1985, Meese was noncommittal as to whether the administration would support the establishment of a deferred amnesty program: ''The provisions of [IRCA], which postpone the effective date of legalization until the effectiveness of enforcement measures has been demonstrated, address some of the concerns that have been raised about legalization and will be the subject of careful discussion and study within the administration.''[55]

However, appearing before the Subcommittee on Immigration and Refugee Policy of the Senate Judiciary Committee following Meese, INS Commissioner Alan Nelson announced that the Reagan administration would support the establishment of a deferred amnesty program.

The provisions of [IRCA] which allow legalization of specified aliens who are presently illegally in the United States are a realistic response to a circumstance which we intend not to allow to recur in the future. Your approach is reasonable to establish a Legalization Commission with responsibility to assess and confirm the existence of effective enforcement measures before allowing commencement of the legalization program.

Once the Legalization Commission has concluded that enforcement measures are in place that are controlling substantially the illegal entry of aliens into the United States and deterring violations of terms of legal admission, as well as substantially eliminating employment of unauthorized aliens, the legalization program would be allowed to begin. This deferred legalization provision should deter persons who otherwise might attempt to enter or remain illegally solely to attempt adjustment through an immediate legalization opportunity.

As President Reagan has stated, this administration favors the concept of legalization. We repeat our support today. We recognize, as Senator Simpson has indicated, that the deferred legalization, endorsed unanimously by the bipartisan blue-ribbon Select Commission on Immigration and Refugee Policy in 1981, is a better approach. It represents a better balance with enforcement [of federal immigration laws]. . . .

The legalization provisions of [IRCA] are designed to ensure that only aliens who are and will be productive members of our society can qualify for residence. The triggering of the legalization provisions by the bipartisan Legalization Commission will preclude the drawing in of new illegal aliens seeking this special benefit, and should help ensure that legalization is a one-time-only program.[56]

CONGRESS GRANTS UNCONDITIONAL AMNESTY TO ILLEGAL ALIENS UNDER IRCA

Liberal Democratic members of Congress, joined by interest groups representing the Latino community, strongly opposed deferred amnesty. Liberal Democrats and Latinos fully recognized that the employer-sanctions provisions of IRCA would fail to stem the flow of illegal immigration to the United States. Illegal aliens could easily circumvent employer sanctions by using fraudulent documents to illegally obtain jobs, IRCA contained no provisions for the establishment of a secure and reliable worker verification system, which would enable employers to detect and crack down on document fraud.

As a result, many employers have accepted as valid fraudulent documents presented to them by illegal aliens, whom they wished to hire, which falsely purport to verify their eligibility to work in the United States. By failing to provide firms any means to determine the authenticity of these documents, the employer sanctions provisions of IRCA were guaranteed to fail in their goal of depriving illegal aliens of jobs. Accordingly, any program which tied the provision of amnesty to the success of employer sanctions in substantially reducing the flow of illegal immigration would effectively prevent the amnesty provisions of IRCA from going into effect.

Recognizing that deferred amnesty meant no amnesty at all, liberal Democratic members of Congress rejected the deferred amnesty provisions of Simpson's latest version of IRCA, insisting on nothing less than unconditional amnesty. Liberal Democrats were supported in their demands for unconditional amnesty by interest groups representing the Latino community. With nearly 90 percent of those obtaining amnesty under IRCA having been born in Latin America, the Latino community strongly supported unconditional amnesty, since a large share of its members, who resided in the United States illegally, stood to become the recipients of amnesty.[57]

The National Security Council (NSC) was actively involved in the development of immigration policy, given the important influence it has on America's relations with the rest of the world, especially the small number of nations which serve as the source of most immigration to the United States. On June 18, 1985, Richard Childress, Director of Public Affairs of the NSC, sent a memo to Robert C. McFarlane, Assistant to the President for National Security Affairs and director of the NSC, informing him of the substantial opposition existing to deferred amnesty. Childress noted that Simpson's latest version of IRCA

establishes a presidentially-appointed commission to determine whether "appropriate immigration enforcement mechanisms" are in place and controlling illegal entry. If the commission makes such a finding, then persons who could prove they have been physically present in the U.S. prior to January 1, 1980, would be eligible for temporary resident status. . . .

Simpson's bill differs in one major respect from last year's legislation that passed the House and Senate, but died in the conference committee. That measure coupled employers' penalties with a program to grant legal status immediately to undocumented workers, who could prove they entered the U.S. prior to January 1, 1981, and had been here since.

Simpson's new bill has drawn fire from Hispanic and civil rights groups, who describe it as a step backwards. Opposition from these groups was one factor that threatened last year's House [immigration reform] bill, which passed 216–211.[58]

Substantial opposition to the deferred amnesty existed among Democratic members of the Judiciary Committee, which exercised jurisdiction over the bill in the Senate. During the committee's deliberations over IRCA, Democratic Senator Kennedy introduced an amendment to the bill which would have granted amnesty to illegal aliens who resided in the United States, immediately following enactment of IRCA into federal law. The Kennedy amendment was defeated on a party-line vote of eight to six, with eight Republicans opposing it and six Democrats supporting it.

However, recognizing that the Democratic Party, which controlled the House and had the votes to mount a successful filibuster in the Senate, would never accept anything which fell short of unconditional amnesty, Republican members of the Senate Judiciary Committee decided to reverse themselves and accept unconditional amnesty. On July 30, 1985, the committee, by a vote of ten to four, approved an amendment, introduced by Democratic Senator Howard Metzenbaum of Ohio, which granted amnesty to illegal aliens who resided in the United States, within three years following the enactment of IRCA into federal law.[59] The final version of IRCA, which Reagan signed on November 6, 1986, reduced the amount of time those illegal aliens would have to wait to receive amnesty to six months following enactment of the bill into federal law.[60]

By rejecting deferred amnesty, and insisting on nothing less than unconditional amnesty, Democratic members of Congress succeeded in forcing their Republican colleagues to grant permanent legal residence to 2.7 million illegal aliens with virtually no prospect that the employer-sanctions provisions of IRCA would succeed in stemming the flow of illegal immigration to this nation. As a result, IRCA gave Democrats what they wanted most—amnesty—without forcing them to make any real and meaningful concessions on the issue of employer sanctions. To be sure, Democrats had to accept employer sanctions as the price they had to pay to win Republican support for amnesty. However, the employer-sanctions provisions of IRCA turned out to be too weak and ineffective to have any discernible impact in stemming the flow of illegal immigration to the United States.

The blame for the failure of employer sanctions must be assigned to the Reagan administration. It rejected the establishment of a fraud-resistant worker verification system, based upon the use of the Social Security card as a secure and reliable means of individual identification.

CONCLUSION

In addition to imposing an employer-sanctions regime, IRCA granted amnesty to illegal aliens who resided in the United States. In many ways, the amnesty program established under IRCA has had a more profound and long-term impact upon the United States than employer sanctions. As we saw in the previous chapter, the employer-sanctions provisions of IRCA have failed to meet the goal of depriving illegal aliens of jobs.

By contrast, IRCA established a liberal and generous amnesty program which granted permanent legal residence to 2.7 million undocumented individuals. Over 80 percent of amnesty recipients were born in Mexico and Central America. Reflecting the socioeconomic characteristics of the Mexican and Central American immigrant communities, amnesty recipients are the least educated and fluent in English, most unskilled, and poorest segment of the foreign-born population who reside in the United States. Trapped in menial employment and earning only meager incomes, amnesty recipients are especially prone to use welfare benefits, since they became eligible to do so five years after being granted temporary legal residence under IRCA.

The purpose of immigration policy should be to allow only the best-educated and highest-skilled aliens—those who can make a vital contribution to the American economy and are unlikely to become dependent upon the welfare system—the opportunity to obtain permanent legal residence in the United States. By granting amnesty to the least educated and fluent in English, most unskilled, and poorest segment of the immigrant community, the amnesty provisions of IRCA did not serve the national economic interest or the aims of a rational, reasoned immigration policy. Accordingly, it is difficult not to conclude that the most important and longest-lasting element of IRCA—its amnesty provisions—represented a significant mistake in the pursuit of immigration policy. By allowing 2.7 million illegal aliens, who represent the most socioeconomically deprived and impoverished segment of the immigrant community, to obtain permanent legal residence, the amnesty provisions of IRCA have almost certainly imposed a substantial financial burden upon the welfare system—an outcome which cannot be anything other than damaging to the national economic interest.

Chapter 6

Ronald Reagan and the Failure of Immigration Policy

> The Immigration and Control Act of 1986 was debated and finally passed, but as those in that battle well understood at the time, its efforts to curtail illegal immigration . . . were bound to fail. And they have.[1]
>
> —Peter Skerry, political scientist

On November 6, 1986, Reagan signed IRCA at a ceremony held in the Roosevelt Room. In his remarks delivered before he signed IRCA, Reagan argued that

The Immigration Reform and Control Act of 1986, that I will sign in a few minutes, is the most comprehensive reform of our immigration laws since 1952. It's the product of one of the longest and most difficult undertakings of the last three Congresses. Further, it's an excellent example of a truly successful bipartisan effort. The administration and the allies of immigration reform on both sides of the Capitol and both sides of the aisle worked together to accomplish these critically important reforms to control illegal immigration. . . .

Future generations of Americans will be thankful for our efforts to humanely regain control of our borders, and thereby preserve the value of one of the most sacred possessions of our people: American citizenship.[2]

As we saw in Chapter 2, nearly three-quarters of all illegal aliens who reside in the United States were born in Latin America, with over half having immigrated from Mexico alone. As a result, the Reagan administration was concerned that the employer-sanctions provisions of IRCA, designed to deprive illegal aliens of jobs, might be construed as targeting Latin Americans, especially those born in Mexico, for punishment, given the fact that citizens born in this region represent an overwhelming share of the undocumented population.

In a memo sent on October 28, 1986 to Thomas F. Gibson III, Special Assistant to the President and Director of Public Affairs, Executive Secretary of the NSC W. Robert Pearson warned that employer sanctions might harm America's relations with Latin America, especially Mexico: "Latin American countries, and Mexico in particular, are very sensitive with regard to U.S. immigration law."

To alleviate Latin American concerns over employer sanctions, Pearson recommended that Reagan's speech writers include in the remarks, which he would make at the signing ceremony for IRCA, words to reassure the nations of the region that the bill was designed to target for punishment not their citizens who reside in the United States illegally, but *all* undocumented individuals, regardless of national origin.

In order to assure them that the law is not aimed at their direction in a discriminatory way, I will be recommending to speech writers words to the following effect:

"Distance has not discouraged illegal immigration to the United States from all around the globe. The problem of illegal immigration should not, therefore, be seen as a problem between the United States and its neighbors. Our objective is only to establish a reasonable, fair, orderly, and secure system of immigration into this country—and not to discriminate in any way against particular nations or peoples."

A few words in summary of these sentiments might be added to the text [of Reagan's remarks].[3]

Pursuant to Pearson's recommendation, Reagan agreed to include the two sentences, containing words of reassurance to Latin America, exactly as they appeared in Pearson's memo, in both the remarks the president delivered at the signing ceremony for IRCA and in the statement he issued following his signing of the bill, which contained his interpretation of its major provisions.[4] In his statement, Reagan noted:

In the past 35 years our nation has been increasingly affected by illegal immigration. This legislation takes a major step toward meeting this challenge to our sovereignty. At the same time, it preserves and enhances this nation's heritage of legal immigration. I am pleased to sign this bill into law.

In 1981 the administration asked the Congress to pass a comprehensive legislative package, including employer sanctions, other measures to increase enforcement of immigration laws, and legalization. The act provides these three essential components. The employer sanctions program is the keystone and major element. It will remove the incentive for illegal immigration by eliminating the job opportunities, which draw illegal aliens here. We have consistently supported a legalization program, which is both generous to the alien and fair to countless thousands of people throughout the world who seek legally to come to America. The legalization provisions of this act will go far to improve the lives of a class of individuals, who must now hide in the shadows, without access to many of the benefits of a free and open society. Very many of these men and women will be able to step out into the sunlight and, ultimately, if they choose, they may become Americans.[5]

THE REAGAN ADMINISTRATION DECEIVES THE PUBLIC
AND CONGRESS OVER THE ISSUE OF EMPLOYER
SANCTIONS

As Reagan noted in the statement he issued following his signing of IRCA, "The employer sanctions program is the keystone and major element" of the federal government's strategy against illegal immigration which the bill defined. "It will remove the incentive for illegal immigration by eliminating the job opportunities which draw illegal aliens here." However, as we have seen, the employer-sanctions provisions of IRCA have had no discernible effect in stemming the flow of illegal immigration to the United States.

How could Reagan have been so utterly wrong in his assurance to the public that the employer-sanctions provisions of IRCA would achieve their goal of removing incentives for aliens to immigrate to the United States illegally by depriving undocumented individuals of jobs? The answer is that Reagan knew those provisions would fail when he signed IRCA into federal law. Indeed, Reagan deceived the public when he assured them in his remarks at the signing ceremony for IRCA that those provisions would work. As we saw in Chapter 3, Smith had made a similarly deceitful statement to members of Congress in 1981 when he assured them that the worker verification procedures, which were eventually contained in IRCA, would be sufficient to deprive illegal aliens of employment. Documents, which the President's Task Force on Immigration and Refugee Policy produced, show that the Reagan administration fully understood that employer sanctions would fail unless they were coupled with the establishment of a fraud-resistant worker verification system.

A worker verification system based upon the use of a single document, preferably the Social Security card, to verify the eligibility of individuals to work in the United States would assure the effective enforcement of the employer-sanctions provisions of IRCA. By depriving illegal aliens of employment, such a system would result in a substantial decline in the flow of illegal immigration to the United States. However, as we saw in Chapter 4, the administration opposed such a system, fearing that it would result in the creation of a national identity card, representing an invasion of individual privacy. In addition, the administration believed that such a system would be too costly to establish and operate. The administration was willing to accept the fraud-ridden worker verification provisions of IRCA, since they would allow individuals to use any combination of a wide array of different documents to verify their eligibility to work in the United States. This would preclude the creation of a national identity card, to which the administration remained adamantly opposed.

IRCA confronted the Reagan administration with a conflict between deterring further illegal immigration and preserving individual privacy and restraining the growth of federal spending. The administration ultimately decided that preserving individual privacy and restraining the growth of federal spending were more important than deterring further illegal immigration to the United States. Accordingly, the administration decided to accept the fraud-ridden worker verification provisions of IRCA as the price it was willing to pay in order to prevent the creation of a national identity card.

However, rather than admitting the fact that the employer-sanctions provisions of IRCA were designed to fail, Reagan deceived the public into believing they would work. This was necessary in order to assure passage of the employer-sanctions provisions of IRCA. Congress was unlikely to have included those provisions in IRCA had the Reagan administration admitted the fact that they would fail to achieve their the goal of depriving illegal aliens of employment. This is especially true, since Congress feared that employer sanctions would result in ethnic discrimination against legal immigrant workers.

However, the Reagan administration made dishonest and deceitful statements to members of Congress on this issue in order to alleviate their concerns over the potential for employer sanctions to result in such discrimination. As we have seen, Smith and Meese denied that employer-sanctions legislation would result in such discrimination. However, documents which the President's Task Force on Immigration and Refugee Policy produced show Smith's and Meese's statements to members of Congress to be false. The documents reveal that the Reagan administration knew that employer-sanctions legislation would result in ethnic discrimination against legal immigrant workers, as the experience with IRCA has confirmed.

Reagan, Smith, and Meese deceived the public and members of Congress on employer sanctions in order to assure passage of the employer-sanctions provisions of IRCA. The Reagan administration engaged in a deliberate and conscious strategy of lying and deceit in order to manipulate Congress into establishing the kind of employer-sanctions regime which the White House wanted: one based upon use of a fraud-ridden worker verification system, which would assure that the employer-sanctions provisions of IRCA would fail in their goal to deprive illegal aliens of jobs. The administration was not interested in establishing a credible and effective employer-sanctions regime which could achieve this goal; rather, the White House saw the employer-sanctions provisions of IRCA as a symbolic, rather than substantive, measure, designed to create the illusion that the federal government was taking steps to stem the flow of illegal immigration, when in fact Washington was actually doing almost nothing about this problem.

The employer-sanctions provisions of IRCA allowed Reagan to have it both ways: satisfying the public's demand for federal action against illegal immigration without violating the president's philosophical commitment to limited government in the process. As we saw in Chapter 2, a 1980 Gallup Poll showed that 91 percent of the public wanted the federal government to launch "an all-out effort" to stem the flow of illegal immigration to the United States. By supporting the imposition of an employer-sanctions regime, Reagan could satisfy the strong public sentiment against illegal immigration.

THE FAILURES OF IRCA

In addition to deceiving the public on the issue of employer sanctions, Reagan created high expectations for IRCA, which the bill has failed miserably to live up to. The boast Reagan made at the signing ceremony for IRCA that it represented "the most comprehensive reform of our immigration laws since 1952" was pure hyperbole. To be sure, IRCA may very well have been the most comprehensive immigration reform bill passed since 1952; but this is only because Congress enacted no comprehensive immigration reform legislation during this period, with the single exception of the Immigration Act of 1965. By unleashing a flood of immigration, both legal and illegal, the Immigration Act of 1965 represents the very source of all the problems in immigration policy which every president since Jimmy Carter has had to confront. IRCA represents the first real effort to achieve comprehensive immigration reform, in terms of addressing and rectifying the disastrous consequences of the Immigration Act of 1965.

However, as we have seen, IRCA failed miserably to meet the challenges of immigration reform, which have continued to go unaddressed since Reagan signed the bill in 1986. IRCA failed to make much-needed reforms in legal immigration, concentrating instead on the more narrow issue of illegal immigration. When measured against its single, central, overriding goal—to address the problem of illegal immigration—IRCA still turns out to be a dismal failure. The employer-sanctions provisions of IRCA have failed to have any discernible effect in stemming the flow of illegal immigration to the United States. The amnesty provisions of IRCA granted permanent legal residence to 2.7 million poorly educated, unskilled, and low-wage workers, who have little to contribute to the American economy, and have almost certainly imposed a substantial financial burden upon the welfare system.

IRCA failed to address the challenges posed by both the excessive and unsustainable levels of legal immigration, combined with the flood of illegal immigration, experienced since 1965. Accordingly, it is difficult not to conclude that IRCA represents a dismal failure; which is why Congress has been forced to confront the issue of immigration reform at least twice since the bill was passed in 1986. In both cases, Congress passed immigration reform legislation— the Immigration Act of 1990 and the Illegal Immigrant Reform and Immigrant Responsibility Act (IIRIRA) of 1996—which have proven to be no more successful than IRCA in confronting the challenges posed by mass immigration to the United States.

REAGAN'S SHARE OF THE BLAME FOR THE FAILURE OF IRCA

Reagan must assume a substantial share of the blame for the failure of IRCA. The bill itself largely reflects the misconceived and incoherent immigration policy which Reagan pursued during his presidency. Reagan's failure to adequately address the issue of immigration reform is based upon his own inability to recognize that the immigration policy pursued since 1965 is inconsistent with the national economic interest.

Indeed, among the most daunting challenges confronting policymakers remains the incongruence between immigration policy and the labor needs of the American economy. Since the early 1970s, the United States has undergone a transition from an economy based upon the production of goods to one dependent upon the dissemination of information. The newly emergent information-based economy demands a substantially better-educated and higher-skilled labor force than the old industrial economy. However, at a time when the United States needs a better-educated and higher-skilled labor force, immigration policy is permitting millions of poorly educated, unskilled, low-wage foreign-born workers to obtain permanent legal residence in this nation. Trapped in low-wage, menial employment, those foreign-born workers have little to contribute to the American economy, and have become dependent upon the welfare system.

The lack of education and skills of a substantial share of the immigrant population, combined with their increasing dependence upon the welfare system, demands major reforms in immigration policy. The deficiencies in the education and skills of the immigrant population is the direct result of Congress's decision to make family reunification the cornerstone of immigration policy through its passage of the Immigration Act of 1965. As a result of the bill, the overwhelming majority of aliens who have immigrated to the United States since 1965 have done so to be reunited with family members residing legally in this nation; only a small fraction have done so as a result of the critically needed skills which they possess.

Family-based immigrants are allowed to obtain permanent legal residence in the United States, regardless of their levels of education and skills; many such immigrants are poorly educated and unskilled. The low levels of education and skills of a substantial share of the immigrant population is the direct result of the family-based immigration policy pursued since 1965. This policy has allowed a virtually unlimited number of poorly educated and unskilled aliens, who are the immediate family members of American citizens, to immigrate to the United States legally.

By fueling the growth of a burgeoning population of poorly educated and unskilled immigrants who are trapped in low-wage, menial employment and have imposed a substantial financial burden upon the welfare system, the family-based immigration policy, pursued since 1965, is inconsistent with the national economic interest and should be reformed. Congress should eliminate family reunification as the primary criterion governing immigration to the United States. Instead, Congress should establish a skills-based immigration policy, which limits immigration to the United States to aliens who possess the highest levels of education and skills, who are capable of earning high incomes and making a contribution to the American economy, and who are highly unlikely to ever use welfare benefits. The most serious error Reagan made in his conduct of immigration policy was his failure to press for the elimination of family reunification as the cornerstone of immigration policy, and urge its replacement with a skills-based immigration policy.

As we saw in Chapter 1, the versions of IRCA which the Senate passed in 1982 and 1983, respectively, included reforms in legal immigration. However, the Democratic majority in the House was completely unwilling to accept any such reforms. In opposing reforms in legal immigration, House Democrats were responding to the interests of the Latino community. Vilma S. Martinez, President of MALDEF, made it clear in the statement she issued before the immigration subcommittees of the Senate and House that her interest group would oppose any reforms in legal immigration. Since Mexico represents the largest source of legal immigration to the United States, any reforms in legal immigration would impose additional restrictions on the ability of Mexicans to immigrate to this nation.

As a result, any reforms in legal immigration which might have been included in the final version of IRCA passed by Congress were sure to have provoked intense opposition from MALDEF and other interest groups representing the Latino community. Responding to the interests of the Latino community, the Democratic majority in the House prevented all efforts to include reforms in legal immigration in IRCA. The Reagan administration was committed to preserving the high levels of legal immigration existing since 1965, believing that immigrants were making a positive contribution to the American economy. Accordingly, the administration made no attempt to revive efforts within Congress to reform legal immigration. Because much of the problems in immigration policy stem from legal, rather than illegal, immigration, the failure of IRCA to even address the issue of legal immigration makes it hard to sustain Reagan's claim that the bill represented genuine and meaningful immigration reform.

In addition to the efforts to reform legal immigration in Congress, in 1981 a prominent expert on the economics of immigration, Barry R. Chiswick, sent Reagan a copy of a paper he authored, which called for the elimination of family-based immigration and its replacement with a skills-based immigration policy, as we saw in Chapter 1. However, Chiswick's recommendation fell on deaf ears at the White House; the economist's proposal failed to elicit any response from the Reagan administration. The effort to reform legal immigration failed largely because it lacked presidential support. Such presidential support was essential to overcome the powerful opposition such reform was sure to confront from the Democratic majority in the House and its allies within the Latino community. The only ''reform'' in legal immigration which the Reagan administration was willing to support was a doubling in the annual number of visas allotted to Mexico, as well as Canada, to relieve the backlog of Mexicans waiting for permission to immigrate to the United States.

In addition to legal immigration, Reagan failed to make much-needed reforms in illegal immigration. To be sure, the Reagan administration was correct in endorsing SCIRP's recommendation for the imposition of an employer-sanctions regime, designed to deprive undocumented individuals of jobs, as the primary means to deter further illegal immigration to the United States. However, employer sanctions alone are insufficient to deny illegal aliens jobs. Illegal aliens can easily circumvent employer sanctions in illegally obtaining jobs through document fraud.

For employer sanctions to serve as an effective means to deny illegal aliens jobs, Congress needs to establish a fraud-resistant worker verification system, which can enable employers to comply with their legal obligations under IRCA, prohibiting them from knowingly hiring undocumented individuals. IRCA failed to establish such a system. IRCA currently allows individuals to choose from among seventeen documents they may use to verify their eligibility to work in the United States; but the bill provides employers no means to determine the authenticity of those documents. This loophole in IRCA has allowed illegal aliens to circumvent employer sanctions in illegally obtaining jobs through document fraud.

During the 1980s, serious consideration was given to establishing a worker verification system based upon the use of the Social Security card as a secure and reliable means to establish the identity of individuals who seek employment. However, the Reagan administration rejected such a system, based upon the fear that it would result in the creation of a national identity card, which would threaten individual privacy and be too costly to implement. As is claimed in Chapter 4, the administration's arguments against a worker verification system, based upon use of the Social Security card as a secure and reliable means of individual identification, are groundless. Such a system would not result in any invasion of individual privacy; nor would it be too costly to implement, when balanced against the enormous sums which the six states with the largest illegal alien populations, especially California, must spend to provide social services to undocumented individuals.

Congress's failure to establish a fraud-resistant worker verification system is the direct result of the Reagan administration's opposition to such a system. The only worker verification procedures the administration was willing to accept were those contained in IRCA which represented an open invitation to document fraud. By rejecting the establishment of a secure and reliable worker verification system, and insisting instead on the fraud-ridden procedures contained in IRCA, Reagan must take direct responsibility for the failure of employer sanctions, and for their failure to have any discernible effect in stemming the flow of illegal immigration since they went into effect in 1987. In signing IRCA, Reagan promised that the bill would enable the United States to regain control of its borders; but the president deliberately emasculated enforcement of the employer-sanctions provisions of the measure by insisting on fraud-ridden worker verification procedures, which have prevented the legislation from achieving its goal of denying illegal aliens jobs.

EXPLAINING THE FAILURES OF REAGAN'S
IMMIGRATION POLICY

Reagan's failures in the conduct of immigration policy are difficult to dispute. The real question is not whether Reagan failed in this regard, but why did he do so. This book has attempted to address this question by arguing that Reagan lacked accurate and reliable information, which was necessary to enable him to develop a credible and effective immigration policy.

The information which existed during the 1980s tended to confirm that the United States benefited from mass immigration. It was fully recognized that most immigrants are poorly educated and unskilled. However, it was assumed that immigrants would be able to overcome their deficiencies in education and skills through hard work and entrepreneurial energy. Through their industriousness, immigrants would be able to reach economic parity with, if not gain an economic advantage over, native-born Americans within a generation. The empirical evidence, which Barry R. Chiswick presented in his influential 1978 study of the economics of immigration, seemed to confirm this. Additional studies conducted during the 1980s reported that immigrants were less prone to use welfare benefits than native-born Americans, further confirming the economic success of immigrants.

Given the economic contributions which immigrants seemed to make to the United States, and the fact that they were enjoying a high rate of economic assimilation, the Reagan administration did not see any reason for major reforms in immigration policy during the 1980s. The only real problem in immigration policy which the administration saw was the flood of illegal immigration existing since 1965. Accordingly, the administration devoted its efforts in immigration reform almost exclusively to addressing the problem of illegal immigration. This was reflected in IRCA, which was exclusively designed to address this problem.

The elimination of family reunification as the primary criterion governing legal immigration to the United States was certain to confront powerful opposition in Congress. The number of immigrants has been rapidly rising as a result of the expansion and liberalization of the legal immigration under the Immigration Act of 1965. Many immigrants are citizens, and have the right to vote. In addition, the American-born children of immigrants are automatically entitled to citizenship under the Fourteenth Amendment, and have the right to vote when they reach the age of eighteen.

Many immigrants wish to be reunited with family members who reside in their native nations. Those immigrants would strongly oppose any effort by Congress to impose additional restrictions upon family-based immigration. Immigrants and their American-born children are likely to organize and target for defeat any member of Congress who seeks to impose such restrictions. Organizations representing the various immigrant ethnic groups have the capacity to mobilize their constituencies to vote against members of Congress who seek to impose such restrictions. Given the fact that immigrants represent a large and growing community, they are sufficiently numerous to have the capacity to defeat members of Congress who represent districts in the six states which have the largest foreign-born populations—California, New York, Texas, Florida, New Jersey, and Illinois.

Given the political backlash which any effort to reform family-based immigration is likely to provoke among America's burgeoning immigrant community, members of Congress are highly reluctant to grant serious consideration to making such reforms. Indeed, as we saw in Chapter 1, serious efforts were undertaken to reform family-based immigration in the 104th Congress. Those efforts went nowhere due to opposition within Congress and organizations representing the various immigrant ethnic groups.

The only possibility that Congress might seriously consider reforming family-based immigration is if the president presents clear and compelling evidence that current federal policy, which makes family reunification the primary criterion governing legal immigration to the United States, has undermined the national economic interest. Such evidence exists today, due in large part to the pioneering work on this issue conducted by George J. Borjas during the 1990s. However, such evidence did not exist during the 1980s when Reagan was in the White House. Instead the evidence available during the 1980s suggested that immigrants were performing well economically.

Why were the experts and policymakers so misinformed about the economic consequences of mass immigration during the 1980s? Why has it been only during the 1990s that the empirical evidence, revealing the negative economic consequences of mass immigration, finally emerged? The answer lies in the dramatic change in the ethnic composition of the immigrant population which has occurred since 1965.

As we saw in Chapter 1, until 1965 the immigrant population was predominantly made up of Europeans and Canadians, who tend to be well-educated, highly skilled, and earn higher incomes which tend to exceed those of native-born Americans. However, as a result of the reforms in legal immigration which Congress imposed under the Immigration Act of 1965, Latin America and Asia have replaced Europe and Canada as the primary sources of legal immigration to the United States. Much of the post-1965 immigration has come from Mexico, Central America, and Indochina, whose citizens tend to be poorly educated, unskilled, and earn low incomes, which is generally less than those of other immigrants, as well as native-born Americans. With Mexico, Central America, and Indochina replacing Europe and Canada as the primary sources of legal immigration to the United States, the average income of aliens has declined substantially since 1970. With their incomes in decline, many immigrants have become dependent upon the welfare system.

Assessments of the economic consequences of mass immigration during the 1980s were based upon 1970 census data. This data showed immigrants to be performing well economically. However, this data was mostly based upon the economic performance of the pre-1965 immigrant population, which was dominated by well-educated, highly skilled, high-income Europeans and Canadians.

Mexicans, Central Americans, and Indochinese have assumed an increasingly dominant share of the immigrant population since 1970. The effect that immigration from those three poor areas has had in reducing the average income of the immigrant population was not fully revealed until the 1980 and 1990 censuses. Census data from 1980 and 1990 revealing the poor economic performance of the post-1965 immigrant population, which has become increasingly dominated by poorly educated, unskilled, and low-income Mexicans, Central Americans, and Indochinese, did not become subject to rigorous analysis, and widely disseminated to the public, until the 1990s.

Reagan could not have acted upon Chiswick's recommendation that family reunification be replaced by skills as the primary criterion governing legal immigration to the United States. Congress would not have granted any serious consideration to making such reforms in immigration policy unless Reagan was able to present a clear and compelling case for such action. Chiswick's argument that such reforms were desirable because they would yield greater economic benefits to the United States was insufficient: he needed to demonstrate that family-based immigration had undermined the national economic interest. Chiswick made no such argument. Indeed, in the paper which he sent Reagan, the economist never challenged the arguments made in his 1978 study that immigrants enjoyed a high rate of economic assimilation.

Lacking any strong evidence to question the wisdom of the mass immigration existing since 1965, and with Congress unwilling to make any reforms in legal immigration, Reagan had no political or economic basis to recommend any changes in legal immigration. Indeed, Reagan would have been politically foolish to recommend reforms in legal immigration, given the opposition it was likely to provoke in Congress, especially in the House. As we have seen, the Democratic majority in the House rejected all efforts to include reforms in legal immigration in IRCA during the 1980s. Given the lack of any clear and compelling evidence for the need to reform legal immigration, and the vociferous opposition to such action existing in Congress, Reagan cannot be held responsible for his failure to recommend such reform. Rather, Reagan's support for the high levels of legal immigration existing since 1965 was rational and fully consistent with the prevailing sentiments on Capitol Hill and among the experts on this issue during the 1980s.

To be sure, the empirical evidence developed since Reagan left the White House provides clear evidence of the need to reform legal immigration. However, it is Bush and especially Clinton, not Reagan, who have had the responsibility to act upon this evidence. The lack of presidential leadership in meeting the challenges posed by mass immigration primarily falls upon the shoulders of Bush and especially Clinton, since they are the ones who have been in the White House during the 1990s, as evidence of the need for major reforms in immigration policy has accumulated. Reagan can only be held responsibile for the information on immigration which existed while he served in the White House; and his actions on this issue were fully consistent with the information available to him.

While Reagan cannot be held responsible for his failure to recommend much-needed reforms in legal immigration, he must be assigned blame for the failure of employer sanctions to have any discernible effect in stemming the flow of illegal immigration to the United States. The issue of whether to reform legal immigration is a complicated issue, which requires the development of a substantial body of accurate and reliable information concerning the economic impact of mass immigration upon the United States. Few question the political legitimacy of maintaining a policy of legal immigration; the only question concerns the appropriate levels of legal immigration the United States should have, and the criteria which should govern the admission of aliens to this nation.

However, unlike legal immigration, illegal immigration is a very simple issue: It represents an abuse of federal immigration law, and a subversion of America's sovereign right to control its own borders and determine the criteria which should govern the admission of aliens to the United States. Virtually every public official, spanning the political spectrum from far Left to far Right, opposes illegal immigration, and supports measures to deter it. That consensus against illegal immigration has prevailed since 1977, when Carter first recommended the imposition of an employer-sanctions regime to deprive undocumented individuals of jobs as the primary means to stem the flow of illegal immigration to the United States.

Given the overwhelming consensus against illegal immigration, Reagan should have been expected to recommend the imposition of a credible and effective employer-sanctions regime, which would stem the flow of illegal immigration to the United States. Reagan failed to do so. Reagan's failure was due to his exaggerated fear of big government.

To be sure, Reagan was not alone in his opposition to a fraud-resistant worker verification system based upon the use of the Social Security card. The libertarian community, spanning the political spectrum from far Left to far Right, shares Reagan's hostility to such a system.[6] Undoubtedly, Congress would have been disinclined to establish such a system. Indeed, as we saw in Chapter 4, Congress failed to act upon the CIR's recommendations calling for the establishment of such a system in 1996 when its members passed the IIRIRA.

However, as president, Reagan had the unique responsibility to assure that federal immigration law is enforced, and that the United States retain its sovereign right to control its borders and determine the legal criteria on which aliens are allowed to immigrate to the United States. The Reagan administration fully recognized its responisibility in this regard. The administration cited the flood of illegal immigration existing since 1965 as evidence that the nation had lost control of its borders. From 1981, when the administration announced its immigration policy, until the passage of IRCA in 1986, the White House continued to urge the enactment of legislation which would enable the United States to regain control of its borders.

By failing to impose effective measures to stem the flow of illegal immigration, Reagan abrogated his responsibility to assure enforcement of federal immigration law, a responsibility that he fully recognized. That failure cannot be blamed on Congress, or opponents of employer sanctions, but on Reagan himself, whose own exaggerated fears of big government prevented him from recommending the establishment of a fraud-resistant worker verification system, which would make employer sanctions enforceable. While Reagan cannot be blamed for his failure to recommend much-needed reforms in legal immigration, he must be assigned responsibility for his failure to make the employer-sanctions provisions of IRCA workable and effective.

IMMIGRATION POLICY AND THE NATIONAL INTEREST

Given Reagan's failure to develop and implement a credible and effective immigration policy, one would be tempted to render a negative judgment on the president's handling of the issue of immigration. However, such a judgment would not be completely warranted. As we have argued, Reagan cannot be responsible for his failure to recommend much-needed reforms in legal immigration, given the lack of information available to him on this issue.

At best, Reagan can only be held responsible for his failure to recommend the establishment of a credible and effective employer-sanctions regime. In fairness to Reagan, however, the president still deserves credit for having supported employer sanctions in the first place. Whatever their shortcomings, the employer-sanctions provisions of IRCA can still be made effective by a future Congress through the imposition of a fraud-resistant worker verification system. At the very least, Reagan must be given credit for having built the foundation of a potentially effective policy to deter further illegal immigration through his support for employer sanctions.

However, given the shortcomings of IRCA, Reagan made no tangible and lasting contribution to the development of immigration policy: The bill failed to effectively address the issues of either legal or illegal immigration, which is why Congress has had to revisit the issue of immigration twice since Reagan left office, resulting in passage of the Immigration Act of 1990 and the IIRIRA. However, Reagan did make one important contribution in terms of setting a precedent for how immigration should be handled by future presidents. Congress has routinely addressed immigration in terms of satisfying the demands of various special-interest groups with a stake in maintaining the status quo on this issue, which is why lawmakers have made no fundamental reforms in immigration policy since it emerged as a major issue on the national agenda with the establishment of SCIRP in 1978.

In contrast to Congress, Reagan was determined to address the issue of immigration in terms of what is good for the national interest. Unlike members of

Congress, who serve rather narrow constituencies, the president is the only elected public official, with real constitutional authority, who is chosen by the entire nation. Accordingly, the president has a unique responsibility to address issues in terms of what is good for the national interest. Reagan took this responsibility seriously in terms of addressing the issue of immigration. No evidence of any kind exists among the voluminous documents on the Reagan administration's immigration policy to suggest that the administration was guided by anything other than its commitment to addressing this issue in terms of serving the national interest. There is no evidence that interest groups on opposing sides of this issue had any influence in the administration's conduct of immigration policy; and interest-group pressures over the White House on this issue, such as they were, were relatively weak anyway.

Reagan's conduct of immigration policy stands in sharp contrast to that of Clinton. As we saw in Chapter 1, the evidence clearly suggests that Clinton's immigration policy was driven by special-interest pressures; more specifically, the need to solicit substantial campaign contributions to assure his reelection to a second term in 1996. It is inconceivable that Reagan would have succumbed to special-interest pressures the way Clinton apparently did in his conduct of immigration policy; and the record clearly shows that the Reagan administration's immigration policy was in no way influenced by interest-group politics. To be sure, immigrants were more numerous and better organized to influence immigration policy during the 1990s than was the case during the previous decade. However, the Reagan administration's consideration of the issue of immigration was completely governed by national interest considerations, which left the White House immune to special-interest pressures, regardless of how heavy they may have been.

To be sure, Reagan made dishonest, deceitful, and misleading statements to the public on the issue of employer sanctions, as we have seen. Moreover, additional dishonest, deceitful, and misleading statements on employer sanctions were made by the two attorneys general who served in office during the five-year effort to pass immigration reform legislation on Capitol Hill—William French Smith and Edwin Meese III. On the whole, the Reagan administration engaged in a deliberate, conscious strategy of lying and deceit in order to manipulate Congress into passing the employer-sanctions provisions of IRCA.

Nevertheless, despite the dishonesty and deceit which the Reagan administration engaged in on the issue of employer sanctions, it pales in comparison to the corruption Clinton apparently undertook in allowing his immigration policy to be governed by campaign contributions from the Asian-American community. Indeed, whatever dishonest, deceitful, and misleading statements the Reagan administration made to Congress on immigration policy, the fact remains that no evidence exists that the president's handling of the issue of immigration was in any way influenced by interest group politics. The fact that the administration's conduct of immigration policy was immune from special-interest pressures is itself a monumental achievement.

As Vernon M. Briggs notes, in a sentence which was quoted at the beginning of Chapter 2, "Immigration . . . is an area of public policy captured by special-interest groups." This has indeed been the case with Congress, as it was with the Clinton administration. This was not the case with the Reagan administration. Whatever his failings as a policymaker, Reagan never succumbed to the corrupt intent, which Clinton apparently did, in his conduct of immigration policy. Reagan always put the interests of the nation, rather than those of the organized constituencies with an interest in immigration, first in his consideration of this issue.

A FINAL WORD ON THE REAGAN PRESIDENCY AND THE ISSUE OF IMMIGRATION

Martin Anderson, who served as Assistant to the President for Policy Development during 1981 to 1982, and is currently a senior fellow at the Hoover Institution, has argued that "Today, looking back over Ronald Reagan's Presidency, there is no correlation between what he accomplished and much of the current conventional wisdom about him. One hundred years from now, however, after the political dust of the twentieth century has settled, the historians of that time will write that Ronald Reagan was one of our greatest Presidents."[7]

Whether Anderson's lofty claims concerning the Reagan presidency prove to be true remains to be seen. This book, limited as it is to the narrow, but important, issue of immigration, can reach no definitive judgment on the Reagan presidency. However, this book can conclude that in an area of public policy which is so permeated with special-interest politics—immigration—Reagan conducted himself with a relatively high degree of honesty and integrity, qualities which Clinton has not shown. In contrast to Clinton, who apparently fell captive to special interests, Reagan placed the national interest first in his conduct of immigration policy.

To be sure, Reagan deceived and misled the public when he assured them that the employer-sanctions provisions of IRCA would work; and he created extraordinarily high expectations for the bill, which he knew that it could not possibly fulfill. However, it is one thing to deceive the public, as Reagan did; it is another to corrupt the policymaking process on an issue as important as immigration, as Clinton apparently did. While Reagan engaged in deceit and misrepresentation to assure the passage of IRCA, he never lost sight of the fact that immigration policy must serve the national interest. In a word, Reagan never sacrificed the national interest on immigration in order to cultivate favor with the dense network of special interests which have a stake in this issue. Accordingly, whatever dishonesty and deceit Reagan engaged in, he still, on balance, demonstrated a relatively high degree of honesty and integrity on this issue, especially when compared to Clinton.

Honesty and integrity are minimum, but not sufficient conditions, to qualify a president for greatness. It is virtually impossible that scoundrels like Richard

Nixon, and possibly even Bill Clinton, will ever be considered great presidents; however qualified Nixon, Clinton, and other scoundrels who have resided in the White House may have been as policymakers and leaders, they lacked the honesty and integrity which are indispensible qualities for greatness. However, to be great, a president must combine honesty and integrity with skills as a leader and policymaker. Despite the dishonest, deceitful, and misleading statements which he and his attorneys general made on IRCA, Reagan still showed a relatively high degree of honesty and integrity in his conduct of immigration policy, but he failed to provide leadership or to demonstrate skills as a policymaker on this issue.

If Reagan is ever to be considered a great president, historians will have to find issues other than immigration, where he combined his reputation for honesty and integrity with his skills as a leader and policymaker. Anderson argues that Reagan "will be remembered for three great things: ending the Cold War with the Soviet Union, and along with it, the threat of global nuclear war; defeating Marxism/Communism; and presiding over one of the greatest economic expansions in history."[8] Anderson and other academic admirers of Reagan may look to issues, pertaining to Soviet–American relations and economic policy, where the president may very well have combined the requisite qualities to qualify him for greatness. However, such greatness cannot be found in immigration policy. Reagan made too many errors in judgment and provided, at best, only minimally acceptable leadership, to demonstrate even a glimmer of greatness in his conduct of immigration policy.

Reagan's conduct of immigration policy shows him to have had a relatively high degree of honesty and integrity, but to have been a relatively weak, disengaged, and detached leader, and an uninformed and disinterested policymaker. Reagan entered the White House disinterested in the issue of immigration. While presidents cannot be interested in every conceivable issue on the national agenda, immigration is obviously an extremely important issue, which has enormous consequences for the United States—politically, economically, fiscally, socially, culturally, demographically, and environmentally. For Reagan to have been disinterested in an issue like immigration, which has enormous consequences for the United States, is evidence enough of his general disinterest in public policy.[9]

Reagan never placed immigration reform as a top priority on the national agenda; rather, the issue was put there by his predecessor, Jimmy Carter, through the thirty-ninth president's own recommendations on immigration reform, which resulted in the establishment of SCIRP in 1978. It was SCIRP's issuance of its final report in 1981, containing its recommendations on immigration reform, that finally forced Reagan to grapple with this issue. However, rather than making recommendations on immigration reform on his own, Reagan delegated this responsibility to members of his administration, especially those who served in the Cabinet, through his establishment of the President's Task Force on Immigration and Refugee Policy.

However, the President's Task Force on Immigration and Refugee Policy was unable to agree on final recommendations on the major issues which pertained to immigration reform, forcing Reagan to take this responsibility himself with the assistance of his Cabinet. And, as this book has argued, the final recommendations on immigration reform, which the Reagan administration finally made, were, at best, inadequate, and at worst, a disastrous failure. The only good thing which can be said about Reagan on the issue of immigration is that he never succumbed to the special-interest pressures on this issue, unlike Clinton, who apparently did; rather, however failed his immigration policy may have been, the fortieth president genuinely attempted to address this issue in a manner consistent with the national interest.

Greatness will only come to the Reagan presidency when historians can find issues where he combined his reputation for honesty and integrity with skills as a leader and policymaker. Only when Reagan can be found to have collectively demonstrated those qualities on issues of fundamental importance to the United States will he be able to lay a legitimate claim to greatness. Uncovering those qualities remains the great unfulfilled task, which Anderson and other academic admirers of Reagan must successfully complete, before their claims concerning Reagan's alleged greatness can be taken seriously, let alone fully accepted.

Notes

PREFACE

1. For an informative analysis of the pivotal role the economy and defense played as issues which determined the outcome of the 1980 presidential election and shaped the domestic policy agenda of the Reagan administration during its first months in office, see John W. Sloan, *The Reagan Effect: Economics and Presidential Leadership* (Lawrence: University Press of Kansas, 1999).

2. For a thorough and comprehensive history of immigration to the United States, from the founding of the American republic to the present, see Vernon M. Briggs, Jr., *Mass Immigration and the National Interest* (Armonk, N.Y.: M. E. Sharpe, 1996).

3. For a perceptive examination of Congress's strong support for the high levels of legal immigration experienced since 1965, and its equally strong opposition to illegal immigration and backing for measures to deter further illegal immigration to the United States, see Kenneth K. Lee, *Huddled Masses, Muddled Laws: Why Contemporary Immigration Policy Fails to Reflect Public Opinion* (Westport, Conn.: Praeger Publishers, 1998).

4. For the text of Carter's recommendations to Congress to address the problem of illegal immigration, see Jimmy Carter, *Public Papers of the Presidents of the United States 1977* (Washington, D.C.: U.S. Government Printing Office, 1978), pp. 1415–21.

5. For an insightful assessment of the politics of immigration reform since 1981, based upon interviews with the chairmen of the Senate and House immigration subcommittees in the 104th Congress—Alan K. Simpson of Wyoming and Lamar Smith of Texas—as well as key lobbyists on opposing sides of the immigration debate, see Lee, *Huddled Masses, Muddled Laws*.

CHAPTER 1

1. Peter H. Schuck, *Citizens, Strangers, and In-Betweens: Essays on Immigration and Citizenship* (Boulder, Colo.: Westview Press, 1998), p. 93.

2. For an insightful analysis of the mounting problems in immigration policy, which the Immigration Act of 1965 provoked, see Vernon M. Briggs, Jr., *Mass Immigration and the National Interest* (Armonk, N.Y.: M. E. Sharpe, 1996).

3. Ibid., p. 158.

4. The sixteen members of SCIRP included the following individuals: Reverend Theodore Hesburgh, president of the University of Notre Dame, who served as chairman of the commission; Attorney General Benjamin Civiletti; Secretary of Health and Human Services Patricia Roberts Harris; Secretary of Labor F. Ray Marshall; Secretary of State Edmund S. Muskie; Senators Dennis DeConcini of Arizona, Edward M. Kennedy of Massachusetts, Charles Mathias of Maryland, and Alan K. Simpson of Wyoming; Representatives Hamilton Fish and Elizabeth Holtzman of New York, Robert McClory of Illinois, and Peter Rodino, Jr., of New Jersey; Rose Ochi of the Office of the Mayor of Los Angeles; Joaquin Otero, vice president of the Brotherhood of Railway and Airline Clerks; and Associate Justice Jose Cruz Reynoso of the Court of Appeals of California.

5. Select Commission on Immigration and Refugee Policy, "Newsletter," January 1981, Francis S. M. Hodsoll Files, Ronald Reagan Presidential Library.

6. The Immigration Act of 1965 created the framework which governed legal immigration to the United States until passage of the Immigration Act of 1990. The Immigration Act of 1990 retained the four preference categories, which govern family-based immigration, established under the Immigration Act of 1965. The Immigration Act of 1990 also eliminated the preference categories for employment-based immigrants established under the Immigration Act of 1965. Instead, the Immigration Act of 1990 established five new preference categories for independent immigrants: workers of exceptional ability; professional workers with advanced degrees; skilled, professional, and unskilled workers; special immigrants; investors. A sixth preference category was created for aliens born in foreign nations, which supplied less than 50,000 legal immigrants, to the United States during the previous five years.

7. Briggs, *Mass Immigration and the National Interest*, p. 115.

8. Select Commission on Immigration and Refugee Policy, "Newsletter."

9. Briggs, *Mass Immigration and the National Interest*, p. 115.

10. Ibid., p. 111.

11. Ibid., p. 119.

12. Select Commission on Immigration and Refugee Policy, "Newsletter."

13. Briggs, *Mass Immigration and the National Interest*, Appendix B.

14. Select Commission on Immigration and Refugee Policy, "Newsletter."

15. Briggs, *Mass Immigration and the National Interest*, Appendix B.

16. Select Commission on Immigration and Refugee Policy, "Newsletter."

17. Kevin F. McCarthy and Georges F. Vernez, *Immigration in a Changing Economy: California's Experience* (Santa Monica, Calif.: The RAND Corporation, 1997), p. 23.

18. Briggs, *Mass Immigration and the National Interest*, p. 157.

19. Ibid., p. 155.

20. Select Commission on Immigration and Refugee Policy, "Newsletter."

21. Michael Fix and Jeffrey S. Passel, *Immigration and Immigrants: Setting the Record Straight* (Washington, D.C.: The Urban Institute, 1994), p. 23.

22. Select Commission on Immigration and Refugee Policy, "Newsletter."

23. Memorandum from Ronald Reagan to the Attorney General; the Secretaries of State, Defense, Education, Labor, Health and Human Services, Transportation, and the Treasury; the Directors of the Office of Management and Budget and the Federal Emer-

gency Management Agency; and the Deputy Assistant to the President, March 6, 1981, Francis S. M. Hodsoll Files, Ronald Reagan Presidential Library.

24. For a list of studies confirming the economic benefits of mass immigration to the United States by experts on the economics of immigration published during the 1980s and early 1990s, see Fix and Passel, *Immigration and Immigrants*, pp. 52–54.

25. For a presentation of the empirical evidence which documents the transition of the United States from an economy based upon the production of goods to one dependent upon the dissemination of information, see Briggs, *Mass Immigration and the National Interest*, pp. 190–99.

26. Stephen Moore, *A Fiscal Portrait of the Newest Americans* (Washington, D.C.: National Immigration Forum and Cato Institute, 1998), p. 6.

27. Ibid., p. 21.

28. Ibid., p. 7.

29. George J. Borjas, "Know the Flow," in Nicholas Capaldi, ed., *Immigration: Debating the Issues* (Amherst, Mass.: Prometheus Books, 1997), p. 189.

30. Fix and Passel, *Immigration and Immigrants*, p. 26.

31. Briggs, *Mass Immigration and the National Interest*, p. 67.

32. Ibid., pp. 63–64.

33. Ibid., pp. 106–7.

34. Peter Brimelow, *Alien Nation: Common Sense About America's Immigration Disaster* (New York: HarperPerennial, 1996), Appendix 1 (B).

35. Ibid., Appendix 2.

36. McCarthy and Vernez, *Immigration in a Changing Economy*, pp. 89–90.

37. For a citation of studies published during the 1980s finding that immigrants are less prone to use welfare benefits than native-born Americans, see George J. Borjas, "Immigration and Welfare: A Review of the Evidence," in Peter Duignan and Lewis H. Gann, eds., *The Debate in the United States over Immigration* (Stanford, Calif.: Hoover Institution Press, 1998), p. 121.

38. Borjas, "Immigration and Welfare," p. 124.

39. Ibid., p. 133.

40. Ibid., p. 139.

41. Georges Vernez and Kevin F. McCarthy, *The Costs of Immigration to Taxpayers: Analytical and Policy Issues* (Santa Monica, Calif.: The RAND Corporation, 1996), pp. xii–xiii.

42. For an analysis of the impact that Chiswick's influential 1978 study has had on the debate among the experts concerning the economic consequences of mass immigration in the United States during the 1980s and 1990s, see Robert F. Schoeni, Kevin F. McCarthy, and Georges Vernez, *The Mixed Economic Progress of Immigrants* (Santa Monica, Calif.: The RAND Corporation, 1997), pp. 3–5.

43. The Immigration Act of 1990 slightly reduced the share of visas reserved for family-based immigrants, while modestly increasing the share earmarked for employment-based immigrants. The bill reserves 71 percent of all visas for family-based immigrants, and 21 percent for employment-based immigrants. As a result, the Immigration Act of 1990 preserved the central element of the Immigration Act of 1965 in continuing to make family reunification the cornerstone of immigration policy.

44. Briggs, *Mass Immigration and the National Interest*, pp. 167–69.

45. Barry R. Chiswick, "Guidelines for the Reform of Immigration Policy," April 15, 1981, Francis S. M. Hodsoll Files, Ronald Reagan Presidential Library.

46. Barry R. Chiswick to Ronald Reagan, April 27, 1981, Francis S. M. Hodsoll Files, Ronald Reagan Presidential Library.

47. Briggs, *Mass Immigration and the National Interest*, p. 229.

48. Barry R. Chiswick to Ronald Reagan, April 27, 1981.

49. Briggs, *Mass Immigration and the National Interest*, pp. 197, 253.

50. Fix and Passel, *Immigration and Immigrants*, p. 33.

51. Moore, *A Fiscal Portrait of the Newest Americans*, p. 10.

52. Briggs, *Mass Immigration and the National Interest*, pp. 224–25.

53. Ibid., pp. 115–16.

54. Ibid., pp. 250, 253.

55. Ibid., p. 198.

56. Ibid., p. 223.

57. Fix and Passel, *Immigration and Immigrants*, p. 21.

58. Schuck, *Citizens, Strangers, and In-Betweens*, p. 164.

59. McCarthy and Vernez, *Immigration in a Changing Economy*, pp. 114–15.

60. Jeffrey S. Passel and Rebecca L. Clark, *Immigrants in New York: Their Legal Status, Income, and Taxes* (Washington, D.C.: The Urban Institute, 1998), p. 79.

61. Kenneth K. Lee, *Huddled Masses, Muddled Laws: Why Contemporary Immigration Policy Fails to Reflect Public Opinion* (Westport, Conn.: Praeger Publishers, 1998), p. 92.

62. Congressional Quarterly Almanac, 97th Congress, 2nd Session (Washington, D.C.: Congressional Quarterly, 1983), p. 407; Congressional Quarterly Almanac, 98th Congress, 1st Session (Washington, D.C.: Congressional Quarterly, 1984), p. 291.

63. Congressional Quarterly Almanac, 98th Congress, 1st Session, p. 291.

64. Congressional Quarterly Almanac, 98th Congress, 2nd Session (Washington, D.C.: Congressional Quarterly, 1985), p. 68-H.

65. "Testimony of Vilma S. Martinez Before the Joint Committee on Immigration Policy," May 6, 1981, Francis S. M. Hodsoll Files, Ronald Reagan Presidential Library.

66. Peter Skerry, *Mexican Americans: The Ambivalent Minority* (Cambridge, Mass.: Harvard University Press, 1993), p. 325.

67. "Mexican Immigration Policy Opportunities," July 9, 1986, Jan W. Mares Files, Ronald Reagan Presidential Library.

68. Briggs, *Mass Immigration and the National Interest*, p. 240.

69. Ibid., p. 242.

70. Ibid., p. 169.

71. For a study published by the Urban Institute defending the open and liberal immigration policy pursued since 1965, see Fix and Passel, *Immigration and Immigrants*. For a study published by the Cato Institute which provides its own defense of current immigration policy, see Moore, *A Fiscal Portrait of the Newest Americans*.

72. In 1997, RAND published a highly influential study cited earlier, entitled "Immigration in a Changing Economy," which documented the negative economic consequences of mass immigration upon the United States. Unlike the Urban and Cato Institutes, RAND is an objective think tank, not tied to any ideological persuasion, which bases its conclusions on the empirical evidence rather than philosphical leanings of its scholars.

73. Congressional Quarterly Almanac, 104th Congress, First Session (Washington, D.C.: Congressional Quarterly, 1996), pp. 6-12–6-13, 6-16.

74. Lee, *Huddled Masses, Muddled Laws*, p. 113.

75. Briggs, *Mass Immigration and the National Interest*, p. 227.

76. Lee, *Huddled Masses, Muddled Laws*, p. 113.

CHAPTER 2

1. Vernon M. Briggs, Jr., *Mass Immigration and the National Interest* (Armonk, N.Y.: M.E. Sharpe, 1996), p. 10.

2. For a study which argues that mass immigration has had a positive economic, fiscal, and environmental impact upon the United States, by a leading academic supporter of mass immigration, see Julian L. Simon, *Immigration: The Demographic and Economic Facts* (Washington, D.C.: Cato Institute and National Immigration Forum, 1995). For a highly influential study which argues that mass immigration has had negative economic, fiscal, political, cultural, and environmental consequences for the United States, see Peter Brimelow, *Alien Nation: Common Sense About America's Immigration Disaster* (New York: HarperPerennial, 1996).

3. Romano L. Mazzoli to Francis S. M. Hodsoll, March 10, 1981, Francis S. M. Hodsoll Files, Ronald Reagan Presidential Library.

4. Richard W. Day to Francis S. M. Hodsoll, March 16, 1981, Francis S. M. Hodsoll Files, Ronald Reagan Presidential Library.

5. "Statement of Commissioner Alan K. Simpson," Francis S. M. Hodsoll Files, Ronald Reagan Presidential Library.

6. Brimelow, *Alien Nation*, p. 46.

7. Roy Beck, *The Case Against Immigration: The Moral, Economic, Social, and Environmental Reasons for Reducing Immigration Back to Traditional Levels* (New York: W. W. Norton, 1996), p. 32.

8. "Statement of Commissioner Alan K. Simpson," Francis S. M. Hodsoll Files, Ronald Reagan Presidential Library.

9. Kevin F. McCarthy and Georges F. Vernez, *Immigration in a Changing Economy: California's Experience* (Santa Monica, Calif.: The RAND Corporation, 1997), p. 13.

10. Ibid., p. 217.

11. Michael Fix and Jeffrey S. Passel, *Immigration and Immigrants: Setting the Record Straight* (Washington, D.C.: The Urban Institute, 1994), p. 49.

12. For a compilation of articles written by immigration restrictionists, which argue that mass immigration results in substantial job displacement of American workers, see *Immigration 2000: The Century of the New American Sweatshop* (Washington, D.C.: Federation for American Immigration Reform, 1992), pp. 45–68.

13. "Statement of Commissioner Alan K. Simpson," Francis S. M. Hodsoll Files, Ronald Reagan Presidential Library.

14. Peter H. Schuck, *Citizens, Strangers, and In-Betweens: Essays on Immigration and Citizenship* (Boulder, Colo.: Westview Press, 1998), p. 331.

15. "Statement of Commissioner Alan K. Simpson," Francis S. M. Hodsoll Files, Ronald Reagan Presidential Library.

16. Memorandum from Francis S. M. Hodsoll to Max Friedersdorf, March 23, 1981, Francis S. M. Hodsoll Files, Ronald Reagan Presidential Library.

17. Jeffrey S. Passel and Rebecca L. Clark, *Immigrants in New York: Their Legal Status, Incomes, and Taxes* (Washington, D.C.: The Urban Institute, 1998), p. 79.

18. Brimelow, *Alien Nation*, Appendix 2.

19. Passel and Clark, *Immigrants in New York*, p. 81.

20. McCarthy and Vernez, *Immigration in a Changing Economy*, p. 291.

21. Memorandum from Francis S. M. Hodsoll to Max Friedersdorf, March 23, 1981, Francis S. M. Hodsoll Files, Ronald Reagan Presidential Library.

22. Memorandum from Max Friedersdorf to Ronald Reagan, May 29, 1981, Francis S. M. Hodsoll Files, Ronald Reagan Presidential Library.

23. "Suggested Talking Points for Meeting with Senator Alan Simpson (R-Wyoming)," Francis S. M. Hodsoll Files, Ronald Reagan Presidential Library.

24. Schuck, *Citizens, Strangers, and In-Betweens*, pp. 105–6.

25. Ibid., p. 97.

26. Federation for American Immigration Reform, "What Is the Federation for American Immigration Reform?" Brochure.

27. Federation for American Immigration Reform, "Are You Concerned About Immigration? You Should Be." Fact sheet.

28. Roger Conner to Francis S. M. Hodsoll, April 8, 1981, Francis S. M. Hodsoll Files, Ronald Reagan Presidential Library.

29. Federation for American Information Reform Fact Sheet, "Public Opinion on Immigration," February 1981, Francis S. M. Hodsoll Files, Ronald Reagan Presidential Library.

30. Federation for American Information Reform, "The FAIR Way," Francis S. M. Hodsoll Files, Ronald Reagan Presidential Library.

31. Brimelow, *Alien Nation*, p. 54.

32. Briggs, *Mass Immigration and the National Interest*, p. 5.

33. Brimelow, *Alien Nation*, p. 54.

34. Ibid., p. 163.

35. Francis S. M. Hodsoll to Roger Conner, April 27, 1981, Francis S. M. Hodsoll Files, Ronald Reagan Presidential Library.

36. Schuck, *Citizens, Strangers, and In-Betweens*, p. 394.

37. Robert H. McBride and David D. Gregory to Martin Anderson, March 30, 1981, Francis S. M. Hodsoll Files, Ronald Reagan Presidential Library.

38. Walter D. Huddleston and Alan K. Simpson to Ronald Reagan, July 8, 1981, Francis S. M. Hodsoll Files, Ronald Reagan Presidential Library.

39. Robin Beard to Ronald Reagan, June 17, 1981, Francis S. M. Hodsoll Files, Ronald Reagan Presidential Library.

40. Ibid., pp. 36–37.

41. For an inside account of Swartz's lobbying activities during the 1990s, based upon an interview conducted with him, see Kenneth K. Lee, *Huddled Masses, Muddled Laws: Why Contemporary Immigration Policy Fails to Reflect Public Opinion* (Westport, Conn.: Praeger Publishers, 1998), pp. 103–13.

42. Rick Swartz, "Shortcomings of Select Commission on Immigration and Refugee Policy's Recommendations on Enforcement Options," Francis S. M. Hodsoll Files, Ronald Reagan Presidential Library.

43. Rick Swartz, "Cost-Benefit Analysis of Methods for Preventing Employment and Illegal Immigration of Undocumented Aliens," Francis S. M. Hodsoll Files, Ronald Reagan Presidential Library.

44. Juan F. Perea, "Introduction," in Juan F. Perea, ed., *Immigrants Out! The New Nativism and the Anti-Immigrant Impulse in the United States* (New York: New York University Press, 1997), pp. 2–3.

Notes

227

45. Ibid., p. 3.

46. Rick Swartz, "Cost-Benefit Analysis of Methods for Preventing Employment and Illegal Immigration of Undocumented Aliens," Francis S. M. Hodsoll Files, Ronald Reagan Presidential Library.

47. For a well-developed argument against the establishment of a worker verification system, based upon use of the Social Security card as a secure and reliable means of individual identification, by two prominent members of the pro-immigration lobby, see John J. Miller and Stephen Moore, "A National ID System: Big Brother's Solution to Illegal Immigration," Cato Institute Policy Analysis No. 237, September 7, 1995.

48. Passel and Clark, *Immigrants in New York*, p. 81.

49. Perea, "Introduction," p. 2.

50. "Testimony of Vilma S. Martinez Before the Joint Committee on Immigration Policy," May 6, 1981, Francis S. M. Hodsoll Files, Ronald Reagan Presidential Library.

51. Ibid.

52. Briggs, *Mass Immigration and the National Interest*, p. 111.

53. Ibid., p. 115.

54. The Immigration Act of 1990 raised the annual ceiling on the number of legal immigrants admitted to the United States from any single foreign nation from 20,000, the level established under the Immigration Act of 1965, to 29,470.

55. "Testimony of Vilma S. Martinez Before the Joint Committee on Immigration Policy," May 6, 1981, Francis S. M. Hodsoll Files, Ronald Reagan Presidential Library.

56. Briggs, *Mass Immigration and the National Interest*, p. 157.

57. The term bracero means one who works with his hands. The term is a variation of the Spanish word brazos, which means arms.

58. Kitty Calavita, "Why Revive an Inhumane Program?" *Los Angeles Times*, July 18, 1999, p. M2.

59. Briggs, *Mass Immigration and the National Interest*, pp. 90–91.

60. Ibid., pp. 178–80.

61. Ronald Reagan, *Public Papers of the Presidents of the United States 1981* (Washington, D.C.: U.S. Government Printing Office, 1982), pp. 201–2.

62. Members of the National Committee for Full Employment included Balfour Brickner of the Union of American Hebrew Congregations; Douglas Fraser, president of the United Auto Workers; Benjamin Hooks, executive director of the National Association for the Advancement of Colored People; Vernon Jordan, president of the National Urban League; Lane Kirkland, president of the American Federation of Labor–Congress of Industrial Organizations; Francis Lally, of the United States Catholic Conference; Lloyd McBride, president of the United Steel Workers of America; Claire Randall, general secretary of the National Council of Churches; Eleanor Smeal, president of the National Organization of Women; and Raul Yzaguirre, director of the National Council of La Raza.

63. "Statement of the Task Force on Undocumented Workers of the National Committee for Full Employment," Francis S. M. Hodsoll Files, Ronald Reagan Presidential Library.

64. David S. North to Francis S. M. Hodsoll, March 20, 1981, Francis S. M. Hodsoll Files, Ronald Reagan Presidential Library.

65. Francis S. M. Hodsoll to David S. North, March 31, 1981, Francis S. M. Hodsoll Files, Ronald Reagan Presidential Library.

66. "Testimony of Vilma S. Martinez Before the Joint Committee on Immigration Policy," May 6, 1981, Francis S. M. Hodsoll Files, Ronald Reagan Presidential Library.

67. Vilma S. Martinez to Edwin Meese III, May 1, 1981, Francis S. M. Hodsoll Files, Ronald Reagan Presidential Library.

68. Memorandum from Francis S. M. Hodsoll to Martin Anderson, May 18, 1981, Francis S. M. Hodsoll Files, Ronald Reagan Presidential Library.

69. Memorandum from George Bush to William French Smith, June 22, 1981, Francis S. M. Hodsoll Files, Ronald Reagan Presidential Library.

70. Susan Gonzalez Baker, *The Cautious Welcome: The Legalization Programs of the Immigration Reform and Control Act* (Washington, D.C. and Santa Monica, Calif.: The Urban Institute and The RAND Corporation, 1990), p. 41.

71. "Foreign Worker Issue Paper for the President's Meeting with GOM President Lopez Portillo, April 26–28, 1981," March 30, 1981, Francis S. M. Hodsoll Files, Ronald Reagan Presidential Library.

72. Memorandum from Marion F. Houstoun to David Hiller, March 30, 1981, Francis S. M. Hodsoll Files, Ronald Reagan Presidential Library.

73. Memorandum from Kate Moore to Francis S. M. Hodsoll, May 6, 1981, Francis S. M. Hodsoll Files, Ronald Reagan Presidential Library.

74. "Questions/Comments from Mexicans," Francis S. M. Hodsoll Files, Ronald Reagan Presidential Library.

75. Memorandum from Kate Moore to Francis S. M. Hodsoll, May 6, 1981, Francis S. M. Hodsoll Files, Ronald Reagan Presidential Library.

76. Vernon M. Briggs, Jr., "Foreign Labor Programs as an Alternative to Illegal Immigration into the United States: A Dissenting View," April 30, 1980, Francis S. M. Hodsoll Files, Ronald Reagan Presidential Library.

77. Robin Beard to Ronald Reagan, June 17, 1981, Francis S. M. Hodsoll Files, Ronald Reagan Presidential Library.

CHAPTER 3

1. Peter H. Schuck, *Citizens, Strangers, and In-Betweens: Essays on Immigration and Citizenship* (Boulder, Colo.: Westview Press, 1998), pp. 97–98.

2. Memorandum from Francis S. M. Hodsoll to James A. Baker III, April 30, 1981, Francis S. M. Hodsoll Files, Ronald Reagan Presidential Library.

3. Schuck, *Citizens, Strangers, and In-Betweens*, p. 179.

4. Jeffrey S. Passel and Barry Edmonston, *Immigration and Race: Recent Trends in Immigration to the United States* (Washington, D.C.: The Urban Institute, 1992), Table 3.

5. Peter Brimelow, *Alien Nation: Common Sense About America's Immigration Disaster* (New York: HarperPerennial, 1996), p. 63.

6. The Gallup Poll, "Majority Favors Law Against Hiring Illegal Aliens," November 30, 1980, Francis S. M. Hodsoll Files, Ronald Reagan Presidential Library.

7. Memorandum from Francis S. M. Hodsoll to James A. Baker III, April 30, 1981, Francis S. M. Hodsoll Files, Ronald Reagan Presidential Library.

8. Memorandum from Francis S. M. Hodsoll to Martin Anderson, May 4, 1981, Francis S. M. Hodsoll Files, Ronald Reagan Presidential Library.

9. "Notes on Trip to Mexico," Francis S. M. Hodsoll Files, Ronald Reagan Presidential Library.

10. Memorandum from James A. Baker III and Edwin Meese III to Ronald Reagan, June 3, 1981, Francis S. M. Hodsoll Files, Ronald Reagan Presidential Library.

11. Kevin F. McCarthy and Georges F. Vernez, *Immigration in a Changing Economy: California's Experience* (Santa Monica, Calif.: The RAND Corporation, 1997), p. 291.

12. Memorandum from James A. Baker III and Edwin Meese III to Ronald Reagan, June 3, 1981, Francis S. M. Hodsoll Files, Ronald Reagan Presidential Library.

13. Michael Fix and Jeffrey S. Passel, *Immigration and Immigrants: Setting the Record Straight* (Washington, D.C.: The Urban Institute, 1994), p. 23.

14. Schuck, *Citzens, Strangers, and In-Betweens*, p. 177.

15. Memorandum from James A. Baker III and Edwin Meese III to Ronald Reagan, June 3, 1981, Francis S. M. Hodsoll Files, Ronald Reagan Presidential Library.

16. Ibid.

17. "Talking Points on Immigration," Francis S. M. Hodsoll Files, Ronald Reagan Presidential Library.

18. Memorandum from James A. Baker III and Edwin Meese III to Ronald Reagan, June 3, 1981, Francis S. M. Hodsoll Files, Ronald Reagan Presidential Library.

19. Memorandum from Richard V. Allen to Francis S. M. Hodsoll, Francis S. M. Hodsoll Files, Ronald Reagan Presidential Library.

20. Memorandum from James A. Baker III and Edwin Meese III to Ronald Reagan, June 3, 1981, Francis S. M. Hodsoll Files, Ronald Reagan Presidential Library.

21. Memorandum from Richard V. Allen to Francis S. M. Hodsoll, Francis S. M. Hodsoll Files, Ronald Reagan Presidential Library.

22. Charles P. Smith, "Immigration Policy Opportunities," March 14, 1986, Jan W. Mares Files, Ronald Reagan Presidential Library.

23. Memorandum from Richard B. Wirthlin to Dick Richards, June 18, 1981, Francis S. M. Hodsoll Files, Ronald Reagan Presidential Library.

24. Memorandum from James A. Baker III and Edwin Meese III to Ronald Reagan, June 3, 1981, Francis S. M. Hodsoll Files, Ronald Reagan Presidential Library.

25. Memorandum from Richard B. Wirthlin to James A. Baker III, Edwin Meese III, and Michael Deaver, June 18, 1981, Francis S. M. Hodsoll Files, Ronald Reagan Presidential Library.

26. "Political Variables: National Identity Card," June 1981, Francis S. M. Hodsoll Files, Ronald Reagan Presidential Library.

27. The individuals which the Justice Department consulted on immigration policy included the chairmen of the Senate and House Judiciary Committees, Strom Thurmond of South Carolina and Peter Rodino of New Jersey, respectively; the chairmen of the Senate and House immigration subcommittees, Alan Simpson of Wyoming and Romano L. Mazzoli of Kentucky, respectively; Lane Kirkland, president of the American Federation of Labor–Congress of Industrial Organizations (AFL-CIO); Antonia Hernandez of the Mexican American Legal Defense and Education Fund (MALDEF); Rick Swartz of the Lawyers' Committee for Civil Rights Under Law; and Roger Conner, executive director of the Federation for American Immigration Reform (FAIR).

28. Memorandum from David D. Hiller to William French Smith, June 30, 1981, Francis S. M. Hodsoll Files, Ronald Reagan Presidential Library.

29. Ibid.

30. Memorandum from Francis S. M. Hodsoll to Ronald Reagan, July 1, 1981, Francis S. M. Hodsoll Files, Ronald Reagan Presidential Library.

31. "Report of the President's Task Force on Immigration and Refugee Policy," July 1, 1981, Francis S. M. Hodsoll Files, Ronald Reagan Presidential Library.

32. Department of Justice, "U.S. Immigration and Refugee Policy," July 30, 1981, Francis S. M. Hodsoll Files, Ronald Reagan Presidential Library.

33. Memorandum from James A. Baker III to Ronald Reagan, July 24, 1981, Francis S. M. Hodsoll Files, Ronald Reagan Presidential Library.

34. Department of Justice, "U.S. Immigration and Refugee Policy," July 30, 1981, Francis S. M. Hodsoll Files, Ronald Reagan Presidential Library.

35. Ibid.

36. Ronald Reagan, *Public Papers of the Presidents of the United States 1981* (Washington, D.C.: U.S. Government Printing Office, 1982), p. 676.

37. "Testimony of William French Smith, Attorney General, Before the Senate Subcommittee on Immigration and Refugee Policy and the House Subcommittee on Immigration, Refugees, and International Law," July 30, 1981, Francis S. M. Hodsoll Files, Ronald Reagan Presidential Library.

38. Ibid.

39. "Testimony of William French Smith, Attorney General, Before the Senate Subcommittee on Immigration and Refugee Policy and the House Subcommittee on Immigration, Refugees, and International Law," July 30, 1981, Francis S. M. Hodsoll Files, Ronald Reagan Presidential Library.

40. "Report of the President's Task Force on Immigration and Refugee Policy," July 1, 1981, Francis S. M. Hodsoll Files, Ronald Reagan Presidential Library.

41. "Report of the President's Task Force on Immigration and Refugee Policy," June 26, 1981, Francis S. M. Hodsoll Files, Ronald Reagan Presidential Library.

42. "Testimony of William French Smith, Attorney General, Before the Senate Subcommittee on Immigration and Refugee Policy and the House Subcommittee on Immigration, Refugees, and International Law," July 30, 1981, Francis S. M. Hodsoll Files, Ronald Reagan Presidential Library.

43. Ibid.

44. Peter Skerry, *Mexican Americans: The Ambivalent Minority* (Cambridge, Mass.: Harvard University Press, 1993), pp. 325–26.

45. Ibid., pp. 326–27.

46. The Senate passed the conference report on IRCA by a margin of sixty-three to twenty-four; the House did the same by a vote of 238 to 173. As a result, while well over two-thirds of all senators voting supported the conference report on IRCA, substantially less than two-thirds of House members did so. Accordingly, it is highly likely that any presidential veto of IRCA would have been sustained in the House, given the fact that substantially less than two-thirds of its members voted for the bill. To muster the two-thirds majority in the House necessary to override a presidential veto of IRCA, many House members who supported the bill would have had to reverse themselves and vote to sustain the veto. There is little likelihood that this would have occurred.

47. The divisions within the Latino community over IRCA were fully reflected in the vote on the conference report on the bill among the eleven members of the House Hispanic Caucus. Six members of the caucus voted against IRCA, and five voted for it. Members of the caucus opposing IRCA did so primarily because they objected to its employer-sanctions provisions; members supporting the measure did so primarily because they favored its amnesty provisions.

48. For a perceptive analysis of the political obstacles Congress confronted in its long, arduous, but ultimately successful effort to pass IRCA, see Schuck, *Citizens, Strangers, and In-Betweens*, pp. 103–15.

CHAPTER 4

1. Michael Fix, "Employer Sanctions: An Unfinished Agenda," in Michael Fix, ed., *The Paper Curtain: Employer Sanctions' Implementation, Impact, and Reform* (Washington, D.C. and Santa Monica, Calif.: The Urban Institute and The RAND Corporation, 1991), p. 2.

2. Michael Fix and Jeffrey S. Passel, *Immigration and Immigrants: Setting the Record Straight* (Washington, D.C.: The Urban Institute, 1994), p. 23.

3. Kenneth K. Lee, *Huddled Masses, Muddled Laws: Why Contemporary Immigration Policy Fails to Reflect Public Opinion* (Westport, Conn.: Praeger Publishers, 1998), p. 152.

4. Susan Gonzalez Baker, *The Cautious Welcome: The Legalization Programs of the Immigration Reform and Control Act* (Washington, D.C. and Santa Monica, Calif.: The Urban Institute and The RAND Corporation, 1990), p. 11.

5. Ibid., p. 90.

6. Barry Edmonston, Jeffrey S. Passel, and Frank D. Bean, "Perceptions and Estimates of Undocumented Migration to the United States," in Frank D. Bean, Barry Edmonston, and Jeffrey S. Passel, *Undocumented Migration to the United States: IRCA and the Experience of the 1980s* (Washington, D.C. and Santa Monica, Calif.: The Urban Institute Press and The RAND Corporation, 1990), p. 27.

7. Fix, "Employer Sanctions," p. 13.

8. Vernon M. Briggs, Jr., *Mass Immigration and the National Interest* (Armonk, N.Y.: M. E. Sharpe, 1996), p. 165.

9. Memorandum from Charles P. Smith to Charles D. Hobbs, October 20, 1986, Jan W. Mares Files, Ronald Reagan Presidential Library.

10. Michael Fix and Paul T. Hill, *Enforcing Employer Sanctions: Challenges and Strategies* (Washington, D.C. and Santa Monica, Calif.: The Urban Institute and The RAND Corporation, 1990), p. 32.

11. Memorandum from Charles P. Smith to Charles D. Hobbs, October 20, 1986, Jan W. Mares Files, Ronald Reagan Presidential Library.

12. Michael Fix, "IRCA-Related Discrimination: What Do We Know and What Should We Do?" in Michael Fix, ed., *The Paper Curtain: Employer Sanctions' Implementation, Impact, and Reform* (Washington, D.C. and Santa Monica, Calif.: The Urban Institute and The RAND Corporation, 1991), p. 274.

13. Fix and Hill, *Enforcing Employer Sanctions*, pp. 33–34.

14. Shirley J. Smith and Martina Shea, "Employer Compliance with IRCA Paperwork Requirements," in Fix, *The Paper Curtain*, p. 160.

15. Congressional Quarterly Almanac, 99th Congress, 2nd Session (Washington, D.C.: Congressional Quarterly, 1987), p. 61.

16. Briggs, *Mass Immigration and the National Interest*, p. 227.

17. Congressional Quarterly Almanac, 98th Congress, 2nd Session (Washington, D.C.: Congressional Quarterly, 1985), p. 231.

18. Edwin Meese III to Strom Thurmond, September 12, 1985, IM, WHORM: Subject File, Ronald Reagan Presidential Library.

19. "Statement of Administration Policy: S. 1200—The Immigration Reform and Control Act of 1985 (Simpson (R) Wyoming)," September 12, 1985, IM, WHORM: Subject File, Ronald Reagan Presidential Library.

20. Congressional Quarterly Almanac, 99th Congress, 1st Session (Washington, D.C.: Congressional Quarterly, 1986), p. 227.

21. Edwin Meese III to Strom Thurmond, September 12, 1985, IM, WHORM: Subject File, Ronald Reagan Presidential Library.

22. Congressional Quarterly Almanac, 99th Congress, 2nd Session, p. 118-H.

23. Ibid., pp. 118–19-H, 122–23-H.

24. Memorandum from Carol T. Crawford to Donald T. Regan, IM, WHORM: Subject File, Ronald Reagan Presidential Library.

25. "Comparison of Senate and House Immigration Reform Bills," IM, WHORM: Subject File, Ronald Reagan Presidential Library.

26. Statement of Administration Policy, "H.R. 3810—The Immigration Control and Legalization Amendments Act of 1986 (Rodino (D) New Jersey and Mazzoli (D) Kentucky)," October 9, 1986, IM, WHORM: Subject File, Ronald Reagan Presidential Library.

27. Statement of Administration Policy, "S. 1200—Immigration Reform (Simpson (R) Wyoming)," October 14, 1986, IM, WHORM: Subject File, Ronald Reagan Presidential Library.

28. Ronald Reagan, *Public Papers of the Presidents of the United States 1986* (Washington, D.C.: U.S. Government Printing Office, 1989), pp. 1522–23.

29. Fix, "Employer Sanctions," pp. 14–15.

30. Congressional Quarterly Almanac, 99th Congress, 2nd Session, p. 62.

31. Robert Bach and Doris Meissner, "Employment and Immigration Reform: Employer Sanctions Four Years Later," in Fix, *The Paper Curtain*, p. 281.

32. Congressional Quarterly Almanac, 99th Congress, 2nd Session, p. 62.

33. Michael Fix, "IRCA-Related Employment Discrimination: What Do We Know and What Should We Do?," in Fix, *The Paper Curtain*, p. 282.

34. Reagan, *Public Papers of the Presidents of the United States 1986*, p. 1522.

35. Ibid., p. 1523.

36. Terry Eastland, *Ending Affirmative Action: The Case for Colorblind Justice* (New York: Basic Books, 1996), pp. 53–54.

37. Reagan, *Public Papers of the Presidents of the United States 1986*, p. 1523.

38. Ronald Reagan, *Public Papers of the Presidents of the United States 1984* (Washington, D.C.: U.S. Government Printing Office, 1987), p. 1009.

39. Edwin Meese III to Strom Thurmond, September 12, 1985, IM, WHORM: Subject File, Ronald Reagan Presidential Library.

40. Robert Bach and Doris Meissner, "Employment and Immigration Reform: Employer Sanctions Four Years Later," in Fix, *The Paper Curtain*, p. 281.

41. Fix, "IRCA-Related Discrimination," p. 267.

42. Ibid., p. 271.

43. Ibid., p. 273.

44. Briggs, *Mass Immigration and the National Interest*, pp. 240–41.

45. John J. Miller and Stephen Moore, "A National ID System: Big Brother's Solution to Illegal Immigration," Cato Institute Policy Analysis No. 237, September 7, 1995, p. 16.

46. "Report of the President's Task Force on Immigration and Refugee Policy," July 1, 1981, Francis S. M. Hodsoll Files, Ronald Reagan Presidential Library.

47. "Report of the President's Task Force on Immigration and Refugee Policy," June 26, 1981, Francis S. M. Hodsoll Files, Ronald Reagan Presidential Library.

48. Ronald Reagan, *Public Papers of the Presidents of the United States 1981* (Washington, D.C.: U.S. Government Printing Office, 1982), p. 677.

49. Memorandum from James A. Baker III to Ronald Reagan, July 24, 1981, Francis S. M. Hodsoll Files, Ronald Reagan Presidential Library.

50. "Report of the President's Task Force on Immigration and Refugee Policy," June 26, 1981, Francis S. M. Hodsoll Files, Ronald Reagan Presidential Library.

51. "Report of the President's Task Force on Immigration and Refugee Policy," July 1, 1981, Francis S. M. Hodsoll Files, Ronald Reagan Presidential Library.

52. Memorandum from Robert Goldfarb and Thomas Lenard to Martin Anderson, June 28, 1981, Francis S. M. Hodsoll Files, Ronald Reagan Presidential Library.

53. Miller and Moore, "A National ID System," p. 15.

54. Memorandum from Robert Goldfarb and Thomas Lenard to Martin Anderson, June 28, 1981, Francis S. M. Hodsoll Files, Ronald Reagan Presidential Library.

55. Fix, "Employer Sanctions," p. 13.

56. "Report of the President's Task Force on Immigration and Refugee Policy," June 26, 1981, Francis S. M. Hodsoll Files, Ronald Reagan Presidential Library.

57. "Testimony of William French Smith, Attorney General, Before the Senate Subcommittee on Immigration and Refugee Policy and the House Subcommittee on Immigration, Refugees, and International Law," July 30, 1981, Francis S. M. Hodsoll Files, Ronald Reagan Presidential Library.

58. "Report of the President's Task Force on Immigration and Refugee Policy," July 1, 1981, Francis S. M. Hodsoll Files, Ronald Reagan Presidential Library.

59. Memorandum from James A. Baker III to Ronald Reagan, July 24, 1981, Francis S. M. Hodsoll Files, Ronald Reagan Presidential Library.

60. Miller and Moore, "A National ID System," p. 21.

61. Ibid., p. 15.

62. Kevin F. McCarthy and Georges F. Vernez, *Immigration in a Changing Economy: California's Experience* (Santa Monica, Calif.: The RAND Corporation, 1997), p. 23.

63. Executive Department, State of California, "Illegal Immigration—Federal Responsibility and Fairness to State and Local Governments."

64. Jeffrey S. Passel and Rebecca L. Clark, *Immigrants in New York: Their Legal Status, Incomes, and Taxes* (Washington, D.C.: The Urban Institute, 1998), p. 79.

65. Briggs, *Mass Immigration and the National Interest*, p. 245.

66. Executive Department, State of California, Executive Order W-113-94.

67. Miller and Moore, "A National ID System," p. 20.

68. The Personal Responsibility and Work Opportunity Reconciliation Act of 1996 makes illegal aliens ineligible for all federal and state entitlement programs, with the exception of K–12 public education, the school breakfast and lunch programs, emergency health care and disaster relief, immunizations and testing and treatment for communicable diseases, and community services, which the attorney general deems necessary for the protection of human life and public safety.

69. Peter H. Schuck, *Citizens, Strangers, and In-Betweens: Essays on Immigration and Citizenship* (Boulder, Colo.: Westview Press, 1998), pp. 157–58.

70. Ibid., pp. 150–51.

71. The constitutionality of Proposition 187 was never determined, due to Governor Gray Davis's decision in 1999 to abandon the state of California's appeal of a lower federal court decision, issued four years earlier, which declared provisions of Proposition 187, denying state social services to illegal aliens, to be unconstitutional. Davis, a strong

opponent of Proposition 187, was elected in November 1998 to succeed Pete Wilson, an equally strong *supporter* of the initiative. Wilson had been pursuing the state of California's defense of Proposition 187 in federal court from the time the voters approved the initiative in November 1994 until his departure from office four years later.

72. In 1996 the House passed the Gallegly bill twice—both as an amendment to the Illegal Immigrant Reform and Immigrant Responsibility Act and as a separate measure. However, the Senate failed to take any action on the Gallegly bill, and it died with adjournment of the 104th Congress in October.

73. Office of Governor Pete Wilson, "Highlights of Wilson's Actions to Fight Illegal Immigration."

74. For a persuasive case against the establishment of a telephone verification system, see Miller and Moore, "A National ID System."

75. The IIRIRA requires the attorney general to establish worker verification pilot projects to determine their effectiveness in enabling firms to meet their legal obligations under the employer sanctions provisions of IRCA. However, the pilot projects are based upon voluntary, rather than mandatory, employer participation. Since few employers are willing to voluntarily participate in such projects, they will have no effect of any kind in impeding the continued ability of illegal aliens to illegally obtain jobs through document fraud.

CHAPTER 5

1. Susan Gonzalez Baker, *The Cautious Welcome: The Legalization Program of the Immigration Reform and Control Act* (Washington, D.C. and Santa Monica, Calif.: The Urban Institute and The RAND Corporation, 1990), p. 25.

2. "Summary of S. 1200—The Immigration Reform and Control Act of 1986," IM, WHORM: Subject File, Ronald Reagan Presidential Library.

3. Congressional Quarterly Almanac, 99th Congress, 1st Session (Washington, D.C.: Congressional Quarterly, 1986), p. 118-H.

4. Memorandum from Charles P. Smith to Charles D. Hobbs, October 8, 1986, Jan W. Mares Files, Ronald Reagan Presidential Library.

5. Memorandum from Charles P. Smith to Charles D. Hobbs, October 20, 1986, Jan W. Mares Files, Ronald Reagan Presidential Library.

6. Peter Brimelow, *Alien Nation: Common Sense About America's Immigration Disaster* (New York: HarperPerennial, 1996), Appendix 2.

7. Congressional Quarterly Almanac, 99th Congress, 1st Session, pp. 118–19-H, 122–23-H.

8. Ronald Reagan, *Public Papers of the Presidents of the United States 1986* (Washington, D.C.: U.S. Government Printing Office, 1989), p. 1523.

9. Ibid., pp. 1523–24.

10. Congressional Quarterly Almanac, 97th Congress, 2nd Session (Washington, D.C.: Congressional Quarterly, 1983), pp. 407–8; Congressional Quarterly Almanac, 98th Congress, 1st Session (Washington, D.C.: Congressional Quarterly, 1984), p. 289; Congressional Quarterly Almanac, 98th Congress, 2nd Session (Washington, D.C.: Congressional Quarterly, 1985), p. 235.

11. Congressional Quarterly Almanac, 99th Congress, 2nd Session, p. 62.

12. "Testimony of Edwin Meese III, Attorney General, Before the Subcommittee on

Immigration and Refugee Policy, Senate Committee on the Judiciary, Concerning the Immigration Reform and Control Act of 1985," IM, WHORM: Subject File, Ronald Reagan Presidential Library.

13. Edwin Meese III to Strom Thurmond, September 12, 1985, IM, WHORM: Subject File, Ronald Reagan Presidential Library.

14. "Statement of Principles," September 12, 1985, IM, WHORM: Subject File, Ronald Reagan Presidential Library.

15. Congressional Quarterly Almanac, 99th Congress, 1st Session, p. 227.

16. "Statement of Principles," September 12, 1985, IM, WHORM: Subject File, Ronald Reagan Presidential Library.

17. Congressional Quarterly Almanac, 99th Congress, 1st Session, p. 224.

18. Ibid., p. 35-S.

19. Ibid., p. 224.

20. Ibid., p. 37-S.

21. Ibid., pp. 35-S, 37-S.

22. Kitty Calavita, "Why Revive an Inhumane System?," *Los Angeles Times*, July 18, 1999, p. M2.

23. Ibid., p. 224.

24. Congressional Quarterly Almanac, 99th Congress, 2nd Session, pp. 63–64.

25. Baker, *The Cautious Welcome*, p. 43.

26. Calavita, "Why Revive an Inhumane Program?," p. M2.

27. Congressional Quarterly Almanac, 99th Congress, 2nd Session, pp. 63–65.

28. Ibid., p. 65.

29. Ibid.

30. "Summary of S. 1200—The Immigration Reform and Control Act of 1986," IM, WHORM: Subject File, Ronald Reagan Presidential Library.

31. Statement of Administration Policy, "H.R. 3810—The Immigration Control and Legalization Amendments Act of 1986 (Rodino (D) New Jersey and Mazzoli (D) Kentucky)," October 9, 1986, IM, WHORM: Subject File, Ronald Reagan Presidential Library.

32. Congressional Quarterly Almanac, 99th Congress, 2nd Session, p. 65.

33. Memorandum from Carol T. Crawford to Donald T. Regan, IM, WHORM: Subject File, Ronald Reagan Presidential Library.

34. "Major Provisions of S. 1200 as Passed by House and Senate," IM, WHORM: Subject File, Ronald Reagan Presidential Library.

35. Memorandum from Carol T. Crawford to Donald T. Regan, IM, WHORM: Subject File, Ronald Reagan Presidential Library.

36. "Major Provisions of S. 1200 as Passed by House and Senate," IM, WHORM: Subject File, Ronald Reagan Presidential Library.

37. "Comparison of Senate and House Immigration Reform Bills," IM, WHORM: Subject File, Ronald Reagan Presidential Library.

38. Statement of Administration Policy, "S. 1200—Immigration Reform (Simpson (R) Wyoming)," October 14, 1986, IM, WHORM: Subject File, Ronald Reagan Presidential Library.

39. Congressional Quarterly Almanac, 99th Congress, 2nd Session, p. 66.

40. Memorandum from Charles P. Smith to Charles D. Hobbs, October 20, 1986, Jan W. Mares Files, Ronald Reagan Presidential Library.

41. Baker, *The Cautious Welcome*, p. 90.

236 Notes

42. Reagan, *Public Papers of the Presidents of the United States 1986*, p. 1524.

43. Vernon M. Briggs, Jr., *Mass Immigration and the National Interest* (Armonk, N.Y.: M. E. Sharpe, 1996), pp. 163–64.

44. Brimelow, *Alien Nation*, Appendix 2; Passel and Clark, *Immigrants in New York*, p. 79.

45. Kevin F. McCarthy and Georges F. Vernez, *Immigration in a Changing Economy: California's Experience* (Santa Monica, Calif.: The RAND Corporation, 1997), p. 23.

46. Passel and Clark, *Immigrants in New York*, p. 79.

47. For data on the low socioeconomic status of Mexicans and Central Americans, relative to that of other immigrant ethnic groups who reside in California, see McCarthy and Vernez, *Immigration in a Changing Economy*, pp. 38–39. For data on the declining median incomes of Mexicans and Central Americans relative to those of other immigrant ethnic groups, see Robert F. Schoeni, Kevin F. McCarthy, and Georges Vernez, *The Mixed Economic Progress of Immigrants* (Santa Monica, Calif.: The RAND Corporation, 1996), p. 24.

48. McCarthy and Vernez, *Immigration in a Changing Economy*, pp. 89–90.

49. Stephen Moore, *A Fiscal Portrait of the Newest Americans* (Washington, D.C.: National Immigration Forum and Cato Institute, 1998), p. 6.

50. For data on the low socioeconomic status of the amnesty population relative to that of refugee and nonrefugee immigrants, see McCarthy and Vernez, *Immigration in a Changing Economy*, p. 52.

51. For data on the high welfare participation rates of Mexicans, Central Americans, Dominicans, and Cubans relative to those of other immigrant ethnic groups, see George J. Borjas, "Immigration and Welfare: A Review of the Evidence," in Peter Duignan and Lewis H. Gann, eds., *The Debate in the United States over Immigration* (Stanford, Calif.: Hoover Institution Press, 1998), pp. 136–37.

52. Baker, *The Cautious Welcome*, p. 32.

53. Congressional Quarterly Almanac, 97th Congress, 2nd Session, p. 407; Congressional Quarterly Almanac, 98th Congress, 1st Session, pp. 287–88; Congressional Quarterly Almanac, 98th Congress, 1st Session, p. 235.

54. Congressional Quarterly Almanac, 99th Congress, 1st Session, p. 223.

55. "Testimony of Edwin Meese III, Attorney General, Before the Subcommittee on Immigration and Refugee Policy of the Senate Committee on the Judiciary Concerning the Immigration Reform and Control Act of 1985," IM, WHORM: Subject File, Ronald Reagan Presidential Library.

56. "Commissioner Nelson Testimony on S. 1200," June 14, 1985, IM, WHORM: Subject File, Ronald Reagan Presidential Library.

57. Congressional Quarterly Almanac, 99th Congress, 1st Session, p. 223.

58. Memorandum from Richard Childress to Robert C. McFarlane, June 18, 1985, IM, WHORM: Subject File, Ronald Reagan Presidential Library.

59. Congressional Quarterly Alamanac, 99th Congress, 1st Session, p. 223.

60. Baker, *The Cautious Welcome*, p. 82.

CHAPTER 6

1. Vernon M. Briggs, Jr., *Mass Immigration and the National Interest* (Armonk, N.Y.: M. E. Sharpe, 1996), p. 222.

2. Ronald Reagan, *Public Papers of the Presidents of the United States 1986* (Washington, D.C.: U.S. Government Printing Office, 1989), p. 1521.

3. Memorandum from W. Robert Pearson to Thomas F. Gibson III, October 28, 1986, IM, WHORM: Subject File, Ronald Reagan Presidential Library.

4. Reagan, *Public Papers of the Presidents of the United States 1986*, pp. 1521, 1524.

5. Ibid., p. 1522.

6. For a list of the libertarian organizations and individuals opposed to a fraud-resistant worker verification system, based upon the use of the Social Security card as a secure and reliable means of individual indentification, see John J. Miller and Stephen Moore, ''A National ID System: Big Brother's Solution to Illegal Immigration,'' Cato Institute Policy Analysis No. 237, pp. 22–23.

7. Martin Anderson, in Peter Hannaford, ed., *Recollections of Reagan: A Portrait of Ronald Reagan* (New York: William Morrow, 1997), pp. 10–11.

8. Ibid., p. 11.

9. For a persuasive argument that Reagan was a disinterested and detached policymaker, see Lou Cannon, *President Reagan: The Role of a Lifetime* (New York: Simon and Schuster, 1991), pp. 180–85.

Selected Bibliography

Anderson, Martin. *Revolution*. San Diego: Harcourt Brace Jovanovich, 1988.

Baker, Susan Gonzalez. *The Cautious Welcome: The Legalization Programs of the Immigration Reform and Control Act*. Washington, D.C. and Santa Monica, Calif.: The Urban Institute and The RAND Corporation, 1990.

Bean, Frank D., Barry Edmonston, and Jeffrey S. Passel. *Undocumented Migration to the United States: IRCA and the Experience of the 1980s*. Washington, D.C. and Santa Monica, Calif.: The Urban Institute Press and The RAND Corporation, 1990.

Beck, Roy. *The Case Against Immigration: The Moral, Economic, Social, and Environmental Reasons for Reducing Immigration Back to Traditional Levels*. New York: W. W. Norton, 1996.

Berman, Larry, ed. *Looking Back on the Reagan Presidency*. Baltimore, Md.: Johns Hopkins University Press, 1990.

Blumenthal, Sidney, and Thomas Byrne Edsall, eds. *The Reagan Legacy*. New York: Pantheon Books, 1988.

Briggs, Vernon M., Jr. *Mass Immigration and the National Interest*. Armonk, N.Y.: M. E. Sharpe, 1996.

Brimelow, Peter. *Alien Nation: Common Sense about America's Immigration Disaster*. New York: HarperPerennial, 1996.

Cannon, Lou. *President Reagan: The Role of a Lifetime*. New York: Simon and Schuster, 1991.

Capaldi, Nicholas, ed. *Immigration: Debating the Issues*. Amherst, Mass.: Prometheus Books, 1997.

D'Souza, Dinesh. *Ronald Reagan: How an Ordinary Man Became an Extraordinary Leader*. New York: The Free Press, 1997.

Duignan, Peter, and Lewis H. Gann, eds. *The Debate in the United States over Immigration*. Stanford, Calif.: Hoover Institution Press, 1998.

Fix, Michael, ed. *The Paper Curtain: Employer Sanctions' Implementation, Impact, and*

Reform. Washington, D.C. and Santa Monica, Calif.: The Urban Institute and The RAND Corporation, 1991.

Fix, Michael, and Paul T. Hill. *Enforcing Employer Sanctions: Challenges and Strategies*. Washington, D.C. and Santa Monica, Calif.: The Urban Institute and The RAND Corporation, 1990.

Fix, Michael, and Jeffrey S. Passel. *Immigration and Immigrants: Setting the Record Straight*. Washington, D.C.: The Urban Institute, 1994.

Hannaford, Peter, ed. *Recollections of Reagan: A Portrait of Ronald Reagan*. New York: William Morrow, 1997.

Johnson, Haynes. *Sleepwalking through History: America in the Reagan Years*. New York: W. W. Norton, 1991.

Lee, Kenneth K. *Huddled Masses, Muddled Laws: Why Contemporary Immigration Policy Fails to Reflect Public Opinion*. Westport, Conn.: Praeger Publishers, 1998.

McCarthy, Kevin F., and Georges F. Vernez. *Immigration in a Changing Economy: California's Experience*. Santa Monica, Calif.: The RAND Corporation, 1997.

Meese, Edwin III. *With Reagan: The Inside Story*. Washington, D.C.: Regnery Gateway, 1992.

Moore, Stephen. *A Fiscal Portrait of the Newest Americans*. Washington, D.C.: National Immigration Forum and Cato Institute, 1998.

Muir, William Ker, Jr. *The Bully Pulpit: The Presidential Leadership of Ronald Reagan*. San Francisco: Institute for Contemporary Studies Press, 1992.

Pemberton, William E. *Exit with Honor: The Life and Presidency of Ronald Reagan*. Armonk, N.Y.: M. E. Sharpe, 1997.

Perea, Juan F., ed. *Immigrants Out! The New Nativism and the Anti-Immigrant Impulse in the United States*. New York: New York University Press, 1997.

Reagan, Ronald. *An American Life*. New York: Simon and Schuster, 1990.

Schaller, Michael. *Reckoning with Reagan: America and Its President in the 1980s*. New York: Oxford University Press, 1992.

Schieffer, Bob, and Gary Paul Gates. *The Acting President*. New York: E. P. Dutton, 1989.

Schmertz, Eric J., Natalie Datlof, and Alexej Urinsky, eds. *Ronald Reagan's America*. Westport, Conn.: Greenwood Press, 1997.

Schoeni, Robert F., Kevin F. McCarthy, and Georges Vernez. *The Mixed Economic Progress of Immigrants*. Santa Monica, Calif.: The RAND Corporation, 1997.

Schuck, Peter H. *Citizens, Strangers, and In-Betweens: Essays on Immigration and Citizenship*. Boulder, Colo.: Westview Press, 1998.

Simon, Julian L. *Immigration: The Demographic and Economic Facts*. Washington, D.C.: Cato Institute and National Immigration Forum, 1995.

Skerry, Peter. *Mexican Americans: The Ambivalent Minority*. Cambridge, Mass.: Harvard University Press, 1993.

Smith, William French. *Law and Justice in the Reagan Administration*. Stanford, Calif.: Hoover Institution Press, 1991.

Strock, James M. *Reagan on Leadership: Executive Lessons from the Great Communicator*. Rocklin, Calif.: Forum, 1998.

Thompson, Kenneth W., ed. *The Reagan Presidency: Ten Intimate Perspectives of Ronald Reagan*. Lanham, Md.: University Press of America, 1997.

Index

About the Author

NICHOLAS LAHAM is an independent scholar specializing in the study of American politics and public policy. Dr. Laham has published three earlier books, the latest of which is *The Reagan Presidency and the Politics of Race* (Praeger, 1998).

ISBN 0-275-96723-9

HARDCOVER BAR CODE